W9-CPO-113

The Future of Assessment

SHAPING TEACHING AND LEARNING

The Future
of Assessment

SHAPING TEACHING AND LEARNING

EDITED BY
Carol Anne Dwyer

LEA Lawrence Erlbaum Associates
Taylor & Francis Group

New York   London

Lawrence Erlbaum Associates
Taylor & Francis Group
270 Madison Avenue
New York, NY 10016

Lawrence Erlbaum Associates
Taylor & Francis Group
2 Park Square
Milton Park, Abingdon
Oxon OX14 4RN

© 2008 by Taylor & Francis Group, LLC
Lawrence Erlbaum Associates is an imprint of Taylor & Francis Group, an Informa business

Printed in the United States of America on acid-free paper
10 9 8 7 6 5 4 3 2 1

International Standard Book Number-13: 978-0-8058-6397-0 (Hardcover)

Library of Congress Cataloging-in-Publication Data

Dwyer, Carol Anne.
  The future of assessment / Carol Anne Dwyer.
    p. cm.
  Includes bibliographical references and index.
  ISBN-13: 978-0-8058-6397-0 (alk. paper)
  1. Educational evaluation. 2. Educational tests and measurements. I. Title.

LB2822.75.D89 2008
371.26--dc22   2007012765

Visit the Taylor & Francis Web site at
http://www.taylorandfrancis.com

and the LEA Web site at
http://www.erlbaum.com

Contents

Contents

To Miles

Acknowledgments

I would like to thank ETS's president, Kurt Landgraf, for his visionary leadership in promoting the use of sound educational data in classrooms around our country and around the world, and for his unwavering support of this book and the ETS Invitational Conference on which this work is based.

I would also like to express my profound gratitude to the authors. In agreeing to be a part of this effort, they committed enormous amounts of time and effort not only to their own contributions but also to shaping the work as a whole by attending to the interconnections between their own work and that of the other authors. It is truly a privilege to work with such distinguished scholars, and it has been a personal pleasure to work with them in the spirit of warm colleagueship that prevailed.

Finally, I am grateful to Evelyn Fisch and Phyllis Murphy. Ms. Fisch provided editorial support to me and to all the authors, helping each of us in exactly the way that we needed. Her gifts of editorial expertise combined with gentle diplomacy and persistence enabled us all, eventually, to meet her exacting standards. Ms. Murphy was our invaluable partner in this team effort as well, using her vast experience to ensure that every detail of our conference and all the authors' practical needs were attended to.

Carol Anne Dwyer
Princeton, NJ
November 2006

Introduction

Testing has historically been shaped by social forces, and our own era is no exception. In the United States today, these forces include rapidly changing demographics, widening socioeconomic divisions, the continued development of a knowledge-driven economy, public concern about ethics and values (both personal and institutional), and faith in the power of science and technology to cure our individual and collective ills.

These trends help to create the context in which assessments are viewed today, and they are converging with important developments in educational, social, and cognitive science that relate directly to assessment and how it is used. Some of the most relevant of these developments include the practical importance of expectations that all children can learn, and teachers who believe that they can make this happen; increased understanding of the concept of developed abilities by educators, students, and families; and the importance of accurate and timely feedback to increasing student achievement and motivation. This convergence of social trends with scientific developments creates the current context in which assessment takes place, and provides us with an increasing number of research-based tools with which we can create assessments that have the potential to benefit students directly.

We are now at a critical turning point, however, with respect to the continued improvement of assessment as a positive force for learning. A number of unsettling trends are revealed in the contemporary dialogue about assessment. Many policy makers, educators, and members of the public seem to act as if raising test scores were the main point of education, rather than actually increasing student knowledge and skills. Similarly, short-term solutions that focus unduly on tests *per se* often find favor in preference to solutions that have been shown by research to produce important and lasting student learning gains. Such research-based solutions include ensuring that teachers have the requisite knowledge and skills for the setting in which they are teaching; and using assessment data on a daily basis to judge student progress toward clearly identified learning goals. Perhaps most disturbing is the frequent recourse, without benefit of data, to the unexamined assumption that a test "can do it all," with little or no further action required: holding institutions and individuals accountable for student learning, influencing curricula, enabling teachers to fine-tune their instruction, ensuring states that they will meet their No Child Left Behind targets, and perhaps even raising real estate values in your neighborhood in its spare time.

The chapters here were originally commissioned for the ETS Invitational Conference held in New York on October 10–11, 2005, The Future of Assessment: Shaping Teaching and Learning. The authors were asked to expand on their conference presentations for this publication. Because our previous Invitational Conference had focused on measurement and research issues in accountability,[1] our aim with the 2005 conference was to move to the next step and examine the role of assessments in improving student learning.

In addition to the troubling treads noted above, there are promising developments, and it is these that our authors primarily address. Contemporary discourse about assessment, while still including a thread that assigns little or no value to assessments under most circumstances, has, as James Pellegrino notes in his chapter, substantially moved on to calls for assessment that is more useful to students and teachers. It is this shift toward finding solutions that is our focus in the research and commentary provided in this volume. The authors provide us with detailed analyses of the most important issues in meeting the need for assessments that can be used by teachers to increase student learning. They have been asked to address the nature of assessments as they now exist, and to point to new developments that hold promise for the near future.

These developments include technical issues related to emerging technologies that enable more sophisticated and responsive assessments; advances in the design of assessments for diagnosis; the effects of using formative assessments on a wide variety of factors, including, most importantly of course, student learning, as well as student motivation and engagement with learning; on teachers' professional development; curricular improvements; and educational policies at all levels. Exponentially increased computing power, widely available to ordinary educators, psychologists, and researchers, has had a number of ramifications for the design and use of educational assessments, as is reflected in the work of Graesser, VanLehn, and Shute, reported in their chapters.

A wide variety of perspectives and experiences are represented among the authors, of course. As one might expect, some are more sanguine than others about our prospects for continuing to move assessments for learning into the mainstream of American education. In this volume, authors address a host of practical issues related to assessments for learning. Navarro, Paige, Haycock, and others give us a clear picture of the vast amount of time, organization, and political will that is necessary to effect changes in student learning. Shepard and Popham provide some sobering examples of how well-intended efforts to improve learning can be derailed by conflicting objectives and interests. Danielson and Stiggins offer analyses that demonstrate the central role of teacher knowledge, beliefs, and actions in making assessment for learning a daily reality.

At the beginning of this book, Gordon offers us a long-term perspective on measurement, society, and social justice. He makes clear that deeply engrained attitudes about who can learn have affected much decision making in education in the past, and continue to present a threat to progress today. Our collective recognition of this reality enables us to move forward, however, harnessing data and theory in service of improved education for all students. Measurement itself has broadened its definitional horizons in a fundamental way, through the reconceptualization of validity. Modern views of validity emphasize the importance of examining tests within their total context. The validity of a test is no longer conceived of as a correlation coefficient, but as a judgment, over time, about the inferences that can be drawn from test data, including the intended or unintended consequences of using the test. Measurement has been moving toward forms and uses of testing that attempt to incorporate new knowledge of intellectual functioning into testing, and into the instruction that is becoming more nearly an intrinsic part of testing. That is why we have entitled this volume, in a hopeful spirit, *The Future of Assessment: Shaping Teaching and Learning.*

Endnotes

1. See our previous volume, *Measurement and Research in the Account-ability Era*, 2005, Lawrence Erlbaum Associates.

Section I

Assessment in the Service of Learning: Why, What, and How

1

The Transformation of Key Beliefs That Have Guided a Century of Assessment

Edmund W. Gordon
Yale University and Teachers College,
Columbia University (Emeritus)

Assessment as we know it in education today is in large measure a product of 20th-century thinking, and has been greatly influenced by conceptions of the educability of individuals and of the functions of education that had currency at the end of the 19th and the beginning of the 20th centuries. At that time, the prevailing thinking in education and psychology was guided by such beliefs as the fixed nature of intelligence and the limited educability of low-status populations such as recent immigrants and the descendants of slaves. These views were also influenced by the limited opportunities for schooling that existed in that era, and the limited need for advanced levels of education in order for individuals to fulfill their responsibilities as productive members of society.

The functions of assessment were thus generally limited to classification, prediction, and sorting. The principal functions of education were thought to be the transfer of knowledge, skills, and values to those thought to be capable of benefiting from it. By the end of the 20th century, however, educators and the general public began to be confronted with important research-based notions from the field of psychology that were directly relevant to pedagogy. These included the view of intellect as a developed ability and the related idea of intellect as a capacity modifiable by education. With the realization that most human beings are educable came social and economic phenomena that in turn influence pedagogy: the almost universal demand for high levels of intellective competence in most spheres;

and, ultimately, the conceptualization of education as a civil right due to all the nation's people.

These changes have confronted the field of educational assessment with new challenges. Beyond such functions as classification, prediction, and sorting, assessment is increasingly being called upon to complement and serve these transformative ideas concerning education. By the end of the 20th century, assessment was under heavy pressure to serve the purposes of governmental accountability. At the same time, some of us were asserting that educational assessment should also be the principal vehicle for advancing the processes of teaching and learning. Despite the current strong emphasis on accountability, and the sorting function that continues to be imposed on assessment, I predict that the educational assessments of the future will be increasingly concerned with the improvement of teaching and learning as its principal purpose.

The president of Educational Testing Service (ETS), Kurt Landgraf, has said that he would like to see the term "testing" disappear from ETS's name. If this is not apocryphal, I think he correctly anticipates that the assessment industry of the future will be concerned with testing only as it serves and advances education. This view is in the tradition of the brilliant young educational psychologist, Michael Martinez, who wrote the wonderful book *Education as the Cultivation of Intelligence* (2000); or from the perspective of the distinguished cognitive psychologist, Robert Sternberg, who titled one of his many books *Teaching for Successful Intelligence: To Increase Student Learning and Achievement* (Sternberg & Grigorenko, 2000). An earlier exponent of these ideas was the eminent developmental psychologist, James McVicker Hunt, whose book, *Intelligence and Experience* (Hunt, 1961), challenged both the fields of education and psychometrics to deal with the mutability of intelligence almost 40 years ago. These and other scholars have influenced my colleague Dr. Beatrice Bridglall and me in the development of a work entitled, "The Affirmative Development of Academic Ability: In Pursuit of Social Justice" (Gordon & Bridglall, 2006). In this work, we demonstrate that academic ability is not so much an aptitude as it is a developed ability. Academic ability is a specialized ability developed as the result of exposure to special experiences—special cultures—associated with schooling and are reinforced by experiences with literate, problem solving, technology-utilizing adults and peers.

In such a conceptual climate, educational tests in the future will fall into disuse unless they are capable of effectively supporting a range of pedagogical functions, including:

1. The diagnosis of what it is possible through teaching and learning. In clinical psychology, we once spoke of "testing the limits" to determine what kinds of performances are evoked under different conditions (see, for example, Feuerstein, 1985; or Haeussermann, 1958).
2. The exploration of performance capabilities in different contexts and under different circumstances and demand situations.
3. The examination of aptitude as a function of time on tasks appropriate to the demands of the material and skills to be learned (see, for example, Carroll, 1993).
4. The iterative exposure to probation, mediation, mediated probation, re-probation as in the dynamic assessment procedures of Feuerstein (1985), Gordon (Gordon, Bridglall, & Meroe, 2004), and Armour-Thomas (Armour-Thomas & Gopaul-McNicol, 1998).
5. Assessments embedded in teaching and learning experiences, where the assessment data are extracted from the record of the teaching and learning transaction.
6. The analysis of the relational adjudication of competing conceptual or social phenomena.
7. The deconstruction of the test items to reveal the learning tasks demands or processual features of the required performance.
8. Relational analysis of teaching, learning, and assessment data that can inform the teaching, learning, and re-assessment processes.

In this context, the central purpose of testing will be to inform and improve teaching and learning. Prediction and selection will be downplayed, in part because the validity of the predictions will be sabotaged by the interventions these data inform. Prescription, development, habilitation, mediation, and remediation will be privileged.

In C. Wright Mills' beautiful little book, *The Sociological Imagination* (1967), Mills challenges the social scientist to ask the "what if" and "why not" questions. As we contemplate the future of psychometrics in the shaping of teaching and learning, we ask: What if we viewed the assessment process as developmental, as a part of the treatment? Why not use testing as a dimension of education, to cultivate the intellect rather than simply to measure it?

References

Armour-Thomas, E., & Gopaul-McNicol, S-A. (1998). *Assessing intelligence: Applying a bio-cultural model.* Thousand Oaks, CA: Sage.

Carroll, J. B. (1993). *Human cognitive abilities: A survey of factor-analytic studies.* Cambridge, UK: Cambridge University Press.

Feuerstein, R. (1985). *Instrumental enrichment: An intervention program for cognitive modifiability.* New York: Scott Foresman.

Gordon, E. W., & Bridglall, B. L. (2006). The affirmative development of academic ability: In pursuit of social justice. In A. Ball (Ed.), *With more deliberate speed: Achieving equity and excellence in education—realizing the full potential of Brown v. Board of Education.* Yearbook of the National Society for the Study of Education, *105*(2), 58-70.

Gordon, E. W., Bridglall, B. L., & Meroe, A.S. (2004). *Supplementary education: The hidden curriculum of high academic achievement.* Lanham, MD: Rowman & Littlefield.

Haeussermann, E. (1958). *Developmental potential of preschool children: An evaluation of intellectual, sensory and emotional functioning.* New York: Grune & Stratton.

Hunt, J. M. (1961). *Intelligence and experience.* New York: Ronald Press.

Martinez, M. E. (2000). *Education as the cultivation of intelligence.* Mahwah, NJ: Lawrence Erlbaum.

Mills, C. W. (1967). *The sociological imagination.* Oxford, UK: Oxford University Press.

Sternberg, R. J., & Grigorenko, E. L. (2000). *Teaching for successful intelligence: To increase student learning and achievement.* Arlington Heights, IL: SkyLight Professional Development.

2

Beyond Rhetoric:
*Realities and Complexities of Integrating Assessment into Classroom Teaching and Learning**

James W. Pellegrino and Susan R. Goldman

Center for the Study of Learning, Instruction, and Teacher Development, University of Illinois at Chicago

Introduction

> Needed are classroom and large-scale assessments that help all students learn and succeed in school by making as clear as possible to them, their teachers, and other education stakeholders the nature of their accomplishments and the progress of their learning.
>
> National Research Council,
> Committee on the Foundations of Assessment, 2001, pp. 1-2[†]

In this era of educational accountability it has become increasingly common to hear calls, like the one above, for better large-scale and classroom-based assessments that not only measure but also improve student learning (e.g., Commission on Instructionally Supportive Assessment, 2001; Shepard, 2000; Wiggins, 1998). Policy makers, educators, and the public are looking to assessments to serve a variety of purposes, including gauging student learning, holding education

---

* The work described in this chapter was supported by a contract from the Chicago Board of Education and was conducted by a research team from the Center for the Study of Learning, Instruction, and Teacher Development that included Matthew Brown, Rona Gepstein, Kate Julian, Cathy Kelso, Traci O'Day, Banu Oney, and Adam Tarnoff. The authors are indebted to the members of that research team for their thoughtful and careful contributions to this project.

† In Pellegrino, Chudowsky, & Glaser, 2001.

systems accountable, signaling worthy goals for students and teachers to work toward, and providing useful feedback for instructional decision making.

Despite all that has been written, both negatively and positively, about assessment over the past several decades, it is only recently that some of the rhetoric surrounding the use of assessments in the educational system has moved away from a primary focus on the purportedly negative impact of large-scale achievement tests on classroom teaching and learning processes, to a discussion of the role of classroom assessment in affecting those processes. For example, Shepard (2000) discussed ways in which classroom assessment practices need to change to better support learning: the content and character of assessments need to be significantly improved to reflect a contemporary understanding of learning; the gathering and use of assessment information and insights must become a part of the ongoing learning process; and assessment must become a central concern in methods courses in teacher preparation programs. Her messages are reflective of a growing belief among many educational assessment experts that if assessment, curriculum, and instruction were more integrally connected, student learning would improve (e.g., Pellegrino, Baxter, & Glaser, 1999; Pellegrino, Chudowsky, & Glaser, 2001; Stiggins, 1997; Wilson & Sloane, 2000). This chapter continues that line of argument by focusing on an analysis of the assessments embedded within major instructional programs for K–8 mathematics.

An Inquiry Into Curriculum-Embedded Assessments

Wise instructional decision making and differentiated instruction depend on teachers being able to take evidence of what students know and can do, compare it to standards-based learning outcomes, and create learning opportunities that reflect appropriate "next steps" for individual students (Donovan & Pellegrino, 2004; NCTM, 1995, 2000; Webb, 1997). Quality curriculum- and classroom-based assessment can support such a process and serve as a critical component of effective teaching, typically leading to enhanced student learning outcomes (Black et al., 2004; Pellegrino et al., 2001; Shepard, 2000; Stiggins, 2001, 2002). For example, there is a substantial body of evidence showing that quality formative assessment practices enhance teaching effectiveness and produce student academic achievement gains ranging from a half to a full course grade, reflecting effect sizes of .4 to .7 or higher (Black & Wiliam, 1998).

This chapter reports on an ongoing attempt to examine whether and how the assessments embedded in four contemporary standards-based curriculum materials have the capacity to support teachers' instructional practices and student learning. We have been focusing on a detailed analysis of four comprehensive mathematics curricula designed for students in grades kindergarten through 8: *Everyday Mathematics* (Bell et al., 2004), Math Trailblazers (Chambers-Boucher et al., 2003), the *Connected Mathematics* project (Lappan, Fey, Fitzgerald, Friel, & Phillips, 1998), and Math *Thematics* (Billstein et al., 1999). Each of these programs was originally developed with National Science Foundation support, is designed to be aligned with the standards developed by the National Council of Teachers of Mathematics (NCTM, 1989, 1995, 2000), and is grounded in research supporting their applicability to a range of students including those attending schools in major urban districts such as the Chicago Public Schools.

There are several reasons for selecting mathematics curricula as targets for research on the effects of classroom assessment processes. One reason is fairly obvious—mathematics is a cornerstone of the educational system and student achievement in mathematics is one of the main indicators of educational quality. Starting with the 2005–2006 academic year, the mathematics achievement of every student in grades 3 through 8 will be assessed as part of the federal No Child Left Behind (NCLB) legislation. More importantly, learning and assessment standards have been clearly specified for mathematics for some time (NCTM, 1989, 1995, 2000). Since the early 1990s the National Science Foundation has supported the development of several standards-based curricula, including the four that are the focus of our investigations. Each of these curricula has been designed to include a variety of embedded assessments, although the developers freely admit that the measurement and cognitive properties of these assessments are largely unknown, a situation more the rule than the exception for curriculum-embedded assessments. In addition, each of these curricula has a substantial base of implementation around the country as well as in the Chicago Public Schools, making the findings of our research important on both the local and national levels. Collectively, these four curricula are in use in over 3,000 districts across our nation, which encompass over 200,000 classrooms representing well over 4 million students. Thus, the four curricula provide exemplary cases in which to examine the instructional and learning affordances of curriculum-embedded assessment.

Our study of curriculum-embedded assessment is concerned with *assessment for learning*, a formative process, as well as the *assessment of learning*, a summative process (e.g., Black & Wiliam, 1998; NRC, 2003; Pellegrino et al., 2001; Shepard, 2000; Stiggins, 2001, 2002). Summative assessment, especially in the context of large-scale, high-stakes tests, has been the primary focus of research on the relationships among assessment, instruction, and learning (e.g., NRC, 2003; Pellegrino et al., 2001). Our effort, with its focus on *assessment for learning* at the classroom and curricular level, is particularly important in light of the paucity of research on the processes of integrating such assessment into instructional practice. Black and Wiliam's work with classroom teachers is one notable exception (Black & Wiliam, 1998; Black et al., 2004). Indeed, systematic study of the integration of assessment into standards-based instructional programs is in its infancy, and the work that is being done is primarily focused on science, not mathematics. For example, Mark Wilson and his colleagues have pursued research on the design and use of curriculum-embedded assessments in instructional units of the SEPUP science curriculum (e.g., Roberts & Wilson, 1998a, 1998b; Roberts, Wilson, & Draney, 1997; Sloane, Wilson, & Samson, 1996; Wilson & Sloane, 2000). To our knowledge, no similar systematic work is underway for any major mathematics curriculum.

The Broader Context Surrounding the Analysis Effort

Many of the Chicago Public Schools' students are failing to perform at or above grade level in mathematics and science, as is the case in many other urban districts. As a result, the district has launched their Mathematics and Science Initiative (CMSI), a comprehensive, system-wide plan to bring about improvement in educational outcomes for all students in the Chicago Public Schools. At the heart of the CMSI plan is a focus on district-wide coherence in mathematics and science. For example, before initiation of the plan, at least 86 different elementary mathematics curricula were being used across the district, often with several in use in the same school. Under CMSI, the district is increasing programmatic coherence by adopting the four elementary mathematics curricula that have been the focus of our analysis efforts. Cognizant of the fact that successful use of these materials requires a strong system of teacher support, CMSI involves a substantial, ongoing, professional development component to assist teachers in implementing these curricula.

Another distinguishing feature of the CMSI is recognition by its leadership of the need for the design, implementation, and evaluation of a comprehensive system of assessments focused on important processes and products of student learning in mathematics. Such a system is needed to support implementation of standards-based curricular and instructional practices and to effectively evaluate student achievement over time. Teachers and administrators must have access to high-quality and appropriate types of information about students' levels of understanding, their thinking strategies, and the nature of their misunderstandings. Current large-scale standardized tests of the type used by most states, and in use in Chicago (e.g., Iowa Test of Basic Skills [ITBS]), to assess academic achievement will not suffice. The models of learning and measurement underlying such tests are rather shallow, raising doubts about the quality of the evidence they can provide about student learning or the impact of instructional programs. Such concerns about the use of standardized test data also apply to the tests in reading, mathematics, and science currently being developed by many states under the No Child Left Behind legislation.

Given the issues noted above, the Center for the Study of Learning, Instruction, and Teacher Development at the University of Illinois at Chicago has been collaborating with the Office of Mathematics and Science (OMS) of the Chicago Public Schools to explore issues in the development and implementation of a comprehensive assessment system that complements the instructional reform agenda at the center of CMSI. The goal of this collaborative effort is to create a context where effective, coherent, and coordinated assessment practices can be set in place and operate at levels from the classroom to the school to the instructional area to the district office.

Chapter Overview

The present chapter provides information about one critical component in building and using such an assessment system within the

CMSI and within Chicago more broadly, namely, the nature and quality of the assessment materials and opportunities built into the existing reform curricula in mathematics that the CMSI has begun implementing. If assessment is to function well in support of the teaching and learning of mathematics, it is essential that the district understand the assessment tools already available to its teachers, and the issues that surround their quality, utility, and implementation. This chapter provides an overview of information about the types of assessments found within the various mathematics curricula and the quality and utility of those assessments based on detailed analyses of their properties. The information we report here is based on systematic content and conceptual analyses of the assessment materials found within each of the curricula, as well as interviews with mathematics specialists who were engaged in supporting teachers at CMSI schools who were implementing these curricula as part of the first year of the CMSI effort. Additional details about the structure and details of the analyses can be found in two lengthy reports (Pellegrino & Goldman, 2004, 2005).

The remainder of this chapter consists of two major sections that consider the results of our analyses and their implications. The next section reports on the nature of the conceptual and content analysis that was applied to each of the four mathematics curricula and the results obtained to date. Within this section, we provide a description of the types of assessments found within and across the four curricula, and then illustrate the outcomes from application of a multilevel analysis system to one of the four curricula. Overall results that come from looking more broadly across the four curricula are also presented. The latter discussion is framed in terms of three very important problems of practice and focus on what we know as well as what we need to know through further empirical study. The final major section of the chapter attempts to put the results of our analysis of the curriculum-embedded assessments in the broader context of a system of assessments. Here we consider what such a system should look like and how it should function. Implications for the design of a benchmark assessment component, as well as for professional development and technology tools and infrastructure, are also given serious consideration within such a systems perspective. We conclude the chapter with some final thoughts about the complexity of the overall design and policy space, and how much effort it will ultimately take if we are to move beyond the rhetoric of recognizing the importance of assessment but doing little to change things. Just what are the prospects for implementing activities designed to ensure that assessment is an ongoing and integral component of the teaching and learning enterprise in classrooms, schools, districts, and states?

Curriculum-Embedded Assessment: Analysis, Outcomes, and Implications

Multiple Forms and Types of Assessments

The four mathematics curricula structure their assessment systems differently, in addition to using different names for the various tasks. In order to analyze and compare both individual assessment instances and assessment systems more generally, a generic set of "assessment types" was initially developed. Table 2.1 illustrates the assessment task "types," provides a general description of each type, and identifies the curriculum-specific examples of each type that are the focus of our analyses. Notice that each curriculum uses a very different nomenclature for its specific examples of each assessment type.

The Analysis Process: An Organizing Framework

Our conceptual and content analysis has been designed to focus on the quality of the assessment types outlined in Table 2.1 and the system of assessments as a whole within each curriculum. It provides an appraisal of how students might understand and respond to the tasks, what their responses may mean, how likely teachers are to understand and use these tools, and what might be done to improve the quality and utility of these materials. To meet such analytic goals, a process and system for analyzing individual assessment tasks and entire systems needed to be put in place. Furthermore, to guide the content and conceptual analysis, multiple perspectives on assessment and its role in teaching and learning needed to be brought to bear in the design of our analysis framework. Figure 2.1 provides an illustration intended to represent the various levels of analysis and the direction of aggregation of data and inferences for a single curriculum.

The primary level of analysis, called Item Analysis, involves a detailed appraisal of the specific assessment instances embedded

TABLE 2.1   Assessment Types and Curriculum-Specific Instances

Assessment Type	Type/Description	Everyday Mathematics	Math Trailblazers	Connected Mathematics	Math *Thematics*
Question(s)	Oral or written word problem(s) contained in the curriculum and specified by the teacher-support materials as assessment	Mental Math, Math Messages, Home/Study Links, Journal Pages, Student Reference Pages, and Ongoing Assessment Boxes	Assessment Pages, Homework Questions, and Home Practice	Applications-Connections-Extensions, Unit Reflections, Question Bank, and Oral Question suggestions	Performance/Portfolio Tasks; Try This as a Class and Discussion Questions
Observation(s)	Opportunities for teacher observation of student performance explicitly identified within the teacher support materials	Ongoing Assessment Boxes and Games/Activities	Assessment Indicators, Observational Assessment Record, Individual Assessment Record Sheet, and Suggestions for Teaching the Lesson: Assessment		
Problem set	Oral or written "naked math" problem(s) contained in the curriculum and specified by the teacher-support materials as assessment	Mental Math, Home/Study Links, Math Journal Pages, Math Master Pages, and Student Reference Pages	Home Practice and Daily Practice and Problems		Warm-Up, Embedded Assessment, and Checkpoint Questions

Journal	Question(s) that ask students to reflect on their learning, make connections, or reason about mathematics	Self-Assessments/ Interviews, Math Logs, and Interest Inventories	Journal Prompts	Mathematical Reflections and Self-Assessment	Closure Question(s) and Reflecting on the Section
Quiz	Mid-unit assessment that summarizes a concept or several concepts and is shorter than a test	Math Boxes	Assessment Pages, Daily Practice and Problems, Home Practice, and Fact Quiz	Check-Up and Quiz	Quick Quiz and Mid-Module Quiz
Test	End-of-unit assessment that summarizes concept(s) taught in the unit	End-of-Unit Test, Mid-Year Test, and End-of-Year Test	Mid-Year Test, End-of-Year Test, and Assessment Pages	Unit Test	Module Test and Performance Assessment
Open-ended response problem(s)	Open-ended problem that takes 1 or 2 days for students to complete	Activities and Explorations	Assessment Lessons		Extended Exploration
Project	Long-term, open-ended activity that may take several days to complete	Project	Laboratory Investigations	Unit Project	Module Project
Portfolio	Collection of student work that must be clearly specified within the teacher-support materials	Portfolio	Assessment Lessons and Suggestions for Teaching the Lesson: Assessment		Portfolio

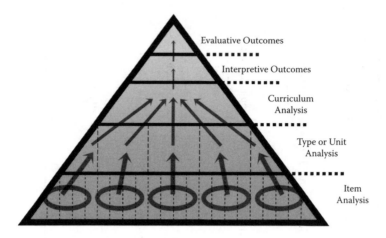

Figure 2.1   Representation of the levels of analysis of assessment materials.

within an instructional unit of a given curriculum. This analysis was conducted by applying a detailed framework and protocol to individual assessment instances. This level of analysis allowed the description and evaluation of the merits of a particular assessment instance in relation to national and local standards, to issues of teacher and student usability, and questions of curriculum coherence.

The second level of analysis, called Type or Unit Analysis, involves aggregation of the Item Analysis data into a common framework, which was slightly different for mathematics and science. For mathematics, this level, called Unit Analysis, involved aggregating the information gathered from the Item Analysis level for a given Unit or Module, which allowed for both the description of the Unit or Module's assessment system and an evaluation of the system's strengths and weaknesses. For science, this level, called Type Analysis, involved aggregating the information gained from the Item Analysis level by assessment type for a given unit and allowed for both the description of the assessment type and an evaluation of the type's strengths and weaknesses.

The third level of analysis, called Curriculum Analysis, involves combining the information generated at the Type or Unit Analysis level. For math this meant consolidating all of the Unit Analysis level information for a given curriculum into a common framework, resulting in a representation for the entire curriculum. This level allows for both the description of the curriculum's assessment system and an evaluation of its strengths and weaknesses.

The fourth level of analysis, called Interpretive Outcomes, involved evaluating the information generated at the Curriculum Analysis level using a framework that addressed issues of the alignment of curriculum, instruction and assessment. The fifth and final level, called Evaluative Outcomes, also involved evaluating the information generated in the Curriculum Analysis level but used a framework that addressed issues of the curriculum's assessment system's cognitive, observational, and interpretive components in light of contemporary advances in the science of learning and measurement. In the example application that follows for the Math Trailblazers curriculum, we provide more detail about the conceptual frameworks guiding the Interpretive and Evaluative outcome levels and illustrate the results for Math Trailblazers.

One result of this analysis process is that curricula can be compared at multiple levels as shown in Figure 2.2.

An Example Application: Results From the Analysis of Math Trailblazers

Although we conducted an analysis of the assessment types and systems embedded within each of the four curricula, it is well beyond the scope of this chapter to provide details about each one and the specific results obtained in each case. Rather, for purposes of illustration, we will focus on one example: application of our analysis system and frameworks to the Math Trailblazers curriculum. We start by providing some general information about the structure of the Math Trailblazers curriculum across the K–5 grade range, how assessment is operationalized within that context, and the specifics of the assessment types and their apparent function and frequency in the instructional program. We then turn to the results of our analysis at the Interpretive and Evaluative Outcome level.

Overview of the Instructional and Assessment Materials   For descriptive purposes it is necessary to break the Math Trailblazers curriculum into two separate grade spans—kindergarten versus grades 1–5—because the curriculum varies across those spans. Kindergarten is organized into 10 Months and three thematic Units. Each Month includes Lessons from the Patterns, Number Sense, Geometry, and/or Measurement strands. Daily calendar, number,

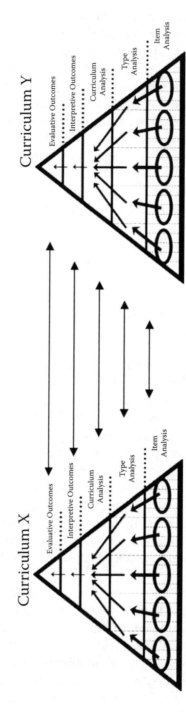

Figure 2.2   Representation of possible cross-curricular comparisons.

data, and problem solving activities are included as Ongoing Content. Teacher materials include a *Teacher Resource Book* with lessons and blackline masters; and a *Teacher Implementation Guide* that includes an overview of the grade and background on pedagogy and math content.

For grades 1–5, each grade is organized into Units subdivided into Lessons. Lessons take 1 to 5 days to complete. Most can be completed in 1 to 3 days. Grades 1–3 contain 20 units each. Grades 4–5 contain 16 units each. Teacher materials include a *Unit Resource Guide* for each unit, a *Teacher Implementation Guide*, and a *Facts Resource Guide*. Student materials include a consumable *Student Guide* in grades 1 and 2, and a nonconsumable *Student Guide* with a consumable workbook in grades 3–5. Each grade includes an *Adventure Book* with original stories that put math in a real-world or fictional context.

Assessment in Math Trailblazers is included within the Units in grades 1 through 5 and within the Months in kindergarten. Within the Lessons, activities are designated as possible assessments. These activities include observations, Daily Practice and Problems items, Home Practice items, homework questions, Journal Prompts, and short-answer quizzes and tests. Not every unit contains the same set of assessments. Some units contain assessment lessons, Open-Response Problems, that take one or two class sessions to complete; other units designate labs (or parts of labs) as assessments that may take three or four class sessions, while others include short-answer tests or quizzes.

Grades 1–5 include two or three Assessment Units that contain a variety of assessments, including observations, Open-Response Problems, Assessment Labs, and/or short-answer tests. The Assessment Units provide baseline data at the beginning of the year, provide opportunities to track student progress at midyear, and supply summative assessments at the end of the year.

The *Teacher Implementation Guide* includes a section on assessment that describes the philosophy and components of the assessment program in Math Trailblazers. This section includes a multidimensional rubric for teachers used to score open-response items. For each of the three dimensions, Knowing, Solving, and Telling, a corresponding Student Rubric is included for students to use as a guide as they complete tasks. Also included in the *Teacher Implementation Guide* is a section describing the use of journals and portfolios as part of a complete assessment system.

Each unit in grades 1–5 includes a set of Assessment Indicators that highlight key concepts and skills to be assessed. These are listed on an Observational Assessment Record that teachers can use to record student progress throughout the Unit. All Assessment Indicators for all the Units are listed together in the *Teacher Implementation Guide* for each grade so that teachers can track individual student progress throughout the year.

To obtain a sense of the totality of the assessment materials woven into the curriculum, Table 2.2 provides an expansion of the assessment types presented in Table 2.1. The table provides a range of information about each assessment type including its apparent purpose, its name, the type of information provided to the teacher and/or student, and the frequency of appearance across grades.

Given the totality of the assessment materials available within the Math Trailblazers curriculum, it would be unwieldy to attempt an analysis of every task within every instructional unit across the entire K–5 grade span. Thus, for analysis sampling purposes, the curriculum was broken into three grade bands: K, 1–2, and 3–5. These bands were chosen because it was hypothesized that the assessment systems within each band would be similar but would vary from band to band. In order to fairly represent the assessments contained within the curriculum, Assessment Units (which contain most of the baseline and summative assessments) were differentiated from regular units. Within a particular grade band, regular and assessment units were randomly selected for evaluation. In kindergarten, one month was randomly selected. In each of the units selected for detailed analysis, all activities recommended by the curriculum as assessments were evaluated. The following are the Units and Month actually evaluated in detail.

- *Month 8*—Kindergarten Month that includes content on number sense, geometry, and measurement
- *Unit 3 Buttons*—Grade 2 baseline Assessment Unit
- *Unit 10 Numbers and Patterns*—Grade 3 midyear Assessment Unit
- *Unit 16 Volume*—Grade 3 Unit that focuses on volume measurement and uses it as a context for developing number concepts
- *Unit 7 Patterns in Multiplication*—Grade 4 Unit that focuses on multiplication concepts and procedures, order of operations, divisibility rules, and estimation strategies

TABLE 2.2 Description of Assessment Types in Math Trailblazers

Purpose	Assessment Type	Assessment Name (MTB)	Description	Information for the Teacher	Information for the Student	Frequency/Change Across Grades
Formative/ Summative	Question(s) or Problem Set	Assessment Page	Short-answer paper-and-pencil assessments	Checks skills or concepts developed in a unit. They may serve as quizzes on one or two skills or summative assessments for a unit. Possible student responses are often included in Answer Keys for questions that require students to explain strategies		K: None G1–5: 0–3/unit
Formative	Journal	Math Journal and Journal Prompt	A small, bound book in which students write regularly (not furnished with the curriculum). Journal Prompts are included in some lessons	Tracks student progress writing about mathematics to document long-term progress. Some are specifically recommended as assessment within a lesson. The *Teacher Implementation Guide* in each grade provides information on organizing and using journals. Lesson Guides in grades 1–5 include Journal Prompts		K: None G1–5: 0–3/unit (Note: In the sampled units, no Journal Prompts were recommended as assessments)

(continued)

TABLE 2.2 (CONTINUED)   Description of Assessment Types in Math Trailblazers

Purpose	Assessment Type	Assessment Name (MTB)	Description	Information for the Teacher	Information for the Student	Frequency/Change Across Grades
Formative/ Summative	Open-Ended Response Problems	Assessment Lesson or Question	Assessment Lessons in which students complete a task that requires them to demonstrate problem-solving skills individually or in groups. The tasks take 1 to 2 days to complete. Open-response problems also appear as questions that require data analysis in labs	Provides information on students' problem-solving and communication skills. A rubric is provided for teachers to score student work.	Student Rubrics make expectations clear to students. They are used with other assessment components	GK–2: None G3: 3/year G4–5: 5/year
Formative/ Summative	Project	Laboratory Investigation	Lessons in which students collect, organize, and analyze data; usually requires several days to complete. Labs usually include open-response problems that require analysis of data	Used to assess students' measurement skills and abilities to collect, organize, graph, and analyze data. Teacher materials often recommend specific parts of the investigations to use as assessment and provide information on how to score students' work		K: None G1–5: 8–10/year

Formative/ Summative	Project	Assessment Lab	Assessment Lessons that are Laboratory Investigations; takes several days to complete in which students collect and organize data and use it to solve problems	Used to assess students' abilities to work with a group on an investigation that takes several days. Teacher materials often recommend specific parts of the investigations to use as assessment and provide information on how to score students' work		K: None G1–2: no complete labs G3: 2/year G4–5: 3/year
Summative	Test	Test	Mid-Year and End-of-Year tests made up of short items	Provide information on students' conceptual understanding and procedural skills		K: None G1–2: 1 at end of year G3: 1 at mid-year and 1 at end of year G4–5: 3 mid-year and 1 at end of year
Formative	Portfolio	Portfolio	A purposeful collection of students' work that provides evidence of their skills, understanding, or attitudes	Document students' growth over time. *Teacher Implementation Guide* in each grade provides information on organizing and using portfolios. Some lessons contain recommendations for tasks to include in portfolios	Document students' growth over time	G4–5 include lessons at the beginning, middle, and end of the year that provide a structure for the use of portfolios

(continued)

TABLE 2.2 (CONTINUED)   Description of Assessment Types in Math Trailblazers

Purpose	Assessment Type	Assessment Name (MTB)	Description	Information for the Teacher	Information for the Student	Frequency/Change Across Grades
Summative	Observation(s)	Observation	Teacher evaluation of student responses during a lesson. Includes informal evaluation of students' oral responses or formal evaluation of students' performance on tasks, especially measurement task	Used to guide instruction, monitor student growth, or evaluate student achievement. Specific suggestions for observational assessments are included in the Lesson Guides. Assessment Indicators in each unit list important skills, behavior, and knowledge that can be assessed in the unit. All the Assessment Indicators are listed together in *Teacher Implementation Guide* so teachers can track students' growth over the year		Much of the assessment in kindergarten is observational. In G1–2, observations continue to be a major source of assessment information. In G3–5, the number of observations decreases. Many are used to assess measurement skills
Formative	Quiz	Facts Self-Assessment	Students use flashcards to quiz each other on a small group of facts and note which facts they know and can answer quickly, those that they can solve using a strategy, and those they still need to learn	Provides teachers with information on which facts students need to study	Students track their progress on a chart.	GK–2: None G3–4: 1–2/unit (most units) G5: 1/unit in 1st semester

Formative	Quiz	Facts Quiz	Short quizzes on a small group of facts	Provides information on students' progress with the facts	Students record their progress on a chart	GK–1: None G2–4: 1/unit G5: 1/unit in 1st semester
Summative	Test	Facts Test	A test on all the facts studied during a semester	Provides summative information on students' facts knowledge	Students record results on a chart	GK–1: None G2–4: 2/year G5: 1/year
Formative/ Summative	Quiz	Daily Practice and Problem	Short exercises that provide review of math concepts, skills, and facts	Can serve as short quizzes on skills or concepts in the unit		K: None G1–5: 0–2/unit recommended as assessments
Formative/ Summative	Quiz	Home Practice	Series of problem sets that supplement homework	Can serve as a quiz on skills or concepts in the unit		GK–2: None G3–5: 0–2/unit recommended as assessments

Appraisal of the Critical Instructional Properties of the Assessments   Earlier we noted that various perspectives were used to make judgments about the quality of the assessment materials woven into the curriculum. At what we have termed the "Interpretive Outcomes Level," we were concerned with critical instructional properties of the assessments. Two perspectives were incorporated to make judgments about these attributes of the assessments. The first perspective is curriculum- and instruction-specific and can be viewed as relatively local. This perspective focuses on the appropriateness of the assessment materials and tools and their functioning within the overall instructional process and with respect to a given curriculum's content and instructional goals. Questions fitting this perspective probe for evidence of (a) support for teacher use of the assessment materials; (b) meaningfulness for application and use in instruction; (c) support for formative assessment activities; and (d) support for summative assessment activities.

The second perspective moves beyond the local curriculum and instructional level to include questions related to state and national standards for mathematics and science teaching, learning, and assessment (e.g., American Association for the Advancement of Science [AAAS], 1993, 2001; NCTM, 2000; NRC, 1996). The standards documents establish various goals for mathematics and science instruction and learning within and across content strands over time. They also provide guidelines about the forms of knowing and understanding that students should acquire and that should, therefore, be assessed as part of the ongoing instructional process. Relevant questions fitting this perspective probe for evidence of (a) coverage of important content and process standards; (b) assessment of multiple forms of knowing and knowledge types; and (c) a range of tasks and formats allowing students to exhibit and communicate what they know.

What follows is a capsule summary of the strengths and weaknesses of the assessment materials and system incorporated into the Math Trailblazers curriculum. The presentation is organized in terms of key questions and issues derived from the two perspectives described above.

Strengths	Weaknesses
Relation to Important Content and Standards	
• All the evaluated assessments reflect the mathematics content outlined in the CPS Essential Mathematics Standards, the Illinois Learning Standards, and the NCTM's *Principles and Standards for School Mathematics*, although some content may vary by grade level.	• Few of the assessment types provide students with the opportunity to appropriately use technology.
• Many of the assessments, especially the Observations, Open-Response Problems, and Projects provide opportunities for students to	
• Problem solve	
• Communicate mathematically either orally or in writing	
• Reason mathematically	
• Apply their knowledge in a meaningful context	
• Use manipulatives and/or measuring devices	
• Be evaluated on skills and procedural knowledge while problem solving	
• Use multiple solution approaches	
• Use chart, graphs and/or other representations	
• Work on teams	
Teacher Support	
• The majority of assessment types either have clearly written directions or the directions can be readily inferred by students based on their interaction with the curriculum.	• Some of the assessments do not include clearly written scoring procedures.
• The length and activity type of most assessment types are appropriate for most students.	• Inconsistency in the location and type of embedded assessments across units within grades may confuse some teachers.
• The student directions in most assessments provide students with guidance about the desired answer.	

Meaningfulness for Instruction

- Many assessment types make student thinking visible to the teacher.
- Some assessments, primarily Open-Response Problems, Lab Questions, and Facts Quizzes, require students to understand their progress, including what they know and have yet to learn.
- Some assessments, primarily Open-Response Problems and Lab Questions, provide clearly laid out, observable performance criteria.
- Some assessments provide a scoring guide that aids teachers in interpreting the meaning of the information. Examples include the Multidimensional Rubric associated with Open-Response Problems and the developmental framework provided by the Assessment Indicators and the Observational Assessment Record contained in each unit.
- Assessments reflect what students were taught and represent the activities of the curriculum.

- Few assessment types provide opportunities for peer assessment.
- None of the assessments make specific recommendations to support special needs students. However, use of manipulatives, drawings, and other representations along with multiple solution strategies allow these students to show what they know and can do.
- While the rubrics and Assessment Indicators provide some information to teachers on how to interpret and make use of the data on student learning, more structure within the assessment program is needed to assist teachers in making decisions based on the results of the assessments.
- Some teachers want a unit-end summative assessment.

Support for Formative Assessment

- Formative assessments are designed to be a routine and integral part of teaching practice and are embedded throughout the curriculum.
- Formative assessments are designed to provide teachers with the opportunity to provide students with timely and actionable feedback during learning and instruction.
- Formative assessments include as many as 11 different assessments that provide teachers with varying types of information about student learning.

- Formative assessments provide teachers with little specific, structured support to adapt instruction.
- Formative assessments do not provide a simple, structured way to measure student progress over time.

Support for Summative Assessment

- Summative assessments include as many as nine different assessments that provide teachers with varying sources of evidence about student learning.

- Summative assessments do not provide a simple, structured way to measure student progress over time.
- Many summative assessments do not directly refer to or explicitly reflect a student developmental continuum. (The Facts Test refers directly to the Assessment Indicators and the assessment section in the Lesson Guides often point out which Assessment Indicators can be used with the assessments.)
- Some teachers are uncomfortable with the lack of a unit-end summative assessment.

Overall

- Assessment is an integral part of the curriculum. It occurs at regular intervals and directly reflects its content and process.
- Both curriculum and assessment reflect the same mathematical content and process goals.
- Assessment system includes a balance of all assessment types.
- Assessment system includes a balance of both formative and summative assessments.

- While assessment does provide information that can be used to inform instruction, additional support is needed to assist teachers in making decisions based on the results of the assessments.

Appraisal Relative to Elements of the "Assessment Triangle" In addition to an appraisal of the instructional properties of the assessments, we applied yet another perspective to judge the merits and quality of the assessments and the system as a whole. We have termed this the "Evaluative Outcomes Level." This level of analysis moves beyond a local curriculum and instructional perspective as well as a state and national standards perspective to a more general perspective on the nature of assessment, including what constitutes quality and coherent assessment. This perspective employs a framework for assessment design and analysis presented in *Knowing What*

Students Know: The Science and Design of Educational Assessment (Pellegrino et al., 2001). The framework is represented by the "assessment triangle," which includes three connected elements or vertices: (1) cognition, (2) observation, and (3) interpretation, together with the relationships among these elements. Relevant questions fitting this perspective probe for evidence that (a) the underlying conceptualization of mathematical knowledge and learning (the cognition element) is consistent with contemporary theory and research on mathematical understanding and development (e.g., Ball 2003; Kilpatrick, Swafford, & Findell, 2001); (b) there is breadth and richness to the tasks and performances that are required of students (the observation element); and (c) there are systematic ways in which performance is scored and interpreted (the interpretation element). Although each of the three vertices is separately evaluated in terms of relative strengths and weaknesses, the strengths and weaknesses of the linkages among the vertices and the degree of coordination and synchrony exhibited within the overall assessment approach of a given curriculum are equally important.

Appraisal in Terms of Each of the Three Vertices   The cognitive model underlying Math Trailblazers' assessment system reflects the interaction that occurred during the development process. The curriculum was developed by mathematical strand through an iterative process involving the interaction of student work in the labs, published research, and work with teachers. The cognitive model reflects both the content and process standards contained in the NCTM's *Principles and Standards for School Mathematics*, with particular emphasis placed on students' doing mathematics in a meaningful context, student use of the scientific method, and student understanding of measurement and variable and proportional reasoning. Overall, Math Trailblazers has a strong cognitive vertex. The assumed cognitive model reflects current empirical knowledge of student leaning in the domain of mathematics, provides a developmental perspective that can be helpful in understanding student growth, and details varying levels and kinds of student understanding. Its major weakness is its lack of explicitness about the cognitive model, which makes it difficult to identify the underpinnings of the assessment system.

Math Trailblazers' observation vertex is strong in the sense that the assessment system contains a set of observations that are an integral part of instruction and provide multiple sources of evidence about student learning. In addition, many of the tasks permit evaluation of students' ability to engage in communicative practices appropriate to mathematics and make student thinking visible to themselves and teachers.

Math Trailblazers' interpretation vertex has a mixture of strengths and weaknesses. Major strengths include assessment tasks that provide teachers with support that goes beyond the typical answer key, and an assessment system that provides teachers with the opportunity to provide students with timely and informative feedback. Major weaknesses include teacher materials that neither advise teachers about all the important characteristics of student responses nor inform teachers about the connections between work features and student understanding.

Appraisal in Terms of the Linkages Among the Vertices   Math Trailblazers' cognition-observation link has a mixture of strengths and weaknesses. The link's greatest strength is that its assessment tasks are designed to elicit the performance indicated in the cognitive model. This strength is offset by the lack of explicit mapping between the tasks and the cognitive model. Math Trailblazers' cognition-interpretation link also has a mixture of strengths and weaknesses. Although some task-interpretive frameworks can be directly linked to the cognitive model, Math Trailblazers does not provide either scoring methods sensitive to critical differences in levels and types of student understanding, or specific or explicit rules that describe the mapping of student productions to an interpretive framework. Finally, like the other links, Math Trailblazers' observation-interpretation link has a mixture of strengths and weaknesses. Although some assessment tasks are explicitly mapped to their interpretation, many tasks are not. Teachers receive little direction on the interpretation of student performance on specific tasks.

As a way of summarizing the results of our analyses of the assessments embedded within the Math Trailblazers curriculum, it is fair to say that this curriculum has a very well-developed system of assessments that are an integral part of the materials and instructional design. There are, however, questions about the quality and informativeness of the assessments as well as the capacity of teachers to understand, use, and manage the assessment process. These, as well as other issues, are general concerns uncovered in our analyses of all four curricula.

Looking Across All Four Curricula: Framing the
Overall Results in Terms of Problems of Practice

Our detailed analyses of the assessment resources within the four mathematics curricula highlight a number of apparent strengths and weaknesses of the curriculum-embedded assessment materials and resources in each program (Pellegrino & Goldman, 2004, 2005). As a means of organizing and highlighting the major results, they can be presented in the context of three major "problems of practice." All three are critical to the effective use of assessment in the teaching and learning process and in the larger system that Chicago would aspire to build. All three problems of practice are germane to understanding the actual or potential value of the assessment tasks and processes that operate within and across the CMSI curricula, as well as to the likelihood that teachers and students can benefit from the systematic use of the curriculum-embedded assessment materials as part of an overall district assessment system.

The first problem of practice is somewhat obvious but nevertheless thorny: the assessments must be of high quality in terms of their capacity to tap important aspects of student knowledge and skill and reveal meaningful variation in that knowledge. While it is often easy to generate "test" items, it is far harder to generate good items driven by a rich conception of student learning and that can serve as diagnostic probes of student knowledge and understanding. Often, curricula leave the item/task generation process up to the teacher or provide perfunctory problem sets with little coherence and construct validity. Thus, a first set of questions concerns what is assessed in a curriculum, how well, and whether the assessments tap the same knowledge and skills in students from different ethnic and linguistic backgrounds. In this area, five major conclusions seem defensible based on our analyses of the four curricula.

- In each curriculum, a range of knowledge types and cognitive performances are typically assessed, including declarative, procedural, conceptual, and strategic knowledge; problem solving; and communication of mathematical and scientific understandings.

- In each curriculum there is typically a developmental progression in what is assessed within and across content and process strands, although the explicit nature of this progression is often unclear.
- The curricula and assessment types appear to vary tremendously in the linguistic and cognitive load they are likely to place on students, thus calling into question their validity for supporting inferences about learning for ethnically and linguistically diverse subgroups of students.
- There is no evidence provided that the various tasks have construct validity, i.e., that they assess important and well-defined aspects of knowing and understanding and have been derived from detailed conceptual and empirical models of student cognition in mathematics.
- The precise measurement properties of the tasks relative to issues of item difficulty and coherence across problem types over time and within units is generally unknown.

The second major problem of practice concerns the confusion that often arises regarding how multiple assessments, including those contained within a curriculum, as well as those external to the instructional setting, are supposed to relate to each other. A persistent misconception is that all assessments should yield the same or very similar information about student performance, as contrasted with the perspective that assessments of student learning in mathematics vary in a number of ways, including their purpose (formative, summative, or program evaluation), what they assess, and whether they provide evidence of near or far knowledge transfer (Hickey & Pellegrino, 2005; Pellegrino et al., 2001). Ruiz-Primo, Shavelson, Hamilton, and Klein (2002) point out that assessments should be viewed as representing varying "distance" from the enactment of a particular curricular activity. They identified five discrete points on the continuum of assessment distance: *immediate* (e.g., informal observation or artifacts from the enactment of a particular lesson), *close* (e.g., embedded assessments and semi-formal quizzes following several activities), *proximal* (e.g., formal classroom exams following a particular curriculum), *distal* (e.g., criterion-referenced achievement tests such as required by NCLB), and *remote* (broader outcomes measured over time, including norm-referenced achievement tests such as ITBS). Thus, a second set of questions concerns the range of assessments designed into a curriculum's instructional materials; how they work together to reveal what students know;

what supports are available to help teachers make sense of the information; and which, if any, of the assessments are most likely to help teachers predict the performance of their students on distal assessments that address accountability issues, especially in the current NCLB era. With regard to these questions, five major conclusions seem defensible based on our analyses.

- Assessment is an integral part of the curriculum design and instructional process for each mathematics program, as suggested in various standards documents for mathematics.
- Each of the curricula utilizes a range of assessment types and tasks representing both formative and summative assessment functions.
- The multiple assessment types represent a mixture of the first three points captured in the Ruiz-Primo et al. (2002) continuum (immediate, close, and proximal). How they are supposed to fit together remains relatively undefined in each of the curricula.
- The mapping of assessment tasks to standards and knowledge types is often implicit; clear expectations about the possible range of student performance and its meaning are often lacking.
- There is no information provided about how and how well a given type of assessment or collection of assessment types can be used to predict performance on external, high-stakes achievement tests of the type used by states under NCLB.

The third major problem of practice has to do with better balancing the practice of assessment *of learning* (summative) with the practice of assessment *for learning* (formative). To take advantage of curriculum-embedded assessment tools, many teachers must change their conception of their role and the role of assessment in the classroom. They must shift toward placing much greater emphasis on exploring student understanding with various assessment tools and then applying a well-informed understanding of what those assessments have revealed. This means teachers must be prepared to use feedback from classroom and external assessments to guide their students' learning more effectively by modifying instructional activities and differentiating instruction. Evidence shows that implementing such a shift in assessment and instructional practices is difficult and requires extensive professional development support (Black et al., 2004). Thus, our third set of questions concerns the support needed for teachers to make this shift in practice and the types of ongoing support and assessment tools that facilitate teachers understanding and capacity to make use of the information that embedded assessments are able to provide. With regard to these questions, four major conclusions seem defensible based on our analyses.

- Support for teacher use of individual assessments for formative or summative purposes is often weak from an interpretive and management standpoint.
- Support for teacher understanding of the system of assessments and their respective roles in supporting the teaching and learning process is generally weak.
- Interview data suggest that teachers do not understand all the assessment components available to them nor do they know how to use them in a systematic way as part of their instructional practice. This suggests the need for substantial professional development about the assessment components of a given curriculum and their role in the teaching and learning process.
- Interview data also suggest that teachers have difficulty understanding the formative versus summative assessment purpose distinction and that they tend to view assessment primarily as a summative activity. This suggests the need for substantial professional development in general assessment literacy.

What We Still Need to Know and Why

Overall, our analyses of the assessment resources built into the four mathematics curricula suggest many potential strengths in each one, as well as some apparent limitations. It also suggests that many of the possible strengths are likely to be missed without specific professional development and other supports to assist teachers in using the assessment resources available to them. Many issues about the use of these assessments and their mappings to state learning standards and state assessment frameworks have yet to be addressed. Furthermore, confirmation of many of the "hypotheses" listed above regarding strengths and weaknesses, as well as possible directions for improvement, should ultimately depend on the execution of a rigorous, multifaceted program of empirical work focused on evaluating the properties and functioning of these assessment systems at the classroom level. Such a program of research should address the six areas identified below.

1. What various specific types of curriculum-embedded assessments actually reveal about student learning, including what students understand and how they understand it, as well as the relationship of estimates of that knowledge to performance on external, accountability tests.

2. What teachers understand about student learning based on the information derivable from the curriculum-embedded assessments, and how they make use of that information to assist student learning.

3. The particular and unique issues that arise in assessing mathematics learning with linguistically and ethnically diverse populations of children.

4. Assessment types and content areas that are most informative for purposes of instructional decision making and/or for projecting performance on external summative assessments.

5. The common and unique ways that the four curricula approach the integration of assessment and instruction, especially with regard to key mathematics content and process standards.

6. Ways to enhance assessment materials and provide basic technology support tools that facilitate the effective use of assessment in instruction.

Such a program research can make a major contribution to understanding (a) what constitutes quality assessment in K–8 mathematics where the goal of the assessment is to support student learning as part of an ongoing and coherent instructional process tied to nationally defined standards (NCTM, 2000); (b) what teachers need to know to make effective use of such assessments in their practice, and what types of assessment tasks and student performance information are most meaningful and useful to them; and (c) how to investigate these questions by coordinating and integrating psychometric, cognitive, and instructional approaches to the process of data collection and analysis.

In addition to answering questions about how and how well assessment functions in support of teaching and learning in four contemporary mathematics curricula, the results would also contribute to teachers' and mathematics curriculum developers' understandings about the capacity of embedded assessments to reveal variation in important aspects of student knowledge and understanding, especially among diverse student groups. Little is currently understood about how to provide all students with good opportunities to "show what they know" and to support and build on student understanding. Attention to the needs of all students includes providing opportunities for them to (1) reference prior experiences and background knowledge; (2) represent their use of a combination of forms of representations; and (3) explain their understandings using the linguistic forms (e.g., first language or dialect) that serve them well in constructing explanations. Situating such work in contexts, like the Chicago Public Schools with its ethnically and linguistically diverse student population, can provide a major contribution to the research, curriculum design, and professional development literatures relevant to providing equitable and principled opportunities for all students in mathematics learning.

Finally, research focused on the objectives outlined above can also help to advance theory, research, and practice on important linkages between assessment design and student learning, leading to the generation of design principles for effectively designing and embedding assessments into curricular materials and instructional strategies. The research can also yield valuable information to guide the design of professional development programs and policies. For example, careful explication of the relationships that different kinds of embedded assessments have to student understanding will define part of the knowledge base for professional development on the process of effective instructional decision making. Professional development in assessment literacy with respect to classroom and large-scale assessment practices and their integration has been designated as a priority if assessment is to have a positive rather than negative impact on classroom teaching and student learning (e.g., Commission on Instructionally Supportive Assessment, 2001; Wilson & Bertenthal, 2005).

Putting the Curriculum-Embedded Results in Context: Components, Criteria, and Functionality of a Comprehensive Assessment System

At the start of this chapter it was mentioned that the analysis of the assessment practices associated with each of the four curricula being implemented in Chicago under the CMSI is part of a larger effort to connect assessment and instruction at the classroom level to a comprehensive assessment system tied to the state's learning standards in mathematics, a system that works across levels from the classroom, to the school, to the district, to the state. We now return to that theme by considering the curriculum-embedded results in the context of such a larger system.

Across the country there has been a general failure of states and school districts to realize that assessment has a very powerful and beneficial role to play in the instructional process, but only when it is conceived as a system that operates across levels of the educational system from the classroom on up to the district and state level with appropriate information flow in both directions (see, e.g., NRC, 2003; Pellegrino et al., 2001; Wilson & Bertenthal, 2005). Furthermore, there is a general failure to realize that such a system requires multiple components, each of which is designed to assist the key actors at each level of the system by providing appropriate assessment tools that yield actionable information at that level. Assessment at each level should be appropriate to the needs of educational personnel and it should be coordinated and coherent across levels. Such a system has many components and a proper design for the Chicago Public Schools context, or any major district, should have as its target the components, criteria, and functionality listed below.

- Classroom-based formative assessment to monitor and assist learning must constitute a major component of the system's overall design, consistent with results showing that quality formative assessment enhances teaching effectiveness and produces student academic achievement gains (Black & Wiliam, 1998). Such assessment practices will require development and implementation of extensive professional development resources.
- As part of the emphasis on classroom assessment practices, students should also learn how to use assessment information and processes to support their own learning. This includes how to assume responsibility for monitoring their knowledge states and how to self-assess to improve future learning.
- Benchmark assessments of student learning must be developed to provide information useable at multiple levels, ranging from the classroom through the school and system levels, to monitor ongoing success in achieving valued outcomes.
- All assessments must be tied to mastery of the curricular and instructional content that is central to mathematics and science education standards articulated at national (AAAS, 1993, 2001; NCTM, 2000; NRC, 1996) and state levels (Illinois State Board of Education, 1997).
- The assessment system must emphasize growth in student understanding and skill within critical areas of mathematical and

scientific thinking and be designed to track progress longitudi-
nally across grades.

- Assessment development, adaptation, and implementation must
rely on multiple knowledge sources, including the expertise of
teachers, curriculum specialists, learning scientists, mathemati-
cians, scientists, mathematics and science educators, and measurement specialists.
- Assessment development and implementation should serve as a
focal point for system-wide discussion regarding valued educational outcomes and the curricular, instructional, and assessment
tools by which such outcomes can be achieved.
- The system's design and implementation must incorporate advanced
uses of information and communications technologies and support
the creation of an information infrastructure for assessment data
collection, sharing, reporting, and assessment administration.
- Assessment tasks and practices should be shared with the broader
public through forums such as Websites and newspapers to promote public understanding and appreciation of the mathematics and science learning and assessment challenges provided to
Chicago's K–8 students.

The type of system needed has multiple components and it involves
multiple alignments. Figure 2.3 is a simplified representation of the
three principal assessment components of a comprehensive system
that supports both instructional and accountability purposes, and
the alignments of those components with each other and with state
learning standards and the new assessment frameworks that will
guide development of the ISAT for mathematics.

Establishing and mapping the separate and multiple alignments
shown in Figure 2.3 while also ensuring the separate and comple-
mentary roles of the three levels of assessment is a major design
challenge. Nevertheless, failure to consider all the elements is likely
to lead to an incomplete and/or incoherent assessment system with
potentially conflicting sources of information. In the following section we consider what is currently understood about the benchmark assessments, including the design challenges that need to be
addressed and next steps appropriate in building a comprehensive
aligned system that complements the curriculum-embedded assessment component of the larger system. The final two sections then
deal with other critical aspects of the design and operation of a
comprehensive assessment system: professional development of the

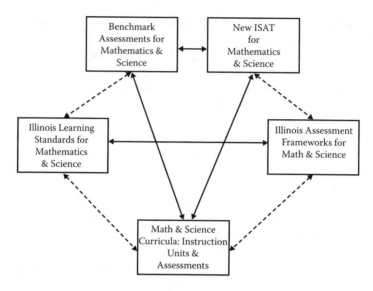

Figure 2.3 Components and alignments of a coordinated instructional and assessment system.

system's educators with respect to specific and general assessment literacies and the technology tools and infrastructure necessary to make the system work as intended.

Benchmark Assessment Components

A perfectly reasonable question to ask is why a benchmark assessment component is needed if there already is a classroom-based assessment component and a state-level accountability component. What purpose is served by an intermediate level of assessment that can add cost and complexity to the system? There are two primary answers to such a question, one of which has to do with the continuum of levels of transfer described earlier. The second has to do with differing time cycles and feedback loops that occur at different levels of the assessment system. The two issues can be taken together to offer the following rationale for development and deployment of a benchmark assessment system. Most classroom-and-curriculum embedded assessments are very near in time and format to the enactment of the instructional process, whereas most state-level assessments are very far in time and format from that same process. Thus, in the former case the assessment is a near-transfer test, whereas in the latter case it is a far-transfer test. There is no guarantee that the near-transfer test will serve as a good proxy or indicator of a student's likely performance on the far-transfer and high-stakes state accountability test. Thus the two forms of feedback differ in what they are likely to reveal about the state of a student's learning and knowledge. They also differ in the time cycle for the arrival of that feedback and the possibility for action—rapid feedback or extremely delayed feedback. An appropriately designed benchmark assessment system provides for an evaluation of student knowledge and performance at an intermediate level of transfer and on a time cycle that still allows for feedback to be used to influence teaching and learning within a school year and prior to administration of the high-stakes state accountability test. It can offer information of use for decision making at the school and classroom level and at the district level.

It is clear that the CMSI's mathematics (and science) curricula provide a variety of assessment resources intended to be used as an integral part of the teaching and learning processes within each of the curricula. Thus, a rich array of information is potentially available to teachers about the state of their students' understandings relative to important learning standards. It is also clear, however, that these assessments are intended to function close to the instructional process and that they vary considerably in how contextualized or "embedded" they are in the language and philosophy of each instructional program. Thus, they are not likely to serve as good measures of far transfer to performance on the ISAT. A further implication is that it is highly unlikely that any of the specific assessments found within a given curriculum can easily be lifted out of the program context to be used as part of a more general and less contextualized benchmark assessment program that would operate at a level above any specific curriculum, either those in use in the CMSI or across the district more generally. At the same time, however, a benchmark assessment program needs to be carefully designed to articulate with what is available at the classroom level, as illustrated in Figure 2.3.

The fact that the CMSI uses multiple curricula in mathematics across each of the two grade spans of K–5 and 6–8 creates a formidable challenge in designing a benchmark assessment program that articulates with the specific curricula and with the sequence of content covered within each curriculum. Not only do any benchmark assessment tasks need to make sense to students who have been engaged in the instructional and assessment practices of their given curriculum, but they need to be timed so that they occur at points where there is a high degree of certainty that students have had the opportunity to learn the specific knowledge and skills that are the focus of the specific assessment tasks. Although it is certainly the case that each mathematics curriculum within a given grade span appears to be well articulated with national and state standards for mathematics learning, the curricula do not necessarily follow the exact same sequence for content and standards coverage within a grade or across successive grades.

Designing an appropriate benchmark assessment system will require a very detailed analysis and mapping within and across curricula of the sequence of content coverage, the alignment with state learning standards and the new Illinois assessment frameworks, and the specific ways in which particular standards and content tend to be assessed. Without such a careful mapping it would be possible to generate and administer a set of benchmark assessments that would be unfair to students and uninformative to the teachers of those students as well as district staff wishing to monitor student progress in attaining the standards.

An additional issue that bears careful scrutiny in the design of a benchmark assessment system is the nature of the standards that would be the focus of the benchmark assessments and the degree of redundancy in information about attainment of standards desired between the benchmark assessments and the curriculum-embedded assessments. In essence, the issue to be resolved is how much the benchmark assessments are intended to serve as an indicator of states of knowledge and understanding not easily derived from the curriculum-embedded assessments, but are deemed developmentally important, versus how much the benchmark assessments are intended as a check on the information available to individual teachers about their students from the curriculum-embedded assessment procedures. Thus, the balance of the standards that are evaluated and the degree of overlap across levels of a system of assessments is not a simple matter. It is further complicated by simultaneous consideration of the relationship of the benchmark assessments to the high-stakes ISAT administered each year for grades 3–8 starting with the 2005–2006 academic year.

Many possible designs can be envisioned for a benchmark assessment system for mathematics; all involve tradeoffs. Participants in the discussion must include OMS leadership and staff, the district academic leadership, and district teachers and principals. Some of the design dimensions are identified below to indicate the areas still in need of discussion and planning.

- The frequency and timing of the administration of benchmark assessments.
- Whether the benchmark program should also include a beginning of the semester pretest and an end of academic year, cumulative posttest. The latter might be designed to focus on learning standards and complex forms of knowledge and skill that will inevitably be missing from the ISAT and are important instructional and learning goals.
- The amount of time to be allocated to the benchmark assessment process, whether it augments the classroom assessment resources or substitutes for some of those resources and activities and the mechanisms for assessment administration, scoring, interpretation, and discussion of results.
- Ways to ensure that teachers understand that the benchmark assessment component is a low-stakes, formative assessment activity while at the same time providing information of use at the district level to monitor performance.
- The role of the benchmark assessment information in professional development and instructional planning processes for teachers within each school.

Professional Development

Several pieces of evidence from our analyses of the mathematics curricula converge on the very strong conclusion that a substantial challenge in the effective use of the curricula chosen by CMSI for implementation at grades K–8 is adequate provision of professional development for teachers and other CMSI personnel targeted on understanding and using the assessment resources built into each of the curricula. There are two separate but related professional development needs with respect to use of curriculum-based assessment.

The first professional development target involves assisting teachers in understanding and using the range of assessment tasks available to them within a given curriculum. Such support needs to deal with two challenges currently facing CMSI teachers: (1) apprehending the nature of each assessment type and the overall system of assessments within the curriculum they are implementing; and (2) assisting teachers in interpreting the results that are likely to be returned from any given assessment, including what constitutes instructional in response to variations in student performance. Providing such professional development will be a challenge. It must be done in coordination with the professional development support staff inside and outside OMS who understand each curriculum in depth. A complicating factor is that these staff may not be able to provide answers to some of the more detailed questions about likely student performance outcomes for given tasks since it is not clear that the curriculum developers and publishers currently have such information available. These staff should, however, be able to provide detailed information and professional development support regarding the overall collection of assessment types within their respective curricula, each assessment's intended role in the instructional process, and where teachers can obtain additional information from the curricular reference materials. This type of professional development is needed not only by the teachers but also by CMSI specialists and OMS facilitators who are trying to support teachers on an ongoing basis. They too need to be fully conversant in the details of the assessment resources available within the various curricula, their intended use, and sources of information to support assessment as part of ongoing classroom instructional processes.

The second professional development need is at a level above a specific curriculum and can be characterized as general assessment literacy. In general, it appears that CPS's teachers and support staff have limited understanding of the distinctions among various purposes of assessment (including formative, summative, and program evaluation), the roles that each type of assessment plays in the educational process, and the differences among them in format and use. This is not intended as a criticism of CPS's teaching force since knowledge of these various roles and functions of assessment is seldom a part of typical teacher education or teacher professional development. Assessment literacy is a national teacher education issue and the local needs reflect national trends (e.g., Commission on Instructionally Supportive Assessment, 2001; Wilson & Bertenthal, 2005). Thus, for teachers to properly apprehend the assessment resources available within the curricula they are implementing, and to then relate assessment at that level to assessment at a benchmark level and at the state's high-stakes annual testing level, is a formidable challenge. Not only do teachers need to understand the distinctions among assessment types, purposes, and levels, but such professional development needs to be provided for a wide range of the district's personnel whose knowledge and actions affect teachers including principals, OMS staff, and members of the district's leadership.

Technology Tools and Infrastructure

Assessment results allow us to address a variety of questions about how a district, school, program, group, or individual is performing. The goal is to make assessment results available to the right people, in the right form, at the right time so that assessment informs decisions and actions. Before we can answer questions, we must have the assessment results to work with. The goal is to collect the results in timely and efficient ways that allow us to answer our most important questions. Finally, it is not enough to answer questions—we must act on those answers. The goal is to help people use assessment results to make decisions about what actions they should take. A *technology infrastructure* is a collection of tools and processes that help people achieve these goals.

Technology might play a variety of roles in this complex process. It is likely that a collection of tools, rather than a single tool, will fulfill these roles. However, information must flow appropriately between tools to support the differing needs of different people. Table 2.3 lists some of the roles that technology might play in the assessment process. Part of designing and implementing an assessment system for Chicago is determining the appropriate roles for technology in that system.

Our analyses of the curriculum-embedded assessments have major implications regarding technology support for the use of assessments at the classroom level and, more generally, in a system of assessments that includes benchmark assessment tasks. Given the

TABLE 2.3 Functions of Technology in Assisting the Assessment Process

Collecting	Reporting	Using
Create assessment	Manage assessment data	Identify resources
Administer assessment	Analyze assessment data	Identify possible actions
Collect assessment data	Create reports	Professional development
Score assessment	Distribute reports	

range of assessment tasks and data on student performance potentially available within each curriculum, it is clear that the processes
of collecting, scoring, and interpreting assessment data and then lon-
gitudinally tracking student performance are formidable. It is highly
unlikely that any teacher would be able to be successful in using all
the assessment data available to them without the support of technology tools to assist in such a process at the curriculum-embedded assessment level. Unfortunately, such tools are largely missing
from all of the curricula we studied. Thus, an important direction
for future development and implementation work is the design of
specific and general technology-based tools that can assist teachers in managing the assessment process within their curriculum.
Ideally, one would like to have a system with extensive diagnostic
assessment capability. That is potentially far off, however, and would
require a considerable development effort. Even so, some very basic
data collection, data entry, and data management tools could be of
great assistance to teachers.*

The design and deployment of even simple technology tools
must ultimately rely on a technology infrastructure that connects
the classroom to powerful database management and information
retrieval systems that operate within and across CPS. This is especially true when the classroom assessment data are viewed as part
of a coordinated system of assessment data that would potentially
include curriculum-embedded assessment information, benchmark
assessment data, and ISAT data. Further work addressing issues of
technology and the design of a comprehensive assessment system
would involve consideration of information and how it needs to
flow through this system. For example: Who needs to use assessment data? What questions need to be answered? In what timeframe
do they need to be answered? What actions might they take based
on these answers? Table 2.4 begins to speculate about some of these
issues, but additional input on specific information needs and data
management goals will be required from each of the major constitu-
encies in order to implement any comprehensive design within an
appropriate infrastructure.

---

* In current revisions of the various curricula, a range of technology-based tools are
  being designed for implementation in new curriculum materials. The nature of
  these tools in terms of quality and efficacy remains to be determined, however.

TABLE 2.4 Timeframes and Needs of Different Users of Assessment Information

	Timeframe					Sample Questions to Ask About Assessment Data
Level	Very Short Day/Week	Short Unit	Mid Semester	Long Year	Very Long Multi-Year	
District				▓	▓	• Is our district meeting its goals? • Are needs of all student groups being addressed? • How effective are different programs (e.g., curricula, initiatives)? • Which schools are making the most/least progress and why? • How is our district performing relative to other groups? • Where should resources be allocated?
School			▓	▓	▓	• Is our school meeting its goals? • How is our school performing relative to other schools? • Are needs of all student groups being addressed? • How well are our students meeting standards? • How effective are different programs in our school (e.g., curricula, initiatives)? • What are our problem areas? • What should we do to address these problems? • Where should resources be allocated?
School Sub-Group (e.g., grade 3 math teachers)		▓	▓	▓	▓	• How well are our students meeting standards? • Which students are having trouble? • What are students having trouble with? • What should we do to help students?

(continued)

TABLE 2.4 (CONTINUED) Timeframes and Needs of Different Users of Assessment Information

Level	Timeframe					Sample Questions to Ask About Assessment Data
	Very Short Day/Week	Short Unit	Mid Semester	Long Year	Very Long Multi-Year	
Classroom/Teacher						• How well are my students meeting standards? • How are my students performing relative to other groups? • Is my teaching effective with these students? • Which students are having trouble? • What are students having trouble with? • How can I adjust my teaching to help my students?
Parents						• How well is my child doing? • How is my child doing relative to other children in the class? • What can I do to help my child? • What can the school do to help my child? • How well is my child's school doing? • How is the school doing relative to other schools? • What can I do to help my child's school?
Public						• How are the schools in our area performing? • Are our schools meeting their goals? • How well are our students meeting standards? • How are they performing relative to other schools?

Concluding Comments

This chapter began by noting that despite all the rhetoric that has surrounded issues of assessment use in the educational system, we know remarkably little about one of the most important uses of assessment to support teaching and learning, namely, assessment at the classroom level embedded within instructional materials and programs. This is despite the fact that the limited evidence that does exist about the impact of classroom assessment on student learning indicates the possibility of profound positive effects. It is within that context that we have embarked on a process of analyzing the assessment materials and systems incorporated into four contemporary mathematics curricula for grades K–8. Our analyses reveal that the potential is there for assessment to have a major impact on teaching practices and student learning in each of the four curricula we studied. There are, however, many questions about the quality and functioning of those assessment materials that demand further empirical study.

Equally important is an understanding of the role of curriculum-embedded and classroom assessment in a larger system of assessments designed to provide coordinated and comprehensive information across levels of the educational system. The Chicago Public Schools have embarked on a path whereby they seek to achieve coherence in their mathematics instruction, and to align assessment with instruction and student learning. As we have argued, curriculum-embedded assessment constitutes one very critical element of a comprehensive system that aligns curriculum, instruction, and assessment, and which coordinates assessment functions across system levels and across time.

This is an ambitious and complicated design space, fraught with policy and practice challenges. Nevertheless, it is the path that needs to be traveled if we are to ever move beyond the debates and rhetoric about proper roles and balance of large-scale accountability tests, benchmark assessments, and classroom and curriculum-embedded assessments. Even more critically, we must recognize the proper role that each type of assessment can play in supporting the teaching and learning process and ensure a proper balance in the influence of assessment on instructional practice.

References

American Association for the Advancement of Science. (1993). *Benchmarks for science literacy.* Washington, DC: Author.

American Association for the Advancement of Science. (2001). *Atlas of science literacy.* Washington, DC: Author.

Ball, D. L. (2003). *Mathematical proficiency for all students.* Santa Monica, CA: RAND.

Bell, M., Bell, J., Bretzlauf, J., Dillard, A., Hartfield, R., Isaacs, A., et al. (2004). *Everyday mathematics.* Columbus, OH: McGraw-Hill.

Billstein, R., Williamson, J., Montoya, P., Lowery, J., Williams, D., Buck, M., et al. (1999). *Middle grades maththematics.* Evanston, IL: McDougal Littell.

Black, P., Harrison, C., Lee, C., Marshall, B., & Wiliam, D. (2004). *Assessment for learning–putting it into practice.* Buckingham, UK: Open University Press.

Black, P., & Wiliam, D. (1998). Assessment and classroom learning. *Assessment in Education, 5*(1), 7-73.

Chambers-Boucher, L. M., Colligan, E., Gartzman, M., Inzerillo, C., Kelso, C. R., Marsh, G. E., et al. (2003). *Math trailblazers* (2nd ed.). Dubuque, IA: Kendall/Hunt Publishing.

Commission on Instructionally Supportive Assessment. (2001). *Building tests to support instruction and accountability: A guide for policymakers.* Report commissioned by NEA, NAESP, NASSP, NMSP, & AASA. Retrieved October 3, 2005, from http://www.nea.org/accountability/buildingtests.html

Donovan, S., & Pellegrino, J. W. (2004). *Learning and instruction: A SERP research agenda.* Washington, DC: National Academy Press.

Hickey, D., & Pellegrino, J. W. (2005). Theory, level, and function: Three dimensions for understanding transfer and student assessment. In J. P. Mestre (Ed.), *Transfer of learning: Research and perspectives.* (pp. 251–293) Greenwich, CT: Information Age Publishing.

Illinois State Board of Education. (1997, July). *Illinois learning standards.* Retrieved October 3, 2005, from http://www.isbe.state.il.us/ils/Default.htm

Kilpatrick, J., Swafford, J., & Findell, B. (Eds.). (2001). *Adding it up: Helping children learn mathematics.* Washington, DC: National Research Council.

Lappan, G., Fey, J. T., Fitzgerald, W. M., Friel, S. N., & Phillips, E. D. (1998). *Connected mathematics.* Glenview, IL: Dale Seymour Publications.

National Council of Teachers of Mathematics. (1989). *Curriculum and evaluation standards for school mathematics.* Reston, VA: Author.

National Council of Teachers of Mathematics. (1995). *Assessment standards for school mathematics.* Reston, VA: Author.

National Council of Teachers of Mathematics. (2000). *Principles and standards for school mathematics*. Reston, VA: Author.

National Research Council. (1996). *National science education standards*. Washington, DC: National Academy Press.

National Council of Teachers of Mathematics. (2003). *Assessment in support of learning and instruction: Bridging the gap between large-scale and classroom assessment*. Committee on Assessment in Support of Learning and Instruction, Board on Testing and Assessment, Center for Education, Division of Behavioral and Social Sciences and Education. Washington, DC: National Academy Press.

Pellegrino, J. W., Baxter, G. P., & Glaser, R. (1999). Addressing the "two disciplines" problem: Linking theories of cognition and learning with assessment and instructional practice. In A. Iran-Nejad & P. D. Pearson (Eds.), *Review of research in education, 24*, 307-353. Washington, DC: American Educational Research Association.

Pellegrino, J. W., Chudowsky, N., & Glaser, R. (Eds.). (2001). *Knowing what students know: The science and design of educational assessment*. Washington, DC: National Academy Press.

Pellegrino, J. W., & Goldman, S. R. (2004). *The assessment resources available within the four standards-based K-8 mathematics curricula of the CMSI: A review, analysis and critique*. (Technical Report, Chicago Public Schools, Center for the Study of Learning, Instruction, and Teacher Development). Chicago: University of Illinois at Chicago.

Pellegrino, J. W., & Goldman, S. R. (2005). *Frameworks and methods for analyzing the assessment resources available within the four standards-based K-8 mathematics curricula of the CMSI*. (Technical Report, Chicago Public Schools, Center for the Study of Learning, Instruction, and Teacher Development). Chicago: University of Illinois at Chicago.

Roberts, L., & Wilson, M. (1998a, January). *Evaluating the effects of an integrated assessment system on science teachers' assessment perceptions and practice*. (BEAR Research Report Series, SA-98-1). Berkeley: University of California. Retrieved October 3, 2005, from http://bear.berkeley.edu/pub.html

Roberts, L., & Wilson, M. (1998b, February). *An integrated assessment system as a medium for teacher change and the organizational factors that mediate science teachers' professional development*. (BEAR Report Series, SA-98-2.). Berkeley: University of California. Retrieved October 3, 2005, from http://bear.berkeley.edu/pub.html

Roberts, L., Wilson, M., & Draney, K. (1997, June). *The SEPUP assessment system: An overview*. (BEAR Report Series, SA-97-1). Berkeley: University of California. Retrieved October 3, 2005, from http://bear.berkeley.edu/pub.html

Ruiz-Primo, M. A., Shavelson, R. J., Hamilton, L., & Klein, S. (2002). On the evaluation of systemic science education reform: Searching for instructional sensitivity. *Journal of Research in Science Teaching, 39,* 369-393.

Shepard, L. A. (2000). The role of assessment in a learning culture. *Educational Researcher, 29*(7), 4-14.

Sloane, K., Wilson, M., & Samson, S. (1996). *Designing an embedded assessment system: From principles to practice.* (BEAR Report Series, SA-96-1). Berkeley: University of California. Retrieved October 3, 2005, from http://bear.berkeley.edu/pub.html

Stiggins, R. J. (1997). *Student-centered classroom assessment.* Upper Saddle River, NJ: Prentice Hall.

Stiggins, R. (2001). The unfilled promise of classroom assessment. *Educational Measurement: Issues and Practice, 20,* 5-15.

Stiggins, R. (2002). Assessment crisis: The absence of assessment for learning. *Phi Delta Kappan, 83*(10), 758-765.

Webb, N. L. (1997). *Criteria for alignment of expectations and assessments in mathematics and science education.* (Research Monograph No. 6). Washington, DC: National Institute for Science Education and Council of Chief State School Officers.

Wiggins, G. (1998). *Educative assessment: Designing assessments to inform and improve student performance.* San Francisco: Jossey-Bass.

Wilson, M., & Bertenthal, M. (2005). *Systems for state science assessment.* Washington, DC: National Academy Press.

Wilson, M., & Sloane, K. (2000). From principles to practice: An embedded assessment system. *Applied Measurement in Education, 13*(2), 181-208.

3

Integrating Assessment with Learning:
What Will It Take to Make It Work?

Dylan Wiliam
Institute of Education, University of London

Marnie Thompson
RPM Data

Introduction

Improving education is a priority for all countries. Increasing the level of educational achievement brings benefits to the individual, such as higher lifetime earnings, and to society as a whole, both in terms of increased economic growth and lower social costs such as health care and criminal justice costs (Gritz & MaCurdy, 1992; Hanushek, 2004; Levin, 1972; Tyler, Murnane, & Willett, 2000). Indeed, the total return on investments in education can be well over $10 for every $1 invested (Schweinhart et al., 2005). This means that even loosely focused investments in education are likely to be cost-effective. Given public skepticism about such long-term investments, however, and given too the reluctance of local, state, and federal governments to raise taxes, there is a pressing need to find the most cost-effective ways of improving student achievement.

Unfortunately, for many years, analysis of school effectiveness focused primarily on easily collected outputs such as average school test scores, and, given the huge differences in the achievement of students entering different schools, between-school differences (what we might call the school effect) appeared to be much larger than within-school differences (such as classroom effects). As disaggregated and longitudinal datasets have become more available, however, it has become possible to look at how much *progress* each student makes (sometimes called "value-added modeling"). Obviously, the estimates of the relative sizes of school and teacher effects will vary according to the models used, but it is quite common to find that the variability of the teacher effect is much greater than the variability of the school effect (although, as Bryk & Raudenbush [1988] note, disentangling these two effects is very difficult). In other words, it seems to matter more which teachers you get in a particular school than which school you go to. Perhaps more importantly, the effect of having a good teacher appears to be far greater than that of being in a small school or even of being in a small class.

Hanushek (2004) estimates that students taught by a teacher who is 1 standard deviation (SD) better than the average—i.e., at the 84th percentile of effectiveness—will achieve .22 SD higher than those taught by the average teacher. Consequently, students taught by a teacher at the 95th percentile of effectiveness will achieve .36 SD higher than those taught by average teachers. Because the annual increase in average achievement found in National Assessment of Educational Progress (NAEP) studies is less than one-third of a standard deviation (see, for example, NAEP, 2006), this means that students taught by one of the best teachers will learn in 6 months what students taught by an average teacher would take a year to learn.

This kind of effect is much greater than is found in most class-size reduction studies. For example, Jepsen and Rivkin (2002) found that reducing elementary school class size by 10 students would increase the proportion of students passing typical mathematics and reading tests by 4% and 3% in math and reading, respectively, equivalent to a standardized effect size of approximately .1 SD for math and .075 for reading. In other words, increasing teacher quality by 1 standard deviation would produce between two and three times the increase in student achievement yielded by reducing class size by 10 students. The challenge of improving student achievement at reasonable cost therefore effectively reduces to a labor force problem with two possible solutions: replacing the teachers we have with better teachers, or improving the teachers we have.

Hanushek (2004) shows that over time even small changes in the way that teachers are hired can lead to large improvements in the quality of the teaching force. Keeping the quality of the teaching force as it is requires hiring at the 50th percentile—this way, the new teachers are just as good as the ones who are leaving. Hiring instead at the 58th percentile would, in 30 years, increase student achievement by 1 SD (and, incidentally, add 10% to per capita GDP). There is, however, little evidence that this would be possible. Some have argued that there are large numbers of prospective teachers who would be effective practitioners but who are deterred by burdensome requirements for certification and/or inadequate remuneration (see, e.g., Hess, Rotherham, & Walsh, 2004). Evidence from recent studies suggests, however, that teachers admitted via alternate routes are no more effective than those who follow traditional certification paths (Darling-Hammond, Holtzman, Gatlin, & Vasquez Heilig, 2005), and there is no evidence yet that raising teacher pay attracts better teachers or results in improvements in student learning. In other words, even if one were motivated solely by economic considerations, any significant improvement in educational outcomes will require developing the capability of the existing workforce rather than looking for ways of replacing it—what might be called the "love the one you're with" approach.

Fifteen or 20 years ago, this would have resulted in a gloomy prognosis. There was little if any evidence that the quality of teachers could be improved through teacher professional development, and certainly not at scale. Indeed, there was a widespread belief that teacher professional development had simply failed to "deliver the goods." "Nothing has promised so much and has been so frustratingly wasteful as the thousands of workshops and conferences that led to no significant change in practice when teachers returned to their classrooms" (Fullan, 1991, p. 315).

Within the past few years, however, a clearer picture of the features of effective teacher professional development has begun to emerge. First, teacher professional development needs to attend to both *process* and *content* elements (Reeves, McCall, & MacGilchrist, 2001; Wilson & Berne, 1999). On the process side, professional development is more effective when it is related to the local circumstances in which the teachers operate (Cobb, McClain, Lamberg, & Dean, 2003), takes place over a period of time rather than being in the form of one-day workshops (Cohen & Hill, 1998), and involves the teacher in active, collective participation (Garet, Birman, Porter, Desimone, & Herman, 1999). It is important to note, however, that some foci for teacher professional development are more productive than others. In particular, professional development is more effective when it has a focus on deepening teachers' knowledge of the content they are to teach, the possible responses of students, and strategies that can be utilized to build on these (Supovitz, 2001). Many approaches satisfy both these process and content considerations, such as lesson study (Fernandez & Yoshida, 2004). In this chapter we will argue that a focus on the use of assessment in support of learning, developed through teacher learning communities (TLCs), promises not only the largest potential gains in student achievement but also provides a model for teacher professional development that can be implemented effectively at scale.

In the following sections, we outline the research on the use of assessment to support learning, sometimes termed formative assessment or assessment for learning, and how the key ideas of formative assessment can be integrated within the broader theoretical framework of the regulation of learning processes. We then summarize briefly the research on teacher learning communities as a powerful mechanism for teacher change, and show how TLCs are perhaps uniquely suited to improving teachers' capabilities in using assessment in the service of learning.

Formative Assessment

In 1967, Michael Scriven proposed the use of the terms "formative" and "summative" to distinguish between different roles that evaluation might play. On the one hand, he pointed out that evaluation "may have a role in the on-going improvement of the curriculum" (p. 41), while on the other, evaluation "may serve to enable administrators to decide whether the entire finished curriculum, refined by use of the evaluation process in its first role, represents a sufficiently significant advance on the available alternatives to justify the expense of adoption by a school system" (pp. 41–42). He then proposed "to use the terms 'formative' and 'summative' evaluation to qualify evaluation in these roles" (p. 43).

Two years later, Benjamin Bloom (1969) applied the same distinction to classroom tests.

Quite in contrast is the use of "formative evaluation" to provide feedback and correctives at each stage in the teaching-learning process. By formative evaluation we mean evaluation by brief tests used by teachers and students as aids in the learning process. While such tests may be graded and used as part of the judging and classificatory function of evaluation, we see much more effective use of formative evaluation if it is separated from the grading process and used primarily as an aid to teaching. (p. 48)

And there, for a while, things rested. Everyone agreed that formative assessment was "a good thing"; people occasionally used the terms "formative" and "summative" to denote different kinds of assessments, and, when asked, teachers typically said that they did indeed use the results of their assessments to make instructional decisions. The kinds of decisions that teachers made, and the kinds of evidence that informed them were rarely examined, however. When the evidence about teacher practice did begin to emerge, it was clear that the way that teachers actually used assessment evidence to inform instruction was rarely in the way that Bloom and others had envisaged.

Stiggins and Bridgeford (1985) found that although many teachers created their own assessments, "in at least a third of the structured performance assessments created by these teachers, important assessment procedures appeared not to be followed" (p. 282); and "in an average of 40% of the structured performance assessments, teachers rely on mental record-keeping" (p. 283). A few years later, two substantial review articles, one by Natriello (1987) and the other by Crooks (1988), provided clear evidence that classroom evaluation practices had substantial impact on students and their learning, although the impact was rarely beneficial. Natriello's review used a model of the assessment cycle, beginning with purposes; and moving on to the setting of tasks, criteria, and standards; evaluating performance and providing feedback; and then discussing the impact of these evaluation processes on students. His most significant point was that the vast majority of the research he cited was largely irrelevant because of weak theorization, which resulted in the conflation of key distinctions such as the quality and quantity of feedback.

Crooks's paper had a narrower focus—the impact of evaluation practices on students. He concluded that the summative function of assessment had been too dominant and that more emphasis should be given to the potential of classroom assessments to assist learning. Most importantly, assessments should emphasize the skills, knowledge, and attitudes regarded as most important, not just those that are easy to assess. The difficulty of reviewing relevant research in this area was highlighted by Black and Wiliam (1998a) in their synthesis of research published since the Natriello and Crooks reviews. The two earlier papers had cited 91 and 241 references, respectively, and yet only 9 references were common to both papers. In their own research, Black and Wiliam found that electronic searches based on keywords either generated far too many irrelevant sources or omitted key papers. In the end, they resorted to manual searches of each issue between 1987 and 1997 of 76 of the journals considered most likely to contain relevant research. Black and Wiliam's review (which cited 250 studies) found that effective use of classroom assessment yielded improvements in student achievement of between .4 and .7 SD. A more recent review focusing on studies in higher education (Nyquist, 2003) found similar results.

Thirty-five years ago, Bloom had suggested that "evaluation in relation to the process of learning and teaching can have strong positive effects on the actual learning of students as well as on their motivation for the learning and their self-concept in relation to school learning…. [E]valuation which is directly related to the teaching-learning process as it unfolds can have highly beneficial effects on the learning of students, the instructional process of teachers, and the use of instructional materials by teachers and learners" (1969, p. 50). At the time, Bloom cited no evidence in support of this claim, but it is probably safe to conclude that the question has now been settled: Attention to classroom assessment practices can indeed have a substantial impact on student achievement. What is less clear is what exactly constitutes effective classroom assessment, and how the gains in student achievement that the research shows are possible can be achieved at scale. These two issues are the main focus of this chapter.

The Nature and Purpose of Assessments

Educational assessments are conducted in a variety of ways and their outcomes can be used for a variety of purposes. There are differences in who decides what is to be assessed, who carries out the assessment, where the assessment takes place, how the resulting responses made by students are scored and interpreted, and what happens as a result. In particular, each of these can be the responsibility of those who teach the students. At the other extreme, all can be carried out by an external agency. Cutting across these differences, there are also differences in the purposes that assessments serve. Broadly, educational assessments serve three functions.

- Supporting learning (formative)
- Certifying the achievements or potential of individuals (summative)
- Evaluating the quality of educational institutions or programs (evaluative)

Through a series of historical contingencies, we have arrived at a situation in many countries in which the *circumstances* of the assessments have become conflated with the *purposes* of the assessment (Black & Wiliam, 2004a). So, for example, it is often widely assumed that the role of classroom assessment should be limited to supporting learning and that all assessments with which we can hold educational institutions to account must be conducted by an external agency, even though in some countries this is not the case (Black & Wiliam, 2005a).

In broad terms, moving from formative through summative to evaluative functions of assessment requires data at increasing levels of aggregation, from the individual to the institution, and from specifics of particular skills and weaknesses to generalities about overall levels of performance. (Although, of course, evaluative data may still be disaggregated in order to identify specific sub-groups in the population not making progress, or to identify particular weaknesses in student performance in specific areas, as is the case in France [see Black & Wiliam, 2005a].) It is also clear, however, that the different functions that assessments may serve are not easy to reconcile. For example, when information about student performance on standardized tests is used to hold schools and districts accountable, there is pressure on teachers to raise student performance even at the expense of narrowing the curriculum. As has been shown by the work of Linn and others (see, for example, Linn, 1995), increases in test scores may indicate only that students are better at doing the specific items in the test. In such cases, the test score provides little information about the aspects of achievement not specifically tested.

For similar reasons, it has been argued that the uses of assessment to support learning and to certify the achievements of individuals are so fundamentally in tension that the same assessments cannot serve both functions adequately (Torrance, 1993). Elsewhere, in a series of papers summarized in Newton (2003) and in Wiliam (2003a), one of us has sketched out how an assessment system might be designed to serve all three functions reasonably well. There are, of course, particular difficulties in implementing such systems where there is a history of students being required to take tests that have little or no consequences for them, as is the case in the United States. For the purposes of this chapter, however, the crucial point is that whatever methods are used for assessing student achievement for summative purposes, assessment still has a role to play in supporting learning. Whether the assessment of student performance for purposes of selection and certification, or for evaluation, is conducted through teacher judgment, external assessments, or some combination of the two, classroom assessment must first be designed to support learning (see Black & Wiliam, 2004b, for a more detailed argument on this point). The remainder of this chapter considers further how this might be done.

What Is Formative Assessment?

In the United States, the term "formative assessment" is often used to describe assessments that are used to provide information on the likely performance of students on state-mandated tests—a usage that might better be described as "early-warning summative." In other contexts, the term is used to describe any feedback given to students, no matter what use is made of it, such as telling students which items they got correct and incorrect (sometimes called "knowledge of results"). These kinds of usages suggest that the distinction between "formative" and "summative" applies to the assessments themselves, but because the same assessment can be used both formatively and summatively, as Scriven and Bloom realized, it suggests that these terms are more usefully applied to the *use* to which the information arising from assessments is put.

In some contexts, assessments that are used to support learning are described under the broad heading "assessment for learning" (in contrast to "assessment *of* learning"). This does suggest a process, rather than being a description of the nature of the assessment itself, but the danger here is that the focus is placed on the intention behind the use of the assessment, rather than action that actually takes place (Wiliam & Black, 1996). Many writers use the terms "assessment for learning" and "formative assessment" interchangeably, but Black, Harrison, Lee, Marshall, and Wiliam (2003, p. 8; Wiliam, Lee, Harrison, & Black, 2004) distinguish between the two as follows.

> Assessment for learning is any assessment for which the first priority in its design and practice is to serve the purpose of promoting pupils' learning. It thus differs from assessment designed primarily to serve the purposes of accountability, or of ranking, or of certifying competence. An assessment activity can help learning if it provides information to be used as feedback, by teachers, and by their pupils, in assessing themselves and each other, to modify the teaching and learning activities in which they are engaged. Such assessment becomes "formative assessment" when the evidence is actually used to adapt the teaching work to meet learning needs.

For the purpose of this chapter, then, the qualifier "formative" will refer not to an assessment, nor even to the purpose of an assessment, but to the function it actually serves. An assessment is formative to the extent that information from the assessment is fed back within the system and actually used to improve the performance of the system in some way (i.e., the assessment *forms* the direction of the improvement).

So, for example, if a student is told that she needs to work harder, and does work harder as a result, and consequently does indeed make improvements in her performance, this would *not* be formative. The feedback would be *causal*, in that it did trigger the improvement in performance, but not *formative*, because decisions about *how* to "work harder" were left to the student. Telling students to "Give more detail" might be formative, but only if the students knew what giving more detail meant (which is unlikely, because if they knew what detail was required, they would probably have provided it on the first occasion). Similarly, a "formative assessment" that predicts which students are likely to fail the forthcoming state-mandated test is not formative unless the information from the test can be used to improve the quality of the learning within the system. To be formative, feedback needs to contain an implicit or explicit recipe for future action. Sometimes this recipe will be explicit, for example, when the feedback identifies specific activities the student is to undertake. At other times, the recipe may be implicit, such as those cases where the teacher has created a culture in the classroom whereby students know they must incorporate any feedback from the teacher into future drafts. Where the teacher relies on implicit recipes, it is of course incumbent on the teacher to check that the students' understanding of the classroom culture is the same as the teacher's.

Another way of thinking about the distinction being made here is in terms of monitoring assessment, diagnostic assessment, and formative assessment. An assessment *monitors* learning to the extent that it provides information about whether the student, class, school, or system is learning or not; it is *diagnostic* to the extent that it provides information about what is going wrong; and it is *formative* to the extent that it provides information about what to do about it. A sports metaphor may be helpful here. Consider a young softball pitcher who has an earned run average of 10 (for readers who know nothing about softball, that's not good). This is the *monitoring* assessment. Analysis of what she is doing shows that she is trying to pitch a rising fastball (i.e., one that actually rises as it gets near the plate, due to the back-spin applied), but that this pitch is not rising, and therefore ends up as an ordinary fastball in the middle of the strike zone, which is very easy for the batter to hit. This is the *diagnostic* assessment, but it is of little help to the pitcher, because she already knows that her rising fastball is not rising, and that's why she is giving up a lot of runs. If a pitching coach is able to see that she is not dropping her pitching shoulder sufficiently to allow her to deliver the pitch from below the knee, then this assessment has the potential to be not just diagnostic, but *formative*. It provides the athlete with some concrete actions she can undertake in order to improve. This use of formative recalls the original meaning of the term. In the same way that an individual's formative experiences are the experiences that shape the individual, formative assessments are those that shape learning. The important point is that not all diagnoses are *instructionally tractable*—an assessment can accurately diagnose what needs attention without indicating what needs to be done to address the issue.

This was implicit in Ramaprasad's (1983) definition of feedback. According to Ramaprasad, a defining feature of feedback was that it had an impact on the performance on the system. Information that did not have the capacity to improve the performance of the system was not feedback. "Feedback is information about the gap between the actual level and the reference level of a system parameter which is used to alter the gap in some way" (p. 4).

In this view, formative assessments (feedback, in Ramaprasad's terminology) cannot be separated from their instructional consequences, and assessments are formative only to the extent that they impact learning (for an extended discussion on consequences as the key part of the validity of formative assessments, see Wiliam & Black, 1996). The other important feature of Ramaprasad's definition is that it draws attention to three key instructional processes.

- Establishing where the learners are in their learning
- Establishing where they are going
- Establishing what needs to be done to get them there

Traditionally, this may have been seen as the teacher's job, but we need also to take account of the role that the learners themselves, and their peers, play in these processes. The framework shown in Table 3.1 provides a way of thinking about the key strategies involved in formative assessment with regard to the "players" or actors in the classroom. Table 3.1 could be extended to include schools, districts, or systems. Because the stance taken in this chapter is that ultimately, assessment must feed into actions in the classroom in order to affect learning, this simplification seems reasonable.

TABLE 3.1   Framework Relating Strategies of Formative Assessment to Instructional Processes

	Where the Learner Is Going	Where the Learner Is Right Now	How to Get There
Teacher	Clarifying and sharing learning intentions and criteria for success	Engineering effective classroom discussions and tasks that elicit evidence of learning	Providing feedback that moves learners forward
Peer	Understanding and sharing learning intentions and criteria for success	Activating students as instructional resources for one another	
Learner	Understanding learning intentions and criteria for success	Activating students as the owners of their own learning	

This framework suggests that formative assessment, or assessment for learning, can be conceptualized as consisting of five key strategies and one "big idea." The five key strategies are:

1. Clarifying and sharing learning intentions and criteria for success
2. Engineering effective classroom discussions, questions, and learning tasks that elicit evidence of learning
3. Providing feedback that moves learners forward
4. Activating students as instructional resources for one another
5. Activating students as the owners of their own learning

The "big idea" is that evidence about student learning is used to adjust instruction to better meet student needs—in other words, that teaching is *adaptive* to the student's learning needs.

Details of how teachers have used these strategies to implement assessment for learning in their classrooms can be found in Leahy, Lyon, Thompson, and Wiliam (2005). In the remainder of this chapter, we discuss how formative assessment may be integrated theoretically with instructional design and implemented in classrooms.

Formative Assessment and the Regulation of Learning

Although the starting point for work on formative assessment was the relatively simple idea of feedback, the formulation above presents a rather complex picture of formative assessment, and the ways in which the elements within Table 3.1 relate to each other are not straightforward. All the elements in Table 3.1 can, however, be integrated within the more general theoretical framework of the *regulation of learning processes* as suggested by Perrenoud (1991, 1998). The word "regulation" has an unfortunate connotation in English, stemming from the idea of "rules and regulations." In French, there are two ways to translate the word regulation—*règlement* and *régulation*. The former has the connotation of rules and regulations, while the latter connotes adjustment, for example, in the way that a thermostat regulates the temperature of a room. It is the latter sense that the word is used in the idea of the regulation of learning, and although the term *regulation* is not ideal to describe this sense in English, in this chapter we will continue its use, not least because of the absence of a suitable alternative.

Within such a framework, the actions of the teacher, the learners, and the context of the classroom are all evaluated with respect to guiding the learning toward the intended goal. In this context, it is important to note that teachers do not create learning; only learners can create learning. In the past, this has resulted in calls for a shift in the role of the teacher from the "sage on the stage" to the "guide on the side." The danger with such a characterization is that it is often interpreted as relieving the teacher of responsibility for ensuring that learning takes place. What we propose here is that the teacher be regarded as responsible for "engineering" a learning environment, both in its design and its operation.

The key features of an effective learning environment are that it creates student engagement and that it is well regulated. As a growing body of research on cognitive development shows, the level of engagement in cognitively challenging environments influences not only achievement but also IQ itself (Dickens & Flynn, 2001; Mercer, Dawes, Wegerif, & Sams, 2004). As well as creating engagement, effective learning environments need to be designed so that, as far as possible, they afford or scaffold the learning that is intended (*proactive* regulation). In addition, if the intended learning is not occurring, then this becomes apparent, so that appropriate adjustments may be made (*interactive* regulation).

It is important to distinguish between the regulation of the activity in which the student engages and the regulation of the learning that results. Most teachers appear to be quite skilled at the former, but have only a hazy idea of the learning that results. For example, when asked, "What are your learning intentions for this lesson?" many teachers reply by saying things such as, "I'm going to have them describe a friend," conflating the learning intention with the activity (Clarke, 2003). In a way, this is understandable, because only the activities can be manipulated directly. Nevertheless, it is clear that in teachers who have developed their formative assessment practices, there is a strong shift in emphasis away from regulating the activities in which students engage, toward the learning that results (Black et al., 2003).

Proactive regulation is achieved "upstream" of the lesson itself (i.e., before the lesson begins), through the setting up of "didactical situations" (Brousseau, 1984). The regulation can be unmediated within such didactical situations, when, for example, a teacher "does not intervene in person, but puts in place a 'metacognitive culture,' mutual forms of teaching and the organisation of regulation of learning processes run by technologies or incorporated into classroom organisation and management" (Perrenoud, 1998, p. 100). For example, a teacher's decision to use realistic contexts in the mathematics classroom can provide a source of regulation, because then students can determine the reasonableness of their answers. If students calculate that the average cost per slice of pizza (say) is $200, provided they are genuinely engaged in the activity, they will know that this solution is unreasonable. In this way, the use of realistic settings provides a "self-checking" mechanism. Similarly, if a teacher spends time creating a culture in the classroom in which students are used to consulting and supporting each other in productive ways, then this contributes to keeping the learning "on track."

On the other hand, the didactical situation may be set up so that the regulation is achieved through the mediation of the teacher—*interactive* regulation—when the teacher, in planning the lesson, creates questions, prompts, or activities that evoke responses from the students that the teacher can use to determine the progress of the learning, and if necessary, to make adjustments. Sometimes, these questions or prompts will be open-ended questions requiring higher-order thinking—indeed, such questions are essential to creating learning environments that create student engagement. But it also important to note that closed questions have a role here too. For example, questions such as "Is calculus exact or approximate?", "What is the pH of 10 molar NaOH?", or "Would your mass be the same on the moon?" are all closed questions, but are valuable because they frequently reveal student conceptions different from those intended by the teacher. Many students believe that calculus is approximate because δx approaches zero, but is not allowed actually to be zero. The pH of 10 molar NaOH is greater than 14, and thus many students think they must have made an error in their calculations because their use of the standard pH indicator has led them to believe that pH cannot be above 14. And although many students know that mass and weight are different, they do not realize that one's mass would be exactly the same on the moon, even though one's weight would be much less. It is possible that these questions may not cause thinking at least for some students, but they do provide the teacher with evidence that can be used to adapt instruction to better meet the students' learning needs.

"Upstream" planning of good questions such as those above therefore creates "downstream" the possibility that the learning activities may change course in light of the student responses. These "moments of contingency"—points in the instructional sequence when the instruction can proceed in different directions according to the responses of the students—are at the heart of the regulation of learning.

These moments arise continuously in whole-class teaching, where teachers are constantly having to make sense of student responses, interpreting them in terms of learning needs, and making appropriate responses. But they also arise when the teacher circulates around the classroom, looking at an individual student's work, observing the extent to which the students are "on track." In most teaching of mathematics and science, the regulation of learning will be relatively tight, so that the teacher will attempt to "bring into line" all learners who are not heading toward the particular goal sought by the teacher—in these subjects, the *telos* of learning is generally both highly specific and common to all the students in a class. In contrast, in much teaching in language arts and social studies, the regulation will be much looser. Rather than a single goal, there is likely to be a broad *horizon* of appropriate goals (Marshall, 2004), all of which are acceptable, and the teacher will intervene to bring the learners "into line" only when the trajectory of the learner is radically different from that intended by the teacher. Having said this, where a science class is considering the ethical impact of scientific discoveries, or a math class is pursuing an open-ended mathematical investigation, then the regulation is likely to be more like that in the typical language arts classroom. Conversely, where the language arts teacher is covering the conventions of grammar, the regulation is likely to be more like the typical mathematics or science lesson.

Finally, it is worth noting that there are significant differences in how such information is used. In the United States, the teacher will typically intervene with individual students when they appear not to be "on track," whereas in Japan the teacher is far more likely to observe all the students carefully while walking around the class and then will select some major issues for discussion with the whole class.

One of the features that makes a lesson "formative," then, is that the lesson can change course in the light of evidence about the progress of learning. This is in stark contrast to the "traditional" pattern of classroom interaction, exemplified by the following extract:

"Yesterday we talked about triangles, and we had a special name for triangles with three sides the same. Anyone remember what it was?... Begins with E...equi-...."

In terms of formative assessment, there are two salient points about such an exchange. First, little is contingent on the responses of the students, except how long it takes to get on to the next part of the teacher's "script," so there is little scope for "downstream" regulation. The teacher is interested only in getting to the word "equilateral" in order that she can move on. The teacher treats all incorrect responses as equivalent in terms of information content; all the teacher learns is that the students didn't "get it."

The second point is that the situation that the teacher set up in the first place—the question she chose to ask—has little potential for providing the teacher with useful information about the students' thinking, except, possibly, whether the students can recall the word "equilateral." This is typical in situations where the questions that the teacher uses in whole-class interaction have not been prepared in advance (in other words, when there is little or no proactive regulation).

Similar considerations apply when the teacher collects the students' notebooks and attempts to give helpful feedback to the students in the form of comments on how to improve rather than grades or percentage scores. If sufficient attention has not been given "upstream" to the design of the tasks given to the students so that they elicit conceptual thinking on the part of students, then the teacher may find that she has nothing useful to say to the students. Ideally, from examining the students' responses to the task, the teacher would be able to judge (a) how to help the learners learn better and (b) what she might do to improve the teaching of this topic to a future class, thus providing a third form of regulation— *retroactive* regulation. In this way, the assessment could be formative for the students, through the feedback the teacher provides, and formative for the teacher herself, in that appropriate analysis of the students' responses might suggest how the lesson could be improved for other students.

A common misconception about assessment—one held by both teachers and administrators—is that testing more frequently makes that testing formative. When, however, we think of formative assessment within the framework of regulation of learning, we can see that frequency alone does not guarantee that the information is used to regulate teaching or learning. Frequent assessment can identify students who are not making as much progress as expected (whether this expectation is based on some notion of "ability," prior achievement, or external demands made by the state). But frequent summative testing—we might call this micro-summative—is not formative unless the information that the tests yield is used in some way to modify instruction (see next section).

System Responsiveness and Timeframes

Although the examples given above have focused on the classroom, it is important to note that assessments can also be formative at the level of the school, district, and state, provided the assessments help to regulate learning. A key issue in the design of assessment systems, if they are to function formatively as well as summatively, is the extent to which the system can respond in a timely manner to the information made available. Feedback loops need to be designed taking account of the responsiveness of the system to the actions that can be used to improve its performance. The less responsive the system, the longer the feedback loops need to be for the system to be able to react appropriately.

For example, analysis of the patterns of student responses on a "trial run" of a state-mandated test in a given school district might indicate that the responses made by students in seventh grade on items involving (say) probability were lower than would be expected given the students' scores on the other items, and lower than the scores of comparable students in other districts. One response to this could be a program of professional development on teaching probability for the seventh-grade mathematics teachers in that district. Since this would take some weeks to arrange, and even longer for it to have an effect, the trial run would need to be held some months before the state-mandated test in order to provide time for the system to interpret the data in terms of the system's needs. The trial run would be formative for the district if, and only if, the information generated were used to improve the performance of the system—and if the data from the assessment actually helped to form the direction of the action taken.

For an individual teacher, the feedback loops can be considerably shorter. A teacher might look through the same students' responses to a trial run of a state test and re-plan the topics that she is going to teach in the time remaining until the test. Such a test would be useful as little as a week or two before the state-mandated test, as long as there is time to use the information to re-direct the teaching. Again, this assessment would be formative as long as the information from the test was actually used to adapt the teaching, and in particular, not only told the teacher which topics needed to be re-taught but also suggested what kinds of re-teaching might produce better results.

Built-in time for pedagogical responses to data from assessment is a central feature of much elementary and middle school teaching in Japan. A teaching unit is typically allocated 14 lessons, but the planned content usually occupies only 10 or 11 of the lessons, allowing time for a short test to be given in the 12th lesson, and for the teacher to use lessons 13 and 14 to re-teach aspects of the unit that were not well understood.

Another example, on an even shorter timescale, is the use of "exit passes" from a lesson. The idea here is that before leaving a classroom, each student must compose an answer to a question that goes to the heart of the concept being taught at the end of the lesson. On a lesson on probability, for example, such a question might be, "Why can't a probability be greater than 1?" Once the students have left, the teacher can look at their responses and make appropriate adjustments in the plan for the next period of instruction.

The shortest feedback loops are those involved in the day-to-day classroom practices of teachers, where teachers adjust their teaching in light of students' responses to questions or other prompts in "real time." The key point in all this is that the length of the feedback loop should be tailored according to the ability of the system to react to the feedback.

This does not mean, however, that the responsiveness of the system cannot be changed. Through appropriate proactive regulation, responsiveness can be enhanced considerably. Where teachers have collaborated to anticipate the responses that students might make to a question and what misconceptions would lead to particular incorrect responses, for example, through the process of Lesson Study practiced in Japan (Lewis, 2002), teachers are able to adapt their instruction much more quickly, even to the extent of having alternative instructional episodes ready. In this way, feedback to the teacher that, in the normal course of things, might need at least a day to be used to modify instruction, could affect instruction immediately.

TABLE 3.2   Cycle Lengths for Different Kinds of Formative Assessment

Type	Focus	Length
Long cycle	Across marking periods, quarters, semesters, years	4 weeks to 1 year
Medium cycle	Within and between instructional units	1 to 4 weeks
Short cycle	Within and between lessons	
Day by day		24 to 48 hours
Minute by minute		5 seconds to 2 hours

In the same way, a school district or state that has thought about how it might use the information about student performance before student results are available (for example, by the preparation of particular kinds of diagnostic reports—see Wiliam, 1999) is likely to reduce considerably the time needed to use the information to improve instruction. As in classroom examples, attention to regulation "upstream" pays dividends "downstream."

All this suggests that the conflicting uses of the term "formative assessment" can be reconciled by recognizing that virtually any assessment can be formative, provided it is used to make instructional adjustments and that a crucial difference between different assessments is the length of the adjustment cycle. A terminology for the different lengths of cycles is given in Table 3.2.

Putting It Into Practice

No matter how elegantly we formulate our ideas about formative assessment, they will be moot unless we can find ways of supporting teachers in incorporating more attention to assessment in their own practice. There are, of course, other ways that educational research can influence practice, such as through the design of curricula and textbooks, although as Clements (2002) notes, these impacts are generally small, perhaps due to the particular ways in which curriculum materials are actually used by teachers (Ball & Cohen, 1996; Remillard, 2005). If educational research is to have any lasting impact on practice, it must be taken up and used by practitioners. Traditionally, researchers have engaged in a process of "disseminating" their work to teachers, or engaging in "knowledge transfer." Both of these metaphors have some utility, but they suggest that all researchers need to do is to "share the results" (English, Jones, Lesh, Tirosh, & Bussi, 2002, p. 805) of their research with practitioners and the findings will somehow be used.

The emerging research on expertise shows, however, that the process of "knowledge transfer" cannot be one of providing instructions to novices or other non-expert teachers in the hope that they will get better (see Wiliam, 2003b, for more on this point). This is because, put simply, all research findings are generalizations and as such are either too general to be useful or too specific to be universally applicable. For example, research on feedback, such as the work of Kluger and DeNisi (1996), suggests that task-involving feedback is to be preferred to ego-involving feedback, but what the teacher needs to know is, "Can I say, 'Well done' to this student, now?" Put crudely, such generalizations underdetermine action.

At the other end of the expertise continuum, expert teachers can often see that a particular recipe for action proposed by a researcher is inappropriate in some circumstances in his or her classroom. Because their reaction is intuitive, however, they may not be able to discern the reason why they believe it is inappropriate in those circumstances, and they conclude that the findings of educational research are not a valid guide to action.

The difficulty of "putting research into practice" is the fault neither of the teacher nor of the researcher. Because our understanding of the theoretical principles underlying successful classroom action is weak, research cannot tell teachers what to do. Indeed, given the complexity of classrooms, it seems likely that the positivist dream of an effective theory of teacher action—which would spell out the "best" course of action given certain conditions—is not just difficult and a long way off, but impossible in principle (Wiliam, 2003b).

What is needed instead is an acknowledgment that what teachers do in "taking on" research is not a more or less passive adoption of some good ideas from someone else but an active process of knowledge *creation*.

> Teachers will not take up attractive sounding ideas, albeit based on extensive research, if these are presented as general principles which leave entirely to them the task of translating them into everyday practice—their classroom lives are too busy and too fragile for this to be possible for all but an outstanding few. What they need is a variety of living examples of implementation, by teachers with whom they can identify and from whom they can both derive conviction and confidence that

they can do better, and see concrete examples of what doing better means in practice. (Black & Wiliam, 1998b, p. 15)

There are, of course, many professional development structures that would be consistent with the emerging research base, but professional learning communities or teacher learning communities (TLCs), as advocated in the *Standards for Staff Development* of the National Staff Development Council (2001), appear to provide the most appropriate vehicle for this work. Numerous authors have contributed to a growing body of literature describing the need for and best ways to build teacher capacity through this school-based collaborative means (Borko, 1997, 2004; Borko, Mayfield, Marion, Flexer, & Cumbo, 1997; Elmore, 2002; Garmston & Wellman, 1999; Kazemi & Franke, 2003; McLaughlin & Talbert, 1993; Putnam & Borko, 2000; Sandoval, Deneroff, & Franke, 2002).

There are several reasons that TLCs are particularly appropriate for the development of teacher expertise in formative assessment. First, formative assessment depends upon a high level of professional judgment on the part of teachers, so it is appropriate to build professional development around a teacher-as-local-expert model. Second, school-embedded TLCs are sustained over time, allowing change to occur developmentally. Third, TLCs are a non-threatening venue allowing teachers to notice weaknesses in their content knowledge and get help with these deficiencies—in discussing a formative assessment practice that revolves around specific content (e.g., by examining student work that reveals student misconceptions), teachers often confront gaps in their own subject matter knowledge, which can be remedied in conversations with their colleagues.

Fourth, TLCs are embedded in the day-to-day realities of teachers' classrooms and schools, and thus provide a time and place where teachers can hear real-life stories from colleagues that show the benefits of adopting these techniques in situations similar to their own. These stories provide "existence proofs" that these kinds of changes are feasible with the exact kinds of students that a teacher has in his or her classroom—which contradicts the common lament, "Well, that's all well and good for teachers at *those* schools, but that won't work here with the kinds of students we get at this school." Without this kind of local reassurance, furthermore, there is little chance teachers will risk upsetting the prevailing "classroom contract" (Brousseau, 1997, p. 31). Although limiting, the old contract at least allows teachers to maintain some form of order and matches the expectations of most principals and colleagues. As teachers adjust their practice, they are risking both disorder and less-than-accomplished performance on the part of their students and themselves. Being a member of a community of teacher-learners engaged together in a change process provides the support teachers need to take such risks.

Fifth, and perhaps most importantly, TLCs allow us to address a fundamental limitation of the formative assessment intervention, which is its (perhaps paradoxical) generality and specificity. The five formative assessment strategies that we identified above are quite general—we have seen each of them in use in pre-kindergarten classes, in graduate-level studies, and at every level in between, and across all subjects. Yet implementing them effectively makes significant demands on subject knowledge. Teachers need good content knowledge to ask good questions, to interpret the responses of their students, and to provide appropriate feedback that focuses on what to do to improve. A less obvious need for subject matter knowledge is that teachers need a good overview of the subject matter in order to be clear about what the "big ideas" are in a particular domain so that these are given greater emphasis. Thus TLCs provide a forum for supporting teachers in converting the broad formative assessment strategies into "lived" practices within their classrooms.

This "bonus" feature of TLCs focused on assessment for learning—attention to the development of teacher content knowledge—is certainly a good thing, given well-documented deficiencies in U.S. teachers' preparation and content knowledge for teaching the subjects they teach (Fennema & Franke, 1992; Gitomer, Latham, & Ziomek, 1999; Kilpatrick, 2003; Ma, 1999; National Commission on Mathematics and Science for the 21st Century, 2000). But it is important to note that the TLCs we describe here are not purposively designed to redress these deficiencies, even as we see evidence of teachers using TLCs to advance their subject matter knowledge in our observations of TLC meetings.

This issue of deficiencies in teachers' subject matter knowledge raises a question for the model we propose here: Are there limits to the effectiveness of TLCs focused on assessment for learning in transforming teacher practice, given preexisting limits on teachers' subject matter knowledge? We do not have a definitive answer to this question, although we can report that we have repeatedly observed groups of teachers improve their practice, even when no teacher in the group has had strong content knowledge. Furthermore, preliminary evidence from one school district in which we are currently working suggests that the students of these teachers are learning better and faster, despite weaknesses in their teachers' content knowledge, because changes in teacher practices have led to students changing their own relationship to their learning and the content they are learning about. If these results bear up under more extensive analysis, they suggest that simply improving teacher pedagogy works to boost student learning, even in the absence of strong content knowledge on the part of the teacher. Whether or when this effect will "top out" remains to be seen in later research. (This is not to say that further gains could not be achieved by deliberately focusing on improving current teacher content knowledge. However, the policy infrastructure and institutional capacity for achieving this goal at scale are not yet in place. We would venture, however, that professional development via TLCs is not an efficient way to accomplish such changes. Rather, we expect that large-scale improvements in teacher content knowledge will be more effectively gained in settings where there is access to identified experts in the field and materials designed for this express purpose, for example, in university classes.)

Creating the conditions and support mechanisms for establishing and sustaining TLCs in schools is non-trivial, and, indeed, challenges long-held structures and assumptions about the nature of teachers' work, teacher learning, and how time should be spent in school. It is our contention, though, that getting teachers to integrate assessment for learning directly into their practice will have such positive effects on student learning, that it is worth investing research and development efforts in support of developing scalable models for helping schools set up and sustain TLCs focused on assessment for learning.

Conclusion

In this chapter, we have argued that the terms *formative* and *summative* apply not to assessments themselves, but to the functions they serve, and as a result, it is possible for the same assessment to be both formative and summative. Assessment is formative when the information arising from the assessment is fed back within the system and is actually used to improve the performance of the system. Assessment is formative for individuals when they use the feedback from the assessment to improve their learning. Assessment is formative for teachers when the outcomes from the assessment, appropriately interpreted, help them improve their teaching, either on specific topics or generally. Assessments are formative for schools and districts if the information generated can be interpreted and acted upon in such a way as to improve the quality of learning within the schools and districts.

The view of assessment presented here involves a shift from quality control in learning to quality assurance in learning. Rather than teaching students and, at the end of the teaching, finding out what has been learned, it seems obvious that what we should do is to assess the progress of learning whilst it is happening, so that we can adjust the teaching if things are not working. In order to achieve this, the length of the cycle from evidence to action must be designed taking into account the responsiveness of the system. Some feedback loops, such as those in the classroom, will be only seconds long, while others, such as those involving districts or state systems, will last months or even years.

More generally, we have suggested that formative assessment be considered as a key component of well-regulated learning environments. From this perspective, the task of the teacher is to not necessarily to teach, but rather to engineer and regulate situations in which students learn effectively. One way to do this is to design the environment so that the regulation is embedded within features of the environment. Alternatively, when the regulation is undertaken through the teacher's mediation, it is necessary to build opportunities for such mediation into the instructional sequence by designing in episodes that will elicit student thinking (proactive regulation) and to use the evidence from these probes to modify the instruction (interactive regulation).

Work with teachers to date suggests that the development of teachers' formative assessment practices through the use of teacher learning communities is manageable and relatively inexpensive to implement. The changes are slow to take effect, however, and it is not yet clear how faithfully the model used here can be scaled up. We have begun to explore what, exactly, changes when teachers develop formative assessment (Black & Wiliam, 2005b), but much more remains to be done. In particular, we do not know whether some of the five key strategies identified above have greater leverage than others, for promoting professional development and for increasing student achievement. Nevertheless, we believe that there are reasons to be optimistic. Perhaps one day we will not talk about "integrating assessment with learning" because the distinction between the two will have become meaningless.

Acknowledgments

We are grateful to Randy Bennet, Carol Dwyer, Laura Goe, and Siobhan Leahy for comments on an earlier version of this chapter.

References

Ball, D. L., & Cohen, D. K. (1996). Reform by the book: What is — or might be — the role of curriculum materials in teacher learning and instructional reform? *Educational Researcher, 25*(9), 6-8.

Black, P., Harrison, C., Lee, C., Marshall, B., & Wiliam, D. (2003). *Assessment for learning: Putting it into practice.* Buckingham, UK: Open University Press.

Black, P. J., & Wiliam, D. (1998a). Assessment and classroom learning. *Assessment in Education: Principles, Policy, and Practice, 5*(1), 7-73.

Black, P. J., & Wiliam, D. (1998b). *Inside the black box: Raising standards through classroom assessment.* London: King's College London School of Education.

Black, P. J., & Wiliam, D. (2004a). Classroom assessment is not (necessarily) formative assessment (and vice-versa). In M. Wilson (Ed.), *Towards coherence between classroom assessment and accountability: 103rd yearbook of the National Society for the Study of Education (part 2).* Chicago: University of Chicago Press.

Black, P. J., & Wiliam, D. (2004b). The formative purpose: Assessment must first promote learning. In M. Wilson (Ed.), *Towards coherence between classroom assessment and accountability: 103rd yearbook of the National Society for the Study of Education (part 2).* Chicago: University of Chicago Press.

Black, P. J., & Wiliam, D. (2005a). Lessons from around the world: How policies, politics and cultures constrain and afford assessment practices. *Curriculum Journal, 16*(2), 249-261.

Black, P. J., & Wiliam, D. (2005b). Developing a theory of formative assessment. In J. Gardner (Ed.), *Assessment and learning.* London: Sage.

Bloom, B. S. (1969). Some theoretical issues relating to educational evaluation. In R. W. Tyler (Ed.), *Educational evaluation: New roles, new means. The 63rd yearbook of the National Society for the Study of Education, part 2.* (Vol. 69, pp. 26-50). Chicago: University of Chicago Press.

Borko, H. (1997). New forms of classroom assessment: Implications for staff development. *Theory Into Practice, 36*(4), 231-238.

Borko, H. (2004). Professional development and teacher learning: Mapping the terrain. *Educational Researcher, 33*(8), 3-15.

Borko, H., Mayfield, V., Marion, S. F., Flexer, R. J., & Cumbo, K. (1997). *Teachers' developing ideas and practices about mathematics performance assessment: Successes, stumbling blocks, and implications for professional development* (Vol. 423). Boulder: University of Colorado, Boulder Center for Research on Evaluations, Standards and Student Testing (CRESST).

Brousseau, G. (1984). The crucial role of the didactical contract in the analysis and construction of situations in teaching and learning mathematics. In H. G. Steiner (Ed.), *Theory of mathematics education* (pp. 110-119). Occasionnel Paper 54, Bielefeld, Germany, University of Bielefeld, Institut für Didaktik der Mathematik.

Brousseau, G. (1997). *Theory of didactical situations in mathematics* (N. Balacheff, M. Cooper, R. Sutherland, & V. Warfield, Trans.). Dordrecht, Netherlands: Kluwer.

Bryk, A. S., & Raudenbush, S. W. (1988). Toward more appropriate conceptualization of research on school effects: A three-level hierarchical linear model. *American Journal of Education, 97,* 65-108.

Clarke, S. (2003). *Enriching feedback in the primary classroom.* London: Hodder & Stoughton.

Clements, D. H. (2002). Linking research and curriculum development. In L. D. English (Ed.), *Handbook of international research in mathematics education* (pp. 599-630). Mahwah, NJ: Lawrence Erlbaum Associates.

Cobb, P., McClain, K., Lamberg, T. d. S., & Dean, C. (2003). Situating teachers' instructional practices in the institutional setting of the school and district. *Educational Researcher, 32*(6), 13-24.

Cohen, D. K., & Hill, H. C. (1998). *State policy and classroom performance: Mathematics reform in California.* Philadelphia: University of Pennsylvania Consortium for Policy Research in Education.

Crooks, T. J. (1988). The impact of classroom evaluation practices on students. *Review of Educational Research, 58*(4), 438-481.

Darling-Hammond, L., Holtzman, D. J., Gatlin, S. J., & Vasquez Heilig, J. (2005). *Does teacher preparation matter? Evidence about teacher certification, teach for America, and teacher effectiveness.* Stanford, CA: Stanford University School of Education.

Dickens, W. T., & Flynn, J. R. (2001). Heritability estimates versus large environmental effects: The IQ paradox resolved. *Psychological Review, 108,* 346-369.

Elmore, R. F. (2002). *Bridging the gap between standards and achievement: Report on the imperative for professional development in education.* Washington, DC: Albert Shanker Institute.

English, L. D., Jones, G., Lesh, R., Tirosh, D., & Bussi, M. B. (2002). Future issues and directions in international mathematics education research. In L. D. English (Ed.), *Handbook of international research in mathematics education* (pp. 787-812). Mahwah, NJ: Lawrence Erlbaum Associates.

Fennema, E., & Franke, M. L. (1992). Teachers' knowledge and its impact. In D. A. Grouws (Ed.), *Handbook of research on mathematics teaching and learning* (pp. 147-164). New York: Macmillan.

Fernandez, C., & Yoshida, M. (2004). *Lesson study: A Japanese approach to improving mathematics teaching and learning.* Mahwah, NJ: Lawrence Erlbaum Associates.

Fullan, M. (1991). *The new meaning of educational change.* London: Cassell.

Garet, M. S., Birman, B. F., Porter, A. C., Desimone, L., & Herman, R. (1999). *Designing effective professional development: Lessons from the Eisenhower program.* Washington, DC: U.S. Department of Education.

Garmston, R., & Wellman, B. (1999). *The adaptive school: A sourcebook for developing collaborative groups.* Norwood, MA: Christopher-Gordon Publishers.

Gitomer, D. H., Latham, A. S., & Ziomek, R. (1999). *The academic quality of prospective teachers: The impact of admissions and licensure testing.* Princeton, NJ: Educational Testing Service.

Gritz, R. M., & MaCurdy, T. (1992). *Participation in low-wage labor markets by young men* (Discussion paper). Washington, DC: Bureau of Labor Statistics.

Hanushek, E. A. (2004). *Some simple analytics of school quality* (NBER working paper No. W10229). Washington, DC: National Bureau of Economic Research.

Hess, F. M., Rotherham, A. J., & Walsh, K. (Eds.). (2004). *A qualified teacher in every classroom? Appraising old answers and new ideas.* Cambridge, MA: Harvard Education Press.

Jepsen, C., & Rivkin, S. G. (2002). *What is the tradeoff between smaller classes and teacher quality?* (NBER working paper No. 9205). Cambridge, MA: National Bureau of Economic Research.

Kazemi, E., & Franke, M. L. (2003). *Using student work to support professional development in elementary mathematics: A CTP working paper.* Seattle, WA: Center for the Study of Teaching and Policy.

Kilpatrick, J. (2003, March). *Teachers' knowledge of mathematics and its role in teacher preparation and professional development programs.* Paper presented at the German-American Science and Math Education Research Conference, Kiel, Germany.

Kluger, A. N., & DeNisi, A. (1996). The effects of feedback interventions on performance: A historical review, a meta-analysis, and a preliminary feedback intervention theory. *Psychological Bulletin, 119*(2), 254-284.

Leahy, S., Lyon, C., Thompson, M., & Wiliam, D. (2005). Classroom assessment: Minute-by-minute and day-by-day. *Educational Leadership, 63*(3), 18-24.

Levin, H. M. (1972). The costs of inadequate education. In Select Committee on Equal Educational Opportunity –United States Senate (Ed.), *Toward equal educational opportunity* (pp. 171-186). Washington, DC: U.S. Government Printing Office.

Lewis, C. C. (2002). *Lesson study: A handbook of teacher-led instructional change.* Philadelphia: Research for Better Schools.

Linn, R. L. (1995). *Assessment-based reform: Challenges to educational measurement* (Report No. PIC-ANG1). Princeton, NJ: William H. Angoff Memorial Lecture Series, Educational Testing Service.

Ma, L. (1999). *Knowing and teaching elementary mathematics: Teachers' understanding of fundamental mathematics in China and the United States.* Mahwah, NJ: Lawrence Erlbaum Associates.

Marshall, B. (2004). Goals or horizons—the conundrum of progression in English: Or a possible way of understanding formative assessment in English. *Curriculum Journal, 15*(2), 101-113.

McLaughlin, M., & Talbert, J. (1993). *Contexts that matter for teaching and learning: Strategic opportunities for meeting the nation's educational goals.* Palo Alto, CA: Stanford University Center for Research on the Context of Secondary School Teaching.

Mercer, N., Dawes, L., Wegerif, R., & Sams, C. (2004). Reasoning as a scientist: Ways of helping children to use language to learn science. *British Educational Research Journal, 30*(3), 359-377.

National Assessment of Educational Progress. (2006). *The nation's report card: Mathematics 2005* (NCES 2006-453). Washington, DC: Institute of Education Sciences.

National Commission on Mathematics and Science for the 21st Century. (2000). *Before it's too late.* Washington, DC: Author.

National Staff Development Council. (2001). *NSDC standards for staff development.* Oxford, OH: Author.

Natriello, G. (1987). The impact of evaluation processes on students. *Educational Psychologist, 22*(2), 155-175.

Newton, P. (2003). The defensibility of national curriculum assessment in England. *Research Papers in Education, 18*(2), 101-127.

Nyquist, J. B. (2003). *The benefits of reconstruing feedback as a larger system of formative assessment: A meta-analysis.* Unpublished Master of Science thesis, Vanderbilt University, Nashville, TN.

Perrenoud, P. (1991). Towards a pragmatic approach to formative evaluation. In P. Weston (Ed.), *Assessment of pupil achievement* (pp. 79-101). Amsterdam, Netherlands: Swets & Zeitlinger.

Perrenoud, P. (1998). From formative evaluation to a controlled regulation of learning. Towards a wider conceptual field. *Assessment in Education: Principles, Policy, and Practice, 5*(1), 85-102.

Putnam, R. T., & Borko, H. (2000). What do new views of knowledge and thinking have to say about research on teacher learning? *Educational Researcher, 29*(1), 4-15.

Ramaprasad, A. (1983). On the definition of feedback. *Behavioural Science, 28*(1), 4-13.

Reeves, J., McCall, J., & MacGilchrist, B. (2001). Change leadership: Planning, conceptualization and perception. In J. MacBeath & P. Mortimore (Eds.), *Improving school effectiveness* (pp. 122-137). Buckingham, UK: Open University Press.

Remillard, J. T. (2005). Examining key concepts in research on teachers' use of mathematics curricula. *Review of Educational Research, 75*(2), 211-246.

Sandoval, W., Deneroff, V., & Franke, M. L. (2002, April). *Teaching, as learning, as inquiry: Moving beyond activity in the analysis of teaching practice.* Paper presented at the 2002 Annual Meeting of the American Educational Research Association, New Orleans, LA.

Schweinhart, L. J., Montie, J., Xiang, Z., Barnett, W. S., Belfield, C. R., & Nores, M. (2005). *Lifetime effects: The High/Scope Perry Preschool study through age 40.* Ypsilanti, MI: High/Scope Educational Research Foundation.

Scriven, M. (1967). *The methodology of evaluation* (Vol. 1). Washington, DC: American Educational Research Association.

Stiggins, R. J., & Bridgeford, N. J. (1985). The ecology of classroom assessment. *Journal of Educational Measurement, 22*(4), 271-286.

Supovitz, J. A. (2001). Translating teaching practice into improved student achievement. In S. H. Fuhrman (Ed.), *From the capitol to the classroom: Standards-based reform in the States* (Vol. 2, pp. 81-98). Chicago: University of Chicago Press.

Torrance, H. (1993). Formative assessment: Some theoretical problems and empirical questions. *Cambridge Journal of Education, 23*(3), 333-343.

Tyler, J. H., Murnane, R. J., & Willett, J. B. (2000). *Estimating the labor market signaling value of the GED* (Research Brief). Boston: National Center for the Study of Adult Learning & Literacy.

Wiliam, D. (1999, May). *A template for computer-aided diagnostic analyses of test outcome data.* Paper presented at 25th annual conference of the International Association for Educational Assessment, Bled, Slovenia.

Wiliam, D. (2003a). National curriculum assessment: How to make it better. *Research Papers in Education, 18*(2), 129-136.

Wiliam, D. (2003b). The impact of educational research on mathematics education. In A. Bishop, M. A. Clements, C. Keitel, J. Kilpatrick, & F. K. S. Leung (Eds.), *Second international handbook of mathematics education* (pp. 469-488). Dordrecht, Netherlands: Kluwer.

Wiliam, D. & Black, P. J. (1996). Meanings and consequences: A basis for distinguishing formative and summative functions of assessment? *British Educational Research Journal, 22*(5), 537-548.

Wiliam, D., Lee, C., Harrison, C., & Black, P. J. (2004). Teachers developing assessment for learning: Impact on student achievement. *Assessment in Education: Principles, Policy, and Practice, 11*(1), 49-65.

Wilson, S. M., & Berne, J. (1999). Teacher learning and the acquisition of professional knowledge: An examination of research on contemporary professional development. In A. Iran-Nejad & P. D. Pearson (Eds.), *Review of research in education* (pp. 173-209). Washington, DC: American Educational Research Association.

Section II

Cutting Edge Technology for Diagnosis and Instruction

4

Conversational Agents Can Provide Formative Assessment, Constructive Learning, and Adaptive Instruction

Arthur Graesser and Bethany McDaniel
University of Memphis

Our vision of the future is to have conversational agents on computers guide all phases of instruction, learning, formative assessment, and testing. The learner will be holding conversations in natural language with multimedia communication channels, just as they have interacted with teachers and mentors for centuries. Unlike teachers, the computer agents will be available 24/7 on the Web. Unlike teachers, computers will be capable of supplying a massive amount of up-to-date information at all scales of depth and breadth. Unlike teachers who manage large classrooms, the computer agents will tailor the conversation and educational experiences to the individual learners. Will the learner become socially detached? Not at all, because the learners will be interacting with a society of other human agents and cyber agents that function as peers, team members, game players, coworkers, teachers, and mentors. Will teachers become extinct? Not at all, because they will be spending more time learning new material, augmenting their expertise, preparing new lessons and assessor facilities with authoring tools, and interacting with students at the deepest depths of knowledge, passion, and wisdom that computers may never achieve.

This vision is not entirely science fiction. A number of computer systems hold conversations in natural language. Some have animated agents (talking heads) with speech recognition, speech generation, facial expressions, gestures, and body movement. One goal of this chapter is to point out some of these systems for the uninitiated. A second goal is to describe a system that we have built and tested, called AutoTutor. AutoTutor is capable of delivering instruction, holding conversations in natural language, performing formative evaluation of subject matter knowledge on the basis of the conversational interaction, and guiding interactions with complex interactive multimedia. AutoTutor adapts to both the learner's knowledge states and, in our current project, the learner's emotions.

Computer Conversations and Agents

Most people are both fascinated by and skeptical about the prospects of having a computer communicate with humans in natural language. Weizenbaum's (1966) ELIZA program was the first conversation system that attracted the attention of researchers in computer science and cognitive science. ELIZA simulated a Rogerian client-centered psychotherapist, as illustrated in the conversation below.

Patient: You are like my father in some ways.
ELIZA: How am I like your father?
Patient: You are very aggressive but I think you don't want me to notice that.
ELIZA: What makes you think I am aggressive?
Patient: You always argue with me.
ELIZA: Why do you think I argue with you?

ELIZA tried to get the patients to express themselves by asking the patients questions about their verbal contributions. ELIZA turned the patients' assertions into therapist's questions by simple syntactic transformational rules. For example, after the patient says, "You always argue with me," ELIZA inserts a question template [*Why do you think X?*], makes appropriate substitutions of pronouns [*I ‡ you, you ‡ I*], and deletes some of the unimportant words (*always*). The only intelligence in ELIZA is the stimulus-response knowledge captured in production rules that operate on keywords and that perform syntactic transformations. Researchers discovered that 100 to 200 rules in ELIZA could create an illusion of comprehension, even though ELIZA had little or no understanding of the patients. One could imagine what might be created from an ELIZA with 20,000 well-selected rules.

Efforts to build conversational systems continued in the 1970s and early '80s. PARRY attempted to simulate a paranoid agent (Colby, Weber, & Hilf, 1971). SCHOLAR tutored students on South American geography by asking and answering questions (Collins, Warnock, & Passafiume, 1975). MOONROCKS (Woods, 1977) and ELINOR (Norman & Rumelhart, 1975) also answered user questions about subject matter knowledge. Schank's research team built computer models of natural language understanding of stories and of simple dialogue about everyday activities, such as eating at a restaurant (Schank & Reisbeck, 1981). SHRDLU scanned a world of simple blocks with an electronic eye, manipulated objects in the blocks world with a rudimentary arm, and generated responses to user commands and questions (Winograd, 1972).

Technical advances in the last decade have encouraged researchers to escalate efforts to build robust dialogue systems (Graesser, Van Lehn, Rose, Jordan, & Harter, 2001; Gratch et al., 2002; Larsson & Traum, 2000; Rich & Sidner, 1998; Rickel, Lesh, Rich, Sidner, & Gertner, 2002). Many of these dialogue systems have been incorporated in learning environments. There are approximately a half dozen intelligent tutoring systems with dialogue in natural language. AutoTutor and Why/AutoTutor (Graesser, Hu, & McNamara, 2005; Graesser, Person, Harter, & Tutoring Research Group, 2001; Graesser, Wiemer-Hastings, Wiemer-Hastings, Kreuz, & Tutoring Research Group, 1999) were developed for introductory computer literacy and Newtonian physics. These systems help college students generate explanations and patterns of knowledge-based reasoning when solving particular problems. Why/Atlas (VanLehn, Jordan, Rose, et al., 2002) also has students learn about conceptual physics from a coach that helps build written explanations of conceptual physics problems. In the CIRCSIM Tutor (Hume, Michael, Rovick, & Evens, 1996; Shah, Evens, Michael, & Rovick, 2002), medical students learn about the circulatory system from a conversational tutor that incorporates strategies of an accomplished tutor with a medical degree. PACO (Rickel et al., 2002) assists learners in interacting with mechanical equipment and completing tasks by interacting in natural language. SCoT (Peters, Bratt, Clark, Pon-Barry, & Schultz, 2004) holds conversations with Navy personnel who need to learn about ship damage.

The development of these dialogue systems would never have occurred without important technical breakthroughs in the fields of computational linguistics, information retrieval, cognitive science, artificial intelligence, and discourse processes. The field of computational linguistics has produced an impressive array of lexicons (word dictionaries), syntactic parsers (which give the structural composition of grammar), semantic interpretation modules (providing analysis of sentence meaning), and dialogue analyzers capable of rapidly extracting information from naturalistic text for information retrieval, machine translation, and speech recognition (Allen, 1995; Harabagiu, Maiorano, & Pasca, 2002; Jurafsky & Martin, 2000; Manning & Schutze, 1999; Moore & Wiemer-Hastings, 2003; Voorhees, 2001). Educational Testing Service has taken a similar path with multidisciplinary research teams that apply advances in computational linguistics, AI, and cognitive science to automated assessments of lengthier text excerpts (Burstein, 2003; Deane, 2005; Leacock & Chodorow, 2003). For example, C-rater analyzes constructed student responses to short answer questions (Leacock & Chodorow, 2003) and E-rater analyses essays (Burstein, 2003).

These sophisticated analyses require some representation of world knowledge in addition to language per se. World knowledge in these systems is represented symbolically, statistically, or by a hybrid of these two computational foundations. For example, Lenat's (1995) CYC system represents a large volume of mundane world knowledge in symbolic forms that can be integrated with many different computer systems. As another example, the world knowledge contained in an encyclopedia can be represented statistically in high dimensional spaces, as in the case of latent semantic analysis (LSA; Landauer, Foltz, & Laham, 1998; Landauer, McNamara, Dennis, & Kintsch, 2007). An LSA space provides the backbone for statistical metrics on whether two text excerpts are conceptually similar; the reliability of these similarity metrics has been found to be equivalent or nearly equivalent to that of human judgments. For example, Landauer's Intelligent Essay Grader assigns grades to student essays as reliably as experts in English composition.

The mechanisms that drive conversational dialogue are also better understood after three decades of research in discourse processing (Clark, 1996; Graesser, Gernsbacher, & Goldman, 2003; Pickering & Garrod, 2004). Discourse analysts have identified frequent conversation patterns in two-party dialogue. Some patterns are context-free in the sense that they occur in most conversational contexts. Context-free patterns include the adjacency pairs in two-party dialogue identified by Schegloff and Sachs (1973) and others, such as [question ‡ answer], [request ‡ acknowledgment], and [offer ‡ {acceptance/refusal}]. Another ubiquitous pattern is an embedded counter-clarification question (Schober & Conrad, 1997), as illustrated in the context of a survey interview.

Person 1 (survey interviewer): How many children live in your home?
Person 2 (interviewee): Should I include the families who rent from us?
Person 1: Yes, all families who live in this residence.
Person 2: Okay, there are four children.

The embedded question is of course constrained by the knowledge state of person 2, namely the uncertainty about who counts as family. Another dialogue pattern that is frequent in classrooms is the [initiate ‡ response ‡ evaluation] sequence (Sinclair & Coulthard, 1975), or more specifically the [question ‡ answer ‡ feedback] sequence.

Teacher: When was America discovered? (initiation, question)
Student: 1492. (response, answer)
Teacher: Very good. (evaluation, feedback)

In tutorial dialogue, this IRE sequence gets expanded into the 5-step tutoring frame introduced by Graesser and Clark (1985).

Teacher: Why is it warmer in the summer than the winter here? (question)
Student: The Earth is closer to the sun? (answer)
Teacher: I don't think so. (short feedback)
Teacher and Student: [Collaborative multi-turn exchange to improve answer]
Teacher: Do you understand? (comprehension gauging question)
Student: Yeah.

One reason why tutoring may produce better learning than classrooms do (Cohen, Kulik, & Kulik, 1982; Graesser & Person, 1994) is step 4, where the student and teacher have a collaborative exchange that scaffolds explanatory reasoning.

Automated computer conversations are often faceless, speechless, and bodiless, as in the case of a chat facility on the Web. Some conversational agents have now progressed to the point where the agents hold conversations very similar to those of humans, so similar, in fact, that it is difficult to distinguish whether particular turns are generated by a human or a computer agent (Person, Erkel, Graesser, & Tutoring Research Group, 2002). Researchers have also designed animated conversational agents that are embodied with a text-to-speech engine, facial expressions, gestures, pointing, and other body movements. Animated agents have become increasingly popular in learning environments on the Web, Internet, and desktop applications (Atkinson, 2002; Baylor, 2002; Cassell & Thorisson, 1999; Cole et al., 2003; Johnson, Rickel, & Lester, 2000; Massaro & Cohen, 1995; Reeves & Nass, 1996). Some of these animated agents use speech recognition (Cole et al., 2003; Gratch et al., 2002; Johnson & Beal, 2005), so there is the capability of a full-fledged face-to-face communication. The Mission Rehearsal system (Gratch et al., 2002) helps U.S. Army personnel interact in a virtual war scenario with several dozens of animated agents. The Tactical Language Training System (Johnson & Beal, 2005) is an interactive game that helps Army personnel learn a new foreign language and culture by holding conversations with virtual agents in a series of realistically depicted microworlds.

Our central proposal is that automated language and discourse technologies have progressed to the point where they can provide the core interface and pedagogical platform to guide all phases of instruction, learning, formative assessment, and testing. The next section illustrates this more concretely by describing a single integrated system that incorporates all these phases. The system is called AutoTutor, developed in the Institute for Intelligent Systems at the University of Memphis.

AutoTutor

AutoTutor simulates a human or ideal tutor by holding a conversation with the learner in natural language (Graesser, Hu, & McNamara, 2005; Graesser, Lu, Jackson, et al., 2004; Graesser, Person, Harter, et al., 2001; Graesser, Weimer-Hastings, Weimer-Hastings, et al., 1999). AutoTutor presents a series of challenging questions/problems that require approximately a paragraph of information to answer correctly. An example question in conceptual physics is: "When a car without headrests on the seats is struck from behind, the passengers often suffer neck injuries. Why do passengers get neck injuries in this situation?" Although a perfect answer to this question is approximately three to seven sentences in length, the initial answers by human learners are typically only one word to two sentences in length. This is where tutorial dialogue is helpful, whether the dialogue is provided by AutoTutor or a human tutor.

AutoTutor assists the learner in the evolution of an improved answer that draws out more of the learner's knowledge that is relevant to the answer. The dialogue between AutoTutor and the learner typically lasts 50 to 200 *turns* (i.e., the learner expresses something, then the tutor, then the learner, and so on), which is on par with the interactivity in human tutoring. There is a *mixed-initiative* dialogue to the extent that each dialogue partner can ask questions and start new subtopics. AutoTutor serves as a *discourse prosthesis* that draws out more of what the learner knows and that adaptively improves answers to questions through collaboration in natural language. During the course of conversation, *formative evaluation* is achieved by tracking the extent to which the learner has mastered the principles associated with the main question or problem.

Dialogue Patterns With AutoTutor

One way to convey what AutoTutor can do is through an example conversational dialogue. The excerpt in Table 4.1 was extracted from a conversation with a student on the topic of Newtonian physics. The conversation begins with a main question selected by AutoTutor from the repertoire of questions in its curriculum.

The example illustrates some of the important dialogue features of AutoTutor. AutoTutor segments the student's turns into speech act units and then classifies these units into categories such as assertion, short answer, metacognition (*I don't follow*), metacommunication (*What did you say?*), definition question (*What does X mean?*), and comparison question (*What is the difference between X and Y?*). There are approximately 20 categories of student speech acts, 16 of which are different categories of student questions. AutoTutor attempts to accommodate virtually any student question, assertion, comment, or extraneous speech act. This requires interpreting the student's speech acts by implementing modules developed in the field of computational linguistics. AutoTutor needs to *generate* language in addition to attempting to *comprehend* the student's language. Each turn of AutoTutor requires the generation of one or more dialogue moves

TABLE 4.1   Excerpts From a Conversation With AutoTutor

AutoTutor-1: When a car without headrests on the seats is struck from behind, the passengers often suffer neck injuries. Explain why. (MAIN QUESTION)

Student-2: I don't know. (This expression by the student is classified as a metacognitive speech act because it conveys what the student knows about his/her own knowledge.)

AutoTutor-3: Could you at least try to give me an answer? That way, we'll have something as a starting place to work from. (PUMP. This dialogue move encourages the student to say more, but does not direct the student to express particular information.)

Let's try this together. (DISCOURSE MARKER. This is a discourse marker that connects different dialogue moves within a turn.)

When the collision provides a large force to accelerate the head, what could happen to the neck? (HINT. This dialogue move leads the student to articulate a particular sentence, clause, or proposition.)

[Later in the conversation.]

Student-4: What is a force? (The student can ask questions during an AutoTutor session.)

AutoTutor-5: I'll take a crack at answering your question. (DISCOURSE MARKER) Force is any influence that tends to accelerate an object, a push or pull, measured in newtons. Force is a vector quantity. (ANSWER. AutoTutor answers the student's direct question. Answers are either accessed from electronic glossaries or a paragraph is dynamically selected from a textbook.)

Was that what you were looking for? (QUESTION SOLICITATION. AutoTutor allows the student the opportunity to rephrase his question.)

[At this point, the dialogue continues until AutoTutor believes it has detected a misconception.]

AutoTutor-20: See if you know the answer to this. (DISCOURSE MARKER. AutoTutor prepares the student for a direct question.)

When the head and body are moving at the same acceleration, they are moving at the same _____? (PROMPT. This dialogue move encourages the student to fill in a particular word or phrase of information, in this case the word "rate." Prompts are needed for students who are low verbal and to elicit a particular noun, verb, or adjective.)

Student-21: Distance.

AutoTutor-22: Moving at the same rate. (PROMPT COMPLETION. AutoTutor splices in the correct information if the student provides an incorrect answer to its prompt.)

[At this point, the dialogue continues until all relevant principles are covered in the conversation, followed by a summary by the tutor.]

that adaptively respond to what the student just expressed and that advance the conversation in a constructive fashion. The dialogue moves within a turn are connected by discourse markers, as illustrated in the example. Some dialogue moves are very responsive to the student's preceding turn, such as the short feedback (positive, neutral, versus negative), the answers to student questions, and corrections of student misconceptions. Other dialogue moves push the dialogue forward in an attempt to cover the expected answers to the main question. These forward-directed dialogue moves include pumps (e.g., *Tell me more, What else?*), hints, prompts for the student to fill in specific words, and assertions.

AutoTutor uses two dialogue mechanisms for guiding the answers to the questions. The first is the 5-step tutoring frame of Graesser and Person (1994) described earlier. The second specifies how step 4 of the tutoring frame is realized, called *expectation and misconception tailored dialogue* (EMT dialogue). Both AutoTutor and human tutors typically have a list of anticipated good answers (called *expectations*) and a list of *misconceptions* associated with each main question. One goal of the tutor is to coach the student in covering the list of expectations. This is accomplished by generating pumps, hints, prompts, and assertions until the student or tutor covers each expectation on the list. A second goal is to correct misconceptions manifested in the student's talk by simply correcting the errors as soon as they are manifested. A third goal is to adaptively respond to the student by giving feedback on the quality of student contributions (positive, negative, or neutral) and by answering the student's questions. A fourth goal is to manage the dialogue in a fashion that appears coherent and accommodates unusual speech acts by learners. As the learner expresses information over many turns, the list of expectations is eventually covered and the main question is scored as answered.

The expectations and principles in the main questions that end up being selected would ideally be aligned with education standards (Dwyer, 2005). For example, an important expectation in physics would be the principle *net force equals mass times acceleration*, one of Newton's laws. The set of main questions presented to the student would have answers that correspond to each of the principles (as defined by educational standards) in several problems so there can be formative assessment of the consistency with which the learner has mastered the principle. Mastery of a principle does

not simply mean that the student can articulate the principle ver-
bally. Mastery also requires that the principle is applied correctly
in the appropriate contexts, and not considered in irrelevant contexts. The knowledge gaps direct subsequent interactions between
the learner and AutoTutor. There can be formative assessment of
specific principles at varying grain sizes, precision, and subtlety. In
addition to formative assessment, it is not at all difficult for Auto-
Tutor to provide instruction and summative assessment, which are
standard technologies in e-learning and computer-based training.
However, the more distinctive, signature contribution of AutoTutor is that it can perform formative assessment by simply holding a
conversation in natural language.

The pedagogical framework of AutoTutor was inspired by three
bodies of theoretical, empirical, and applied research. These include
explanation-based constructivist theories of learning (Aleven &
Koedinger, 2002; Chi, de Leeuw, Chiu, & LaVancher, 1994; VanLehn,
Jones, & Chi, 1992), intelligent tutoring systems that adaptively
respond to student knowledge (Anderson, Corbett, Koedinger, &
Pelletier, 1995; VanLehn, Lynch, Taylor, et al., 2002), and empirical
research that has documented the collaborative constructive activities that routinely occur during human tutoring (Chi, Siler, Jeong,
Yamauchi, & Hausmann, 2001; Fox, 1993; Graesser & Person, 1994;
Moore, 1995; Shah et al., 2002). According to the explanation-
based constructivist theories of learning, learning is more effective
and deeper when the learner must actively generate explanations,
justifications, and functional procedures than when merely given
information to read. Regarding adaptive intelligent tutoring systems, the tutors give immediate feedback to the learner's actions
and guide the learner on what to do next in a fashion that is sensitive to what the system believes the learner knows. Regarding the
empirical research on tutorial dialogue, the patterns of discourse
uncovered in naturalistic tutoring are imported into the dialogue
management facilities of AutoTutor.

AutoTutor delivers its dialogue moves with an animated conversational agent that has a text-to-speech engine, facial expressions, gestures, and pointing. The learner's contributions are currently typed
into AutoTutor, although we do have a prototype version with speech
recognition. Examples of interfaces are provided in Figure 4.1 for the
two subject matters we have investigated most extensively: conceptual physics and computer literacy. The main question is presented

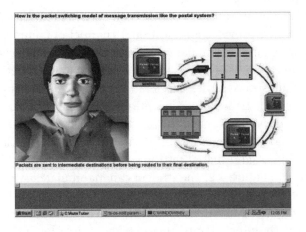

Figure 4.1 Interface of AutoTutor in physics and computer literacy.

in the top or top-right window. This major question remains at the top of the Web page until it is finished being answered during a multi-turn dialogue. The students use the bottom or bottom-right window to type in their contributions for each turn. The dialogue history between tutor and student is shown in the bottom-left window in the left screenshot on conceptual physics, but is not included in the right screenshot on computer literacy. The computer literacy tutor does have a display area for diagrams. The animated conversational agent resides in the upper left area. The agent uses one of three text-to-speech engines from either AT&T, SpeechWorks, or a

Figure 4.2   AutoTutor's interactive simulation.

Microsoft agent (dependent on licensing agreements) to speak the content of AutoTutor's turns.

One version of AutoTutor has an embedded interactive 3D simulation, which provides an additional channel of communication (see Figure 4.2). Each simulation is crafted to cover particular physics principles (e.g., Newton's second law that states that net force on a body equals mass times acceleration) in an ideal answer, or to help correct particular misconceptions about physics (such as the impetus fallacy). For each of the physics problems, we developed an interactive simulation world in *3D Studio Max*. This includes the people, objects, and spatial setting associated with the problem, as illustrated in Figure 4.2. The student can manipulate parameters of the situation (e.g., mass and speed of objects) and then ask the system to simulate what will happen. They can compare their expected outcome with the actual outcome after the simulation is completed. Students can run as many of the simulations as they wish until they feel they understand the relationship between parameters and outcomes of simulations. Interacting with and viewing the simulations is not all there is, however. In order to manage the interactive simulation, AutoTutor gives hints and suggestions, once again scaffolding the learning process with dialogue. Therefore, deep learning of physics is believed to emerge from the combination of interactivity, perceptual simulation, feedback on the simulation, and explaining what happens. Formative evaluation is achieved by collecting performance measures on each of these manifestations of the mastery of particular principles.

Evaluations of AutoTutor on Learning

Different types of performance evaluation can be made when assessing the success of AutoTutor. One type of evaluation assesses whether AutoTutor is successful in producing learning gains, as manifested in tests of summative assessment. Second, technical evaluations assess whether particular components of AutoTutor (e.g., learner speech act classification, coverage of expectations, and identification of learner misconceptions) are producing output that is valid and satisfies the intended specifications. From the standpoint of this chapter, formative evaluation is an important issue so we are interested in the accuracy of AutoTutor in assessing whether a student has mastered particular expectations or expressed particular misconceptions. A third type of evaluation assesses the quality of the dialogue moves produced by AutoTutor. That is, to what extent are AutoTutor's dialogue moves coherent, relevant, and smooth? Expert judges evaluate the quality of particular dialogue moves. The fourth type of evaluation assesses the learners' impressions of the agent and the learning experience by collecting ratings and open-ended evaluations from learners after interacting with AutoTutor. This subsection covers the first of these classes of evaluation of AutoTutor.

AutoTutor has been evaluated on learning gains in over a dozen experiments on the topics of computer literacy (Graesser, Lu, Jackson, et al., 2004; Graesser, Moreno, Marineau, et al., 2003) and conceptual physics (Graesser, Jackson, Mathews, et al., 2003; VanLehn, Graesser, Jackson, et al., 2005). In most of the studies, a pretest is administered, followed by a tutoring treatment, followed by a posttest. The tutoring treatments compare AutoTutor under different types of conditions. The conditions have varied from experiment to experiment because colleagues have had different views on what a suitable control condition would be. AutoTutor's posttest scores have been compared with (a) pretest scores (*Pretest*); (b) students reading nothing (*Read-nothing*); (c) students reading relevant chapters from the course textbook (*Textbook*); (d) students reading the same relevant chapters from the course textbook in *c*, except that content is included only if it is directly relevant to the content trained by AutoTutor (*Textbook-reduced*); and (e) students reading text prepared by the experimenters that succinctly describes the content covered in the curriculum script of AutoTutor (*Script-content*). The dependent measures have been different for computer literacy and physics, but have included multiple-choice tests (on both shallow and deep knowledge), essay answers, a cloze procedure (filling in missing content words in explanations or steps in reasoning), and far transfer problems. Far transfer problems are questions and problems that require verbal reasoning, but the physical surface features of the people, objects, and situation are not similar to the training problems.

Means, standard deviations, and effect sizes (standardized mean differences, signified by) have been collected for several measures in 12 experiments on both computer literacy and physics. In computer literacy, AutoTutor did not facilitate learning on the shallow multiple-choice test questions that had been prepared by the writers of the test bank for the textbook; we discovered that 96% of the textbank questions tapped shallow knowledge. These effect sizes were low or negative (mean d was .05 for 7 comparisons). Shallow knowledge is not the sort of knowledge that AutoTutor was designed for, so this result is not surprising. AutoTutor was built to facilitate deep reasoning, and this was apparent in the effect sizes for deep multiple-choice questions. All 7 ds were positive, with a mean of .49. Similarly, all 6 effect sizes for the cloze tests were positive, with a mean of .50. These effect sizes were generally higher when the comparison condition was Read-nothing or the Textbook (mean = .43 for 9 effect sizes) than when the comparison condition was Textbook-reduced (mean = .22).

Experiments on conceptual physics also have shown the benefits of AutoTutor. Graesser, Jackson, Mathews, et al. (2003) compared AutoTutor, Textbook, or Read-nothing in pretests and posttests that tapped deeper comprehension. There were either multiple-choice questions or essays that answered conceptual physics problems (and graded by PhDs in physics). Additional experiments are described in VanLehn, Graesser, Jackson, et al. (2005), where the same tests were administered, but there were a variety of control conditions. When considering all of the conceptual physics studies to date, and both the multiple-choice and the essay tests, the mean effect sizes of AutoTutor have varied substantially when contrasted with particular comparison conditions: Read-nothing (.67), mediated conversation (.08). The number of participants per condition vary between 18 and 40 in each of the experiments that have been conducted in tests of AutoTutor.

Recent experiments on conceptual physics have compared two new versions of AutoTutor, one with and one without 3D simulations, as illustrated earlier. A student had the freedom to interact with the

3D world several times per scenario. The difference between Auto-Tutor-3D and the normal AutoTutor was subtle ($d = .20$) and non-significant, in part because many of the students did not use the simulation very much. Students who *did* make a minimum number of simulation manipulations showed positive correlations between their learning outcomes and two simulation variables: the number of simulations they received ($r = .51$; $p < .01$) and the relevance of their manipulations to the problem ($r = .47$; $p < .05$). Simply grounding the physics in a visual display is insufficient because many users don't know what to do next or how to effectively manipulate the parameters en route to learning. They need modeling and coaching for effective inquiry (Azevedo & Cromley, 2004; Rieber & Kini, 1995; Winne, 2001).

There are a number of noteworthy outcomes from these analyses. First, AutoTutor is effective in promoting learning gains at deep levels of comprehension, when compared with the typical ecologically valid situations in which students read nothing (all too often), perform at the level of pretest, or read the textbook for an equivalent amount of time as AutoTutor. The mean effect size is .80 when considering these comparison conditions, the deeper tests of comprehension (i.e., not shallow tests), and both computer literacy and physics. Second, it is surprising that reading the textbook is not much different than reading nothing. It appears that a tutor (or some challenging exercise) is needed to help students discern the limits of their knowledge and to encourage them to focus on deeper levels of comprehension. Third, AutoTutor is as effective as a human tutor who communicates with the student over terminals in computer-mediated conversation. The human tutors had doctoral degrees in physics and extensive teaching experience, yet they did not out-perform AutoTutor. Such a result clearly needs replication before we consider it as a well-established finding, but the result is quite provocative. Fourth, interactive 3D simulation does not necessarily improve learning, particularly when students need modeling and coaching on using these simulations. Fifth, the impact of AutoTutor on learning gains is considerably reduced when the comparison consists of students reading text that is carefully tailored to match the exact content covered by AutoTutor. That is, textbook-reduced and script-content controls yielded an AutoTutor effect size of only .22, when combining computer literacy and physics. Of course, in the real world, texts are rarely crafted to copy tutoring content, so the status of this control is uncertain in the arena of practice. But it does suggest that the impact of AutoTutor is dramatically reduced or disappears when there are comparison conditions that present content that has information equivalence to AutoTutor. This does raise the question, of course, of whether the rhetorical structure of texts should be guided by principles of tutoring.

The question that colleagues frequently ask is: What it is about AutoTutor that facilitates learning? For example, is it the dialogue content or the animated agent that explains the learning gains? We suspect that the animated conversational agent fascinates some students and is possibly more motivating. They are fascinated with an agent that controls the eyes, eyebrows, mouth, lips, teeth, tongue, cheekbones, and other parts of the face in a fashion that is meshed appropriately with the language and emotions of the speaker (Reeves & Nass, 1996). The agents provide an anthropomorphic human-computer interface that simulates having a conversation with a human. This will be exciting to some, frightening to a few, annoying to others, and so on. There is some evidence that these agents tend to have a positive impact on learning or on the learner's perceptions of the learning experience, compared with speech alone or text controls (Atkinson, 2002; Moreno, Mayer, Spires, & Lester, 2001; Whittaker, 2003). However, additional research is needed to determine the precise conditions, agent features, and levels of representation that are associated with learning gains. According to Graesser, Moreno, Marineau, et al. (2003), the dialogue content has a substantially larger impact on learning than the talking head, whereas the animated agent can have an influential role on motivation (positive, neutral, or negative). One rather provocative result is that there is a near-zero correlation between learning gains and how much the students like the conversational agents (Moreno, Klettke, Nibbaragandla, Graesser, & Tutoring Research Group, 2002). Therefore, it is important to distinguish liking from learning in this area of research.

AutoTutor's Detection of Expectations and Misconceptions

One important question addresses how well AutoTutor can perform formative evaluation by virtue of tracking whether particular expectations and misconceptions are covered in the conversation.

For example, the collision problem has the following expectations and misconceptions affiliated with it.

Expectations

(E1) The magnitudes of the forces exerted by the two objects on each other are equal.

(E2) If one object exerts a force on a second object, then the second object exerts a force on the first object in the opposite direction.

(E3) The same force will produce a larger acceleration in a less massive object than a more massive object.

Misconceptions

(M1) A lighter/smaller object exerts no force on a heavier/larger object.

(M2) A lighter/smaller object exerts less force on other objects than does a heavier/larger object.

(M3) The force acting on a body is dependent on the mass of the body.

(M4) Heavier objects accelerate faster for the same force than do lighter objects.

(M5) Action and reaction forces do not have the same magnitude.

The learner would ideally articulate all the expectations verbatim, but that far exceeds what would be anticipated by AutoTutor's mechanisms. Natural language is much too imprecise, fragmentary, vague, ungrammatical, and elliptical to require such semantically well-formed and complete responses. LSA (see earlier discussion) or some other semantic analyzer is used to evaluate the extent to which the information within the student turns (i.e., an individual turn, a combination of turns, or collective sequence of turns) matches each of the expectations (E) and misconceptions (M); an E or M is considered articulated by the student if its *match score* (LSA cosine or another type semantic overlap metric) meets or exceeds some threshold (T). AutoTutor's dialogue manager attempts to finesse the student to cover each E by periodically identifying a missing E during the course of the dialogue and posting the goal of covering expectation E. Hints and prompts are generated to get the student to articulate missing words, phrases, or propositions in E. However, sometimes the student fails to do so, and E is considered not mastered. The students may also periodically express misconceptions during the dialogue. This happens when the student input (I) matches a misconception (M) with a sufficiently high match score. At that point AutoTutor corrects the misconception and goes on. When the conversation is finished during the course of answering the main question, there is a formative assessment of the student's performance by computing the proportion of expectations the student articulated and the proportion of misconceptions articulated. In the case of AutoTutor 3D with the interactive simulation, performance is assessed by computing the extent to which the learner manipulates the correct parameters (mass, speed, etc.).

The question arises: How accurate are AutoTutor's match scores in evaluating whether particular expectations and misconceptions are covered? We had experts in physics or computer literacy make judgments about the quality of the student essays. An expert's *quality rating* was operationally defined as the proportion of expectations in an essay that judges believed were covered. Coverage was defined by either a strict criterion (there was a close match between a statement expressed by a student and an expectation) or a lenient criterion (the expectation either explicitly matched an expectation or the expectation could be inferred from what the student articulated). Similarly, AutoTutor's LSA-based match score was used to compute the proportion of expectations covered, using varying thresholds of match scores on whether information in the student essay covered each expectation. Correlations between AutoTutor and human experts were approximately .5 for both conceptual physics (Olde, Franceschetti, Karnavat, Graesser, & Tutoring Research Group, 2002) and computer literacy (Graesser, Wiemer-Hastings P., Wiember-Hastings K., Harter, Person, & Tutoring Research Group, 2000). Correlations between a pair of experts in our studies have varied between .5 and .7, so LSA agrees with experts almost as well as two experts agree with each other.

We also have evaluated match scores between particular expectations and single learner speech acts within a turn during an Auto-Tutor session. This is, in essence, a comparison between a sentence expressed by a student and a sentence-like expectation. An expert physicist rated the degree to which particular speech acts expressed during AutoTutor training matched particular expectations. The question is how well the expert ratings correlate with LSA coverage scores. It should be noted that this analysis involves comparisons between sentential expectations and single student speech acts during training; this is not the same as previous analyses in which a set of expectations is compared with content of an entire student essay. The correlation between an expert judge's rating and the LSA cosine was significant but modest, $r = .29$ (N = 125 pairs). When we scaled the sample of sentence pairs on two other scales of semantic matching, the individual correlations increased to $r \approx .39$. These results support the conclusion that analysis of sentences would benefit from a hybrid model of semantics that considers both LSA and alternative algorithms that capture logical form (Rus & Moldovan, 2002).

Tracking Learner Emotions

One version of AutoTutor attempts to perceive and respond to learner emotions in addition to the learner's knowledge states. In this version, AutoTutor is augmented with sensing devices and signal processing models that classify affective states of learners. Emotions are classified on the basis of dialog patterns during tutoring, the content covered, facial expressions, speech parameters, body posture, haptic mouse pressure, and keyboard pressure. Our project has two specific objectives. First, AutoTutor will analyze patterns of facial, body, and dialog activity that arise while interacting with AutoTutor and will classify this input into basic affective states such as confusion, frustration, boredom, interest, excitement, and insight. Second, we will investigate whether learning gains and learner impressions of AutoTutor are influenced by dialog moves of AutoTutor that are sensitive to the learner's emotions. For example, if the student is extremely frustrated, then AutoTutor presumably should give a good hint or prompt that directs the student in a more positive learning trajectory. If the student is bored, AutoTutor should give more engaging, challenging, and motivating problems. If the student is very absorbed and happy, then AutoTutor should be minimally invasive and stay out of the student's way.

We have already collected some data that illustrate emotions might be intimately interwoven with complex learning. Six different affect states (frustration, boredom, engagement/flow, confusion, delight/ eureka, and neutral) were tracked while college students learned introductory computer literacy with AutoTutor (Craig, Graesser, Sullins, & Gholson, 2004). Expert judges recorded such emotions at random points during the interaction with AutoTutor. Significant relationships were found between learning gains (posttest/pretest scores on multiple-choice tests) and the affective states of boredom ($r = -.33$), engagement/flow ($r = .29$), and confusion ($r = .33$). Correlations with eureka ($r = .03$) and frustration ($r = -.06$) were near zero, but this may be because these behaviors were of very low frequency.

These results fit some available theoretical frameworks that link emotions and cognition. The positive correlation between confusion and learning is consistent with a model that assumes that *cognitive disequilibrium* is one precursor to deep learning (Graesser & Olde, 2003). Cognitive disequilibrium occurs when the learners encounter contradictions, discrepancies, novel input, obstacles to goals, decision deadlocks, and major knowledge gaps. Deeper thought and emotions are experienced until equilibrium is restored. The findings that learning correlates negatively with boredom and positively with engagement/flow are consistent with predictions from Csikszentmihalyi's (1990) analysis of *flow* experiences. Conscious flow occurs when the student is absorbed in the material to the point that time and fatigue disappear. Experiences of eureka were much too rare in the experiment: only one recorded eureka experience in 17 total hours of tutoring among 34 students.

We have assembled and installed many of the emotion-sensing technologies with AutoTutor. Analyses are being performed on the components, features, and representations of the following sensing technologies: dialogue patterns during tutoring, facial expressions, and body posture (Graesser, Chipman, Haynes, & Olney, 2005; D'Mello, et al., 2005). Affective states will be interpreted and classified on the basis of several input channels of information. The computational models being explored have quantitative foundations in Bayesian, hidden Markov, neural network, and/or dynamical systems, which are substantially more complex than the standard architectures.

AutoTutor Script Authoring Tool (ASAT)

It is widely acknowledged that the authoring tools for most intelligent tutoring systems require substantial technical expertise to use (Murray, Blessing, & Ainsworth, 2003). One of the virtues of AutoTutor is that it is possible to develop lessons on a new subject matter in a short amount of time, considerably shorter than in intelligent tutoring systems. The core processing mechanisms of AutoTutor remain constant; only the subject matter changes. In one of our tests with NASA, for example, we developed an AutoTutor version for a small set of questions/problems in only 3 days. Development of AutoTutor on a new topic requires only four components, all of which address the subject matter knowledge: (1) a corpus of texts and articles on the subject matter in electronic form, (2) a glossary of terms in electronic form, (3) a Latent Semantic Analysis (LSA) space, and (4) a curriculum script with lesson content and example main questions/problems. For each main question, there is (a) the ideal answer, (b) a set of expectations, (c) families of potential hints, prompts, and assertions associated with each expectation, (d) a set of misconceptions and corrections for each misconception, (e) a set of key words and functional synonyms, (f) a summary, and (g) a markup language for the speech generator and gesture generator for components in (a) through (f) that require actions by the animated agents. Subject matter experts can create the content of the curriculum script with an authoring tool called the *AutoTutor Script Authoring Tool* (Susarla, Adcock, Van Eck, Moreno, & Graesser, 2003).

AutoMentor

The agent-based technology may be sufficiently advanced to consider the prospects of an *AutoMentor* who guides all phases of the learning process in e-learning. AutoMentor would orchestrate the process of diagnosing student knowledge and ability, formative evaluation of subject matter, instruction, scaffolding of active learning processes, and summative evaluation for high-stakes tests. AutoMentor would be available as a conversation partner to assist the learner 24/7.

An AutoMentor would need some important components. It would need a *learner profile,* a record of the knowledge, skills, and history of the learner, at a suitable grain size. The profile would include an evolving assessment of the student's particular knowledge and skills, as well as other historical data useful for making pedagogical decisions (e.g., time on task, percentage of entries preceded by help requests). It would include the learner's interests, needs, abilities, personality, and preferred learning styles. The mentor will select learning objects and dynamically sequence the content in a fashion tailored to the learner profile. The mentor would stop the learner from becoming overly involved with one topic at the expense of the others, would suggest learning strategies, and would offer suggestions on controlling the learner's emotions. AutoMentor would need a *conversational interface* with an animated agent, controlled by dialog and interface components, that delivers the decisions of the mentoring agent, scaffolds the learning process through tutoring, and guides learner navigation. The agent would sometimes converse in natural language, saying the right thing at the right time, with capabilities of pointing, gesturing, and expressing emotion. For other learners, however, the interface would be more streamlined, at times consisting simply of text to be read. AutoMentor would need to accommodate learner preferences and capabilities.

Closing Comments

We believe the time is right for having 24/7 animated conversational agents guide all phases of learning. Each student would have a personal agent that accumulates a learner profile, diagnoses gaps in knowledge and ability, adaptively and dynamically composes instruction material, performs formative evaluation in many rounds of testing, scaffolds student learning through intelligent tutoring strategies, recommends when the learner is ready for a high-stakes summative evaluation, and recommends long-term goals. The agent would track the emotions of the learner in addition to cognition. The AutoMentor agent would follow the students for weeks, months, or years. This sketch of the future will no doubt be exciting to some, frightening to others, and bewildering to many. In any case, the technologies are ready or well within our grasp.

Author Notes

This research was supported by the National Science Foundation (SBR 9720314, REC 0106965, REC 0126265, ITR 0325428), the Institute for Education Sciences (IES R3056020018-02), and the DoD Multidisciplinary University Research Initiative (MURI) administered by ONR under grant N00014-00-1-0600. Requests for reprints should be sent to Art Graesser, Department of Psychology, 202 Psychology Building, University of Memphis, Memphis, TN 38152-3230.

References

Aleven, V. W. M. M., & Koedinger, K. R. (2002). An effective metacognitive strategy: Learning by doing and explaining with a computer-based cognitive tutor. *Cognitive Science, 26*, 147-179.

Allen, J. F. (1995). *Natural language understanding*. Redwood City, CA: Benjamin/Cummings.

Anderson, J. R., Corbett, A. T., Koedinger, K. R., & Pelletier, R. (1995). Cognitive tutors: Lessons learned. *Journal of the Learning Sciences, 4*(2), 167-207.

Atkinson, R. K. (2002). Optimizing learning from examples using animated pedagogical agents. *Journal of Educational Psychology, 94*, 416-427.

Azevedo, R., & Cromley, J. G. (2004). Does training on self-regulated learning facilitate students' learning with hypermedia. *Journal of Educational Psychology, 96*, 523-535.

Baylor, A. L. (2002). Expanding preservice teachers' metacognitive awareness of instructional planning through pedagogical agents. *Educational Technology Research and Development, 50*(2), 5-22.

Burstein, J. (2003). The E-rater scoring engine: Automated essay scoring with natural language processing. In M. D. Shermis & J. C. Burstein (Eds.), *Automated essay scoring: A cross-disciplinary perspective* (pp. 113-133). Mahwah, NJ: Lawrence Erlbaum Associates.

Cassell, J., & Thorisson, K. (1999). The power of a nod and a glance: Envelope vs. emotional feedback in animated conversational agents. *Applied Artificial Intelligence, 13*(3), 519-538.

Chi, M. T. H., de Leeuw, N., Chiu, M. H., & LaVancher, C. (1994). Eliciting self-explanations improves understanding. *Cognitive Science, 18*, 439-477.

Chi, M. T. H., Siler, S. A., Jeong, H., Yamauchi, T., & Hausmann, R. G. (2001). Learning from human tutoring. *Cognitive Science, 25*, 471-533.

Clark, H. H. (1996). *Using language*. Cambridge, UK: Cambridge University Press.

Cohen, P. A., Kulik, J. A., & Kulik, C. C. (1982). Educational outcomes of tutoring: A meta-analysis of findings. *American Educational Research Journal, 19*, 237-248.

Colby, K. M., Weber, S., & Hilf, F. D. (1971). Artificial paranoia. *Artificial Intelligence, 2*(1), 1-25.

Cole, R., van Vuuren, S., Pellom, B., Hacioglu, K., Ma, J., Movellan, J., et al. (2003). Perceptive animated interfaces: First steps toward a new paradigm for human-computer interaction. *Proceedings of the IEEE, 91*(9), 1391-1405.

Collins, A., Warnock, E. H., & Passafiume, J. J. (1975). Analysis and synthesis of tutorial dialogues. In G. Bower (Ed.), *The psychology of learning and motivation: Advances in research and theory* (pp. 49-87). New York: Academic Press.

Craig, S. D., Graesser, A. C., Sullins, J., & Gholson, B. (2004). Affect and learning: An exploratory look into the role of affect in learning. *Journal of Educational Media, 29*(3), 241-250.

Csikszentmihalyi, M. (1990). *Flow: The psychology of optimal experience*. New York: Harper Row.

Deane, P. (2005). Strategies for evidence identification through linguistic assessment of textual responses. Unpublished manuscript. Educational Testing Service, Princeton, NJ.

D'Mello, S. K., Craig, S. D., Gholson, B., Franklin, S., Picard, R. W., & Graesser, A. C. (2005). Integrating affect sensors in an intelligent tutoring system. In *Affective interactions: The computer in the Affective Loop Workshop at 2005 International conference on Intelligent User Interfaces* (pp. 7-13). New York: AMC Press.

Dwyer, C. A. (Ed.). (2005). *Measurement and research in the accountability era*. Mahwah, NJ: Lawrence Erlbaum Associates.

Fox, B. A. (1993). *The human tutorial dialogue project*. Hillsdale, NJ: Lawrence Erlbaum Associates.

Graesser, A. C., Chipman, P., Haynes, B. C., & Olney, A. (2005). AutoTutor: An intelligent system with mixed-initiative dialogue. *IEEE Transactions in Education, 48*, 612-618.

Graesser, A. C., & Clark, L. C. (1985). *Structures and procedures of implicit knowledge*. Norwood, NJ: Ablex.

Graesser, A. C., Gernsbacher, M. A., & Goldman, S. (Eds.). (2003). *Handbook of discourse processes*. Mahwah, NJ: Lawrence Erlbaum Associates.

Graesser, A. C., Hu, X., & McNamara, D. S. (2005). Computerized learning environments that incorporate research in discourse psychology, cognitive science, and computational linguistics. In A. F. Healy (Ed.), *Experimental cognitive psychology and its applications: Festschrift in honor of Lyle Bourne, Walter Kintsch, and Thomas Landauer*. Washington, DC: American Psychological Association.

Graesser, A. C., Jackson, G. T., Mathews, E. C., Mitchell, H. H., Olney, A., Ventura, M., et al. (2003). Why/AutoTutor: A test of learning gains from a physics tutor with natural language dialog. Proceedings of the 25th annual conference of the Cognitive Science Society. Mahwah, NJ: Lawrence Erlbaum Associates.

Graesser, A. C., Lu, S., Jackson, G. T., Mitchell, H., Ventura, M., Olney, A., et al. (2004). AutoTutor: A tutor with dialogue in natural language. *Behavioral Research Methods, Instruments, and Computers, 36*, 180-193.

Graesser, A. C., Moreno, K., Marineau, J., Adcock, A., Olney, A., & Person, N. (2003). AutoTutor improves deep learning of computer literacy: Is it the dialog or the talking head? In U. Hoppe, F. Verdejo, & J. Kay (Eds.), *Proceedings of artificial intelligence in education* (pp. 47-54). Amsterdam: IOS Press.

Graesser, A. C., & Olde, B. A. (2003). How does one know whether a person understands a device? The quality of the questions the person asks when the device breaks down. *Journal of Educational Psychology, 95*, 524-536.

Graesser, A. C., & Person, N. K. (1994). Question asking during tutoring. *American Educational Research Journal, 31,* 104-137.

Graesser, A. C., Person, N., Harter, D., & Tutoring Research Group. (2001). Teaching tactics and dialog in AutoTutor. *International Journal of Artificial Intelligence in Education, 12,* 257-279.

Graesser, A. C., VanLehn, K., Rose, C., Jordan, P., & Harter, D. (2001). Intelligent tutoring systems with conversational dialogue. *AI Magazine, 22,* 39-51.

Graesser, A. C., Wiemer-Hastings, P., Wiemer-Hastings, K., Harter, D., Person, N., & Tutoring Research Group. (2000). Using latent semantic analysis to evaluate the contributions of students in AutoTutor. *Interactive Learning Environments, 8,* 129-148.

Graesser, A. C., Wiemer-Hastings, K., Wiemer-Hastings, P., Kreuz, R., & Tutoring Research Group. (1999). AutoTutor: A simulation of a human tutor. *Journal of Cognitive Systems Research, 1,* 35-51.

Gratch, J., Rickel, J., André, E., Cassell, J., Petajan, E., & Badler, N. (2002). Creating interactive virtual humans: Some assembly required. *IEEE Intelligent Systems, 17*(4), 54-63.

Harabagiu, S. M., Maiorano, S. J., & Pasca, M. A. (2002). Open-domain question answering techniques. *Natural Language Engineering, 1,* 1-38.

Hume, G. D., Michael, J. A., Rovick, A., & Evens, M. W. (1996). Hinting as a tactic in one-on-one tutoring. *Journal of the Learning Sciences, 5*(1), 23–47.

Johnson, W. L., & Beal, C. (2005). Iterative evaluation of a large-scale, intelligent game for learning language. In C. Looi, G. McCalla, B. Bredeweg, & J. Breuker (Eds.), *Artificial intelligence in education* (pp. 290-297). Amsterdam: IOS Press.

Johnson, W. L., Rickel, J. W., & Lester, J. C. (2000). Animated pedagogical agents: Face-to-face interaction in interactive learning environments. *International Journal of Artificial Intelligence in Education, 11,* 47-78.

Jurafsky, D., & Martin, J. H. (2000). Speech and language processing: An introduction to natural language processing, computational linguistics, and speech recognition. Upper Saddle River, NJ: Prentice Hall.

Landauer, T. K., Foltz, P. W., & Laham, D. (1998). An introduction to latent semantic analysis. *Discourse Processes, 25,* 259-284.

Landauer, T., McNamara, D. S., Dennis, S., & Kintsch, W. (Eds.). (2007). *LSA: A road to meaning.* Mahwah, NJ: Lawrence Erlbaum Associates.

Larsson, S., & Traum, D. (2000). Information state and dialogue management in the TRINDI Dialogue Move Engine Toolkit. *Natural Language Engineering, 6,* 323-340.

Leacock, C., & Chodorow, M. (2003). C-rater: Automated scoring of short answer questions. *Computers and the Humanities, 37*(4), 389-405.

Lenat, D. B. (1995). CYC: A large-scale investment in knowledge infrastructure. *Communications of the ACM, 38*(11), 33-38.

Manning, C., & Schutze, H. (1999). *Foundations of statistical natural language processing.* Cambridge, MA: MIT Press.

Massaro, D. W., & Cohen, M. M. (1995). Perceiving talking faces. *Current Directions in Psychological Science, 4,* 104-109.

Moore, J. D. (1995). *Participating in explanatory dialogues.* Cambridge, MA: MIT Press.

Moore, J. D., & Wiemer-Hastings, P. (2003). Discourse in computational linguistics and artificial intelligence. In A. C. Graesser, M. A. Gernsbacher, & S. R. Goldman (Eds.), *Handbook of discourse processes* (pp. 439-486). Mahwah, NJ: Lawrence Erlbaum Associates.

Moreno, K. N., Klettke, B., Nibbaragandla, K., Graesser, A. C., & Tutoring Research Group. (2002). Perceived characteristics and pedagogical efficacy of animated conversational agents. In S. A. Cerri, G. Gouardères, & F. Paraguaçu (Eds.), *Intelligent tutoring systems: 6th international conference, ITS 2002* (pp. 963-971). Berlin: Springer-Verlag.

Moreno, R., Mayer, R. E., Spires, H. A., & Lester, J. C. (2001). The case for social agency in computer-based teaching: Do students learn more deeply when they interact with animated pedagogical agents? *Cognition and Instruction, 19*(2), 177-213.

Murray, T., Blessing, S., & Ainsworth, S. (Eds.). (2003). *Authoring tools for advanced technology learning environments.* Amsterdam: Kluwer.

Norman, D. A., & Rumelhart, D. E. (1975). *Explorations in cognition.* San Francisco: Freeman.

Olde, B. A., Franceschetti, D. R., Karnavat, A., Graesser, A. C., & Tutoring Research Group. (2002). The right stuff: Do you need to sanitize your corpus when using latent semantic analysis? In W. G. Gray & C. D. Schunn (Eds.), *Proceedings of the 24th annual conference of the Cognitive Science Society* (pp. 708-713). Mahwah, NJ: Lawrence Erlbaum Associates.

Person, N. K., Erkel, M., Graesser, A. C., & Tutoring Research Group. (2002). AutoTutor passes the bystander Turing test. In M. Driscoll & T. C. Reeves (Eds.), *Proceedings for E-Learning 2002: World conference on E-Learning in corporate, government, healthcare, & higher education* (pp. 778-782). Montreal: AACE.

Peters, S., Bratt, E. O., Clark, B., Pon-Barry, H., & Schultz, K. (2004). Intelligent systems for training damage control assistants (Paper No. 1908). In *Proceedings of the Interservice/Industry Training, Simulation, and Education Conference 2004*, Orlando, FL.

Pickering, M. J., & Garrod, S. (2004). Toward a mechanistic psychology of dialogue. *Brain and Behavioral Sciences, 27,* 169-225.

Reeves, B., & Nass, C. (1996). *The media equation: How people treat computers, televisions, and new media like real people and places.* Cambridge, UK: Cambridge University Press.

Rich, C., & Sidner, C. L. (1998). COLLAGEN: A collaboration manager for software interface agents. *User Modeling and User-Adapted Interaction, 8*(3/4), 315-350.

Rickel, J., Lesh, N., Rich, C., Sidner, C. L., & Gertner, A. S. (2002). Collaborative discourse theory as a foundation for tutorial dialogue. In S. A. Cerri, G. Gouardères, & F. Paraguaçu (Eds.), *Intelligent Tutoring Systems: 6th international conference, ITS 2002* (pp. 542-551). Berlin: Springer-Verlag.

Rieber, L. P., & Kini, A. (1995). Using computer simulations in inductive learning strategies with children in science. *International Journal of Instructional Media, 22*(2), 135-144.

Rus, V., & Moldovan, D. I. (2002). High performance logic form transformation. *International Journal on Artificial Intelligence Tools, 11*(3), 437-454.

Schank, R., & Riesbeck, C. (1981). *Inside computer understanding.* Hillsdale, NJ: Lawrence Erlbaum Associates.

Schegloff, E. A., & Sacks, H. (1973). Opening up closings. *Semiotica, 8,* 289-327.

Schober, M. F., & Conrad, F. G. (1997). Does conversational interviewing reduce survey measurement error? *Public Opinion Quarterly, 61,* 576-602.

Shah, F., Evens, M., Michael, J. A., & Rovick, A. A. (2002). Classifying student initiatives and tutor responses in human keyboard-to-keyboard tutoring sessions. *Discourse Processes, 33*(1), 23-52.

Sinclair, J. M., & Coulthard, R. M. (1975). *Towards an analysis of discourse: The English used by teachers and their pupils.* London: Oxford University Press.

Susarla, S., Adcock, A., Van Eck, R., Moreno, K., & Graesser, A. C. (2003). Development and evaluation of a lesson authoring tool for AutoTutor. In V. Aleven, U. Hoppe, J. Kay, R. Mizoguchi, H. Pain, F. Verdejo, & K. Yacef (Eds.), *AIED2003 supplemental proceedings* (pp. 378-387). Sydney, Australia: University of Sydney School of Information Technologies.

VanLehn, K., Graesser, A. C., Jackson, G. T., Jordan, P., Olney, A., & Rose, C. P. (2005). When is reading just as effective as one-on-one interactive tutoring? In B. Bara (Ed.), *Proceedings of the 27th annual meetings of the Cognitive Science Society.* Mahwah, NJ: Lawrence Erlbaum Associates.

VanLehn, K., Jones, R. M., & Chi, M. T. H. (1992). A model of the self-explanation effect. *Journal of the Learning Sciences, 2*(1), 1-60.

VanLehn, K., Jordan, P., Rosé, C. P., Bhembe, D., Bottner, M., Gaydos, A., et al. (2002). The architecture of Why2-Atlas: A coach for qualitative physics essay writing. In S. A. Cerri, G. Gouardères, & F. Paraguaçu (Eds.), *Intelligent Tutoring Systems: 6th international conference, ITS 2002* (pp. 158-167). Berlin: Springer-Verlag.

VanLehn, K., Lynch, C., Taylor, L., Weinstein, A., Shelby, R. H., Schulze, K. G., et al. (2002). Minimally invasive tutoring of complex physics problem solving. In S. A. Cerri, G. Gouardères, & F. Paraguaçu (Eds.), *Intelligent Tutoring Systems: 6th international conference, ITS 2002* (pp. 367-376). Berlin: Springer-Verlag.

Voorhees, E. (2001). The TREC question answering track. *Natural Language Engineering, 7*(4), 361-378.

Weizenbaum, J. (1966). ELIZA – A computer program for the study of natural language communication between man and machine. *Communications of the ACM, 9*(1), 36-45.

Whittaker, S. (2003). Computer mediated communication: A review. In A.Graesser, M. A. Gernsbacher, & S. R.Goldman (Eds.), *The handbook of discourse processes*. Mahwah, NJ: Lawrence Erlbaum Associates.

Winne, P. H. (2001). Self-regulated learning viewed from models of information processing. In B. Zimmerman & D. Schunk (Eds.), *Self-regulated learning and academic achievement: Theoretical perspectives* (pp. 153-189). Mahwah, NJ: Lawrence Erlbaum Associates.

Winograd, T. (1972). *Understanding natural language*. New York: Academic Press.

Woods, W. A. (1977). Lunar rocks in natural English: Explorations in natural language question answering. In A. Zampoli (Ed.), *Linguistic structures processing* (pp. 201-222). New York: Elsevier.

5

Intelligent Tutoring Systems for Continuous, Embedded Assessment

Kurt VanLehn
University of Pittsburgh

This chapter describes how intelligent tutoring systems (ITS) can be used for assessment. It begins by describing intelligent tutoring systems and distinguishing them from an older, more widely available technology. It argues that this newer technology has some intrinsic benefits as a tool for assessment. It then describes a particular type of assessment widely used in the ITS community. The assessment technique is based on a mathematically sound inference method, Bayesian belief networks. The basic technique, an adaptation of Knowledge Tracing (Corbett & Anderson, 1995), is described along with several recent extensions.

An Introduction to Intelligent Tutoring Systems

There are many types of tutoring systems. The oldest and most commonly available technology has students enter the final answer to a question or problem, and gives them feedback and hints based on the answer (Dick & Carey, 1990). For instance, such a system might assign an algebra word problem and expect the student to solve it on scratch paper and enter a numerical answer. If the answer is correct, the system says so; otherwise, it may give a hint. This kind of tutoring system is often called computer-aided instruction (CAI), computer-based training (CBT), or more recently, Web-based homework (WBH).

Perhaps the second largest category of tutoring system has students enter steps leading up to the solution of a problem, and it can give feedback and hints on those steps as well as on the final answer

(VanLehn, 2006; Corbett, Koedinger, & Anderson, 1997; Rickel, 1989; Shute & Psotka, 1996). For instance, after assigning an algebra word problem, such a system would expect the student to enter a sequence of lines, each consisting of a variable definition or an equation. That is, the work that would otherwise be done on scratch paper is instead done on the computer. The system can give the student feedback and hints on the intermediate steps leading up to the final answer. These systems are called intelligent tutoring systems (ITS).

Although the defining feature of this kind of ITS is that it gives feedback and hints on steps as well as final answers, *when* it gives feedback and hints varies. Some ITS (e.g., Mitrovic & Ohlsson, 1999) delay giving feedback and hints on steps until the student has indicated that the solution is complete; this allows the student to practice finding his/her own errors and correcting them. However, many ITS are intended for novices who are still struggling to find any solution at all, so these systems (e.g., Anderson, Corbett, Koedinger, & Pelletier, 1995) give feedback on a step just as soon as it is entered; this prevents long, unproductive trial-and-error searches. In short, the distinguishing feature is not when the feedback and hints are given, but whether the system addresses only the final answer or the intermediate steps as well.

The term "ITS" encompasses systems that don't easily fit the description above, such as a tutoring system that converses with a student in spoken natural language (e.g., Litman et al., in press). However, the field does not yet have an accepted nomenclature for distinguishing the various subtypes of intelligent tutoring systems, so this chapter will use "ITS" to refer only to tutoring systems where a student receives either immediate or delayed feedback and hints on multiple steps that comprise a solution to a problem.

The term "step" will be used for the user interface entries that students are expected to make. Steps can take many forms. For illustration, consider a simulated laboratory task: determining if a particular chemical solution changes its acidity as it is heated. The student's steps might be to (1) get a clean test tube from the (simulated) storage cabinet, (2) decant some of the solution into it, (3) heat it to a specific temperature, (4) measure its acidity (pH), (5) create a blank line graph, (6) label the x-axis "temperature," (7) label the y-axis "acidity," (8) plot a point on the graph, (9) heat the solution some more, (10) plot a second point on the graph, and (11) enter "true" as the final answer. Each of these 11 user interface gestures is a step. Let us suppose that the tutoring system is a delayed feedback system, so as soon as the student has entered "true," it gives feedback by suggesting that more than two data points are needed for reliability, and that "pH" would be a more accurate label for the y-axis than "acidity." Thus, its feedback and hints are at the level of steps.

For most ITS, the user interface is designed so that steps are entered frequently. That is, the student only has to think for a few seconds or perhaps a minute at most to decide how to do the next step. If a step is so complex that it tempts the student to use scratch paper, then the ITS designers might redesign the user interface to break down that step into substeps. However, the size of steps is an ITS design variable just like immediate/delayed feedback. More competent students should probably be given a user interface that requires larger, more complex steps, whereas novices probably learn best from a user interface with frequent, small, simple steps (Greer & McCalla, 1989).

Based on studies of human tutors (Douglas, 1991; Fox, 1993; Hume, Michael, Rovick, & Evens, 1996; Lepper, Woolverton, Mumme, & Gurtner, 1993; McArthur, Stasz, & Zmuidzinas, 1990; Merrill, Reiser, Ranney, & Trafton, 1992; VanLehn, Siler, Murray, Yamauchi, & Baggett, 2003; Wood & Middleton, 1975), ITS give feedback and hints in sequences of increasing specificity. Suppose a student enters an incorrect step into a tutoring system that gives feedback and hints immediately. The minimal-information feedback is simply to say, "that's incorrect." Systems often do this by turning the step red or beeping. This minimal-information response comprises the first "hint" in the system's sequence. If the student either asks for a hint or makes a second incorrect attempt at the step, the system gives the next hint in the sequence, which is usually designed to jog the student's memory or to point out some critical feature of the problem that the student may have overlooked. If the student again asks for a hint or enters the step incorrectly, the system gives the third hint in the sequence, which reveals further information. This continues until the student either enters the step correctly or the system reaches the last hint in its sequence. The last hint, which is called the "bottom out hint," tells the student exactly what to enter. Although most ITS use hint sequences exclusively, some use even more complicated hint dialogues for some steps (e.g., VanLehn, Lynch, Schultz, et al., 2005).

Some basic concepts of ITS have been introduced: A *task* is solved by entering many *steps* leading up to a *final answer.* The student can get *feedback* and *hints* on individual steps either *immediately* or *delayed* until they have submitted their final answer. The feedback and hints are often given in a *hint sequence* that ends with a *bottom-out hint.*

An Illustrative ITS

In order to illustrate these concepts in an integrated fashion, let us use a college physics tutoring system, Andes (VanLehn, Lynch, Schultz, et al., 2005). Andes is in regular use at the U.S. Naval Academy (USNA). It is used by students in their dorm rooms to help them do their assigned homework. When Andes was adopted, all the other instructional activities in the course were almost entirely unaffected. In particular, the instructors continued to use the same textbooks, lectures, labs, and exams.

Indeed, the USNA course is taught by a team of instructors, and only some of them have adopted Andes. The other instructors' students still do homework on paper. This has allowed us to compare students who do homework on Andes with those who do homework on paper while holding all other instructional activities constant. The Andes students learned significantly more (effect size, .61).

Figure 5.1 shows the Andes screen, which is divided into four windows. (1) The upper left window shows the homework problem, which is often illustrated with a picture. A box for entering the final answer is also displayed. Below the picture is some white space in which the student can draw diagrams. In this case, the student has drawn a diagram with a body (the dot), a Cartesian coordinate system (tilted slightly), a vector pointing downward representing the weight force Fw on the car, and a vector pointing leftward representing the displacement d of the car. (2) The upper right window lists the variables the student has defined so far. Most were defined as side effects of drawing vectors, etc. (3) The lower right window is a list of equations that the student has defined so far. (4) The lower left window is for hint dialogues between the tutoring system ("T:…") and the student ("S:…").

There are several different kinds of steps. Entering an equation is a step, and it consists of clicking in a box in the lower right window,

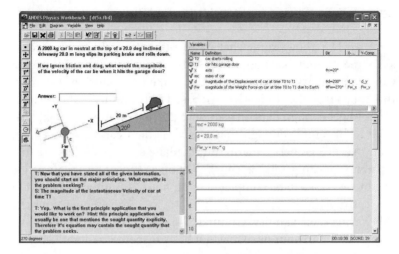

Figure 5.1   User interface of the Andes physics tutoring system.

typing the equation, and pressing the Enter key. Defining a scalar variable is a step, and it is done by pulling down a menu, selecting the type of variable, and filling out a dialogue box that defines the variable precisely and names it. Drawing a vector is a step, and it is done by clicking on the vertical menu bar on the left side of the screen, dragging out a vector, then filling out a dialogue box to complete a precise definition of the vector. There are several other kinds of steps as well.

Whenever the student enters a step, it turns green if it is correct and red if incorrect. In the figure, only equation 3 is incorrect; all the other steps are correct. Andes will give hints only if asked, and students ask for a hint by clicking on a button in the top menu bar. In most cases, Andes uses a hint sequence. On a few especially important cases, it uses a more complex hint dialogue, wherein it asks the students a question and provides menus for answering it. A fragment of such a hint dialogue is shown in the lower left window of the figure.

Why Use an ITS for Assessment?

There are several reasons for using ITS for assessment. This section lists them, dividing them into those that flow from the intrinsic operation of ITS, and those that arise from their routine use in instruction.

Benefits Due to the Multistep Nature of ITS

First, an ITS allows somewhat more authentic tasks to be used for assessment, and that may increase the validity of the assessment. Conventional assessment methods are like CAI tutoring systems in that they judge the student's work based only on the final answer. In order to get enough data on a student during a testing session, tasks need to be simple enough that many of them can be solved in an hour. An ITS gathers data on intermediate steps as well as the final answer, so it can get just as much data on a student by assigning just one or two tasks to be completed in an hour. It is often thought that short, simple tasks are not as authentic as complex ones, and that this harms their validity. Granted, a single student working with a computer for an hour or so may not be as authentic as a multi-person team working on a project over a semester, but moving from a 30-second task to a 30-minute task is at least a step toward authenticity and increased validity.

Second, an ITS can provide strategic and meta-cognitive assessments. Because an ITS monitors the steps leading up to a solution, an ITS can observe a student's problem-solving strategy, which is difficult or impossible to observe when only the final answer is entered. If the ITS includes reference information, such as a glossary, worked example problems, principles, or even the textbook itself, then it can monitor the student's use of this information as the student solves problems. This can reveal the student's meta-cognitive strategies for learning. Even the student's use of the ITS's hints can reveal their meta-cognitive strategies (Aleven & Koedinger, 2000). This allows an assessment to measure not only what a student knows, but how they use it and how they learn it.

Third, the consequential validity (Messick, 1994) of using an ITS for assessment is probably positive. It has been argued that conventional assessments based on final answers to many relatively short, inauthentic problems have caused students and instructors to focus too much on becoming proficient in this kind of problem solving. That is, the societal consequences of the assessment are negative. On the other hand, when students and instructors adapt their instruction in order to raise ITS scores, they are probably improving the student's meta-cognitive and problem-solving strategies. Thus, the consequential validity of an ITS assessment is probably more positive than that of conventional assessment.

Benefits of Embedded Assessment

With a few exceptions, ITS have *not* been used to take over or replace classroom instruction. As mentioned earlier, the Andes physics tutoring system (VanLehn et al., 2005) only helps students do their homework; all other instructional activities are carried out by the instructors as usual. As another example, Carnegie Learning's popular Cognitive Algebra Tutor (www.carnegielearning.com) is used by high school students 2 days a week in computer labs; the other 3 days are regular algebra classes.

Let us assume that our assessment ITS is used only to coach students as they solve complex tasks, and that the course contains many other instructional activities besides problem solving. To put it in a slightly old fashioned way, we are assuming that the ITS grades students' homework and seatwork. This saves the instructor a great deal of time and effort, but can it really change classroom practices very much?

Unlike a human grader, the ITS is objective, indefatigable, and completely reliable. It is reliable in the sense that given the same log of student actions (i.e., all user interface events, in chronological order, with the same pauses), it will generate exactly the same assessment.[1]

Moreover, the assessment can be standardized, in that the same measures can be used in all classes. The assessment can be nationally or internationally normed. Norming is particularly easy because the ITS is viable as an instructional tool, which allows one to collect calibration data on student behavior over extended periods of time from many sites prior to releasing it as a normed assessment tool. Lastly, the ITS can send its assessments over a secure connection to an impartial judge, such as a testing company, as well as to the instructor and/or student. These are some of the same benefits that standardized testing achieves.

At first glance, it might appear that using an ITS for high-stakes assessment would require the same kind of authentication used at testing centers. When an ITS is used for homework or seatwork, the ITS cannot really tell who is at the keyboard. A student could log in and then have a friend sit down and solve the problems. However, even if an ITS is used for high-stakes decision making, it would be used to gather data over a whole year or semester. Only rarely would someone be willing to do a whole year of homework and/or seatwork for their friend and not get caught.

A much more important issue is that conventional testing is usually sequestered problem solving (Bransford & Schwartz, 1999), but
ITS problem solving is not. That is, conventional testing is done in a
situation where students cannot receive help, do not receive feedback
on their answers, and in general are prevented from learning. However, an ITS has exactly the opposite goal—it tries to get students
to learn. As will be described in the subsequent section, algorithms
have been developed that can track students' evolving competence
even when the tutoring system is giving them hints and helping them
learn. However, the ITS cannot detect when the student is receiving
help from a human. Clearly, we do not want to prevent ITS students
from obtaining help from instructors, friends, and family whenever
they need it. Thus, we need to know how often such help is likely to
occur and how much impact it might have on the accuracy of the ITS
assessment. Let us consider seatwork first, then homework.

Ethnographic studies of the Cognitive Tutors indicate that even
though students doing seatwork get most of their help from the
tutoring system, they still ask for help from the instructor (Schofield,
1995). However, the instructors and students report that their conversations are often mathematically deeper than they were before the
tutoring system was adopted. The tutoring system takes care of the
simple help requests, leaving the instructor to deal with the complex
ones. Both instructors and students prefer this mode of interaction.

When an ITS is used for homework, it is harder to conduct the
appropriate ethnographic studies to determine how it is really used,
but it appears that ITS homework is like ITS seatwork in that the ITS
deepens human help but does not eliminate it. The Andes instructors
still get many visits from students during office hours, and we can
draw a few inferences from their experiences (D. Treacy, personal
communication, 2000–2005). The instructors report that Andes
makes it much easier for them to diagnose the student's difficulties.
When a student reports having trouble with a particular homework
problem, the instructor downloads the student's (partial) solution
from a server. If the partial solution doesn't immediately identify the
student's difficulty, the instructor can replay the log data in order to
find out what kinds of mistakes were made and erased, what kind
of hints were given by Andes, etc. The instructor can also examine
Andes's analysis of the student's work. For diagnosing the student's
misconceptions, these new sources of data seem much more effective
than the student's self-reports.

Although more ethnographic studies are clearly needed, it appears that doing seatwork and homework with an ITS deepens human help but certainly does not eliminate it. Thus, an issue for future research, which can probably only be addressed by field studies, is determining if the existing ITS assessment algorithms gracefully accept sharp changes in competence due to human help.

Assuming that the existing assessment algorithms suffice (or that new ones do), we have a mode of assessment that does not require sequestered problem solving. Students are expected and encouraged to learn as they are being assessed, and they are working on complex, more authentic problems. Moreover, the assessments can be standardized, normed, and secured just like conventional tests are now. This suggests that standardized tests may be superfluous if an ITS is used to grade seatwork and homework. If so, then a major advantage of ITS assessment is that it would eliminate sequestered testing.

Elimination of sequestered, standardized testing in favor of continuous, embedded assessment could bring several practical advantages.

- It would free up the time currently used on taking tests that are deliberately designed to prevent learning during the test.
- Students could not be absent on the day of the test, because with ITS assessment, almost every day is a "test day."
- Students' assessed performance would not be atypically higher or lower than their "ordinary" performance, because the ITS measures their ordinary performance. It would no longer make sense to say that a student "doesn't test well" or "is good at tests, but nothing else."
- Test anxiety would disappear (or be indistinguishable from general anxiety).
- Cramming for the test no longer makes sense.
- Instead of measuring students' competence a few times a year, instructors could track students' knowledge growth continuously. For instance, if the instructor wants to create pairs comprised of a knowledgeable student and less knowledgeable student for tomorrow's discussions, the instructor can read the student's current state of knowledge today. The instructor can also detect more rapidly those students who are falling behind and those that are not sufficiently challenged.

However, before deciding to eliminate conventional testing, it needs to be repeated that an ITS measures performance during only part of the student's instructional activities. Students may also participate in class discussions, engage in group projects, write essays, or give presentations. The assessment derived from an ITS should be combined with other measures in order to get a complete and well-rounded picture of the student's evolving strengths and weaknesses.

Bayesian Assessment of Knowledge Component Mastery

Having described ITS and their potential benefits as assessments, this section defines a particular kind of assessment, reflected in the section's title, and argues for its utility. In order to define this kind of assessment, a few technical terms need to be introduced.

The first technical term is "knowledge component," which has its roots deep in the history of ITS and artificial intelligence (AI) more generally. After a few decades of working with relatively general reasoning methods, AI researchers realized that effective problem solving requires large quantities of domain-specific knowledge. Knowledge was represented in various notations, including production rules, frames, Prolog clauses, and so on. The knowledge was operational, in that it was specific enough to be used to solve problems. It was also represented in many small pieces, such as rules, frames, etc. The term *knowledge component* has emerged as a notation-neutral term for a small piece of operational domain knowledge.

When used in the context of an ITS, knowledge component denotes a small piece of domain knowledge *that the student should learn.* For instance, in late 2005, Andes contained 308 knowledge components and covered about 75% of the AP Physics B curriculum. A typical textbook for that curriculum has about 35 chapters, so this works out to about 12 knowledge components per chapter. Most of the knowledge components are well-known principles, such as Newton's second law or Ohm's law. However, some knowledge components are needed for reasoning but do not have names. For instance, in electrical circuits, there is a knowledge component that says that the current through a switch is zero if the switch is open, and the voltage drop across a switch is zero if the switch is closed. This knowledge component is mentioned in the textbook, but is not treated as a "named" principle like Ohm's law.

The second technical term that needs to be defined is the set of knowledge components that are *relevant* to a step. Suppose a student is solving a problem and takes a correct step. The knowledge components relevant to the step are those that an ideally competent student would need to apply in order to generate that step in that context. For instance, suppose a physics problem is partially solved, as in Figure 5.1, and the student draws a zero-length vector representing the car's initial velocity. There is just one relevant knowledge component: "If an object is at rest at a certain time, then its instantaneous velocity at that time is zero." When an ITS is intended to be used by novice learners, then the number of relevant knowledge components per step is usually small—under five, typically, and often just one. When the ITS is intended for use by more competent students, then the number of relevant knowledge components per step is often somewhat larger—perhaps five or 10. As mentioned earlier, the average step size is an important ITS design parameter, similar to immediate vs. delayed feedback.

The third technical term that needs definition is "step attempt history." Because the ITS can give feedback and hints on steps, students sometimes make several attempts before successfully entering a step. In the earlier illustration of a simulated chemistry lab, instead of simply labeling the x-axis with "temperature," the following events might occur:

1. The student labels the x-axis "acidity."
2. The system's speech generator says, "OK, but I wouldn't choose axes that way."
3. The student clicks on the Hint button.
4. The system's speech generator says, "The question asks whether acidity varies as temperature is varied. So temperature is the independent variable."
5. The student clicks on the Hint button again.
6. The system says, "It is conventional to put the independent variable on the x-axis, so I would advise putting 'temperature' on the x-axis and 'acidity' on the y-axis."
7. The student enters "temperature" as the x-axis label.

In other words, it took seven user interface events to get this step entered correctly. When tutoring systems are used for assessment, it matters whether a step was entered correctly on the first try or only after receiving several hints. For future reference, let us use "step attempt history" to refer to the sequence of user interface events leading up to the student's final entry of the step.[2]

The last technical term that needs definition is *mastery* of a knowledge component. ITS assessment was often developed with mastery learning in mind, and some ITS actually do implement mastery learning (Bloom, 1984). That is, they choose the tasks that the student should do, and they keep assigning tasks from an instructional unit until the student has mastered all the unit's knowledge components. However, mastery learning causes students to proceed at different paces. After a few weeks, some students may be in chapter 10 while others are still struggling with chapter 3. Thus, instructors often turn mastery learning off, and assign all students the same tasks. Nonetheless, the concept "mastery of a knowledge component" has been retained and is the last of our technical terms.

The concept is actually quite subtle. Intuitively, mastery means that the knowledge component is known so well that the instructor and ITS no longer need to focus on teaching it. However, this intuitive definition refers to instructional policy (how the mastery judgment is used) rather than the evidence used to define or infer mastery. As evidence of mastery, one intuitively expects the following:

- The knowledge component is always applied in situations where it should be applied.
- The knowledge component is never applied in situations where it should not be applied.
- When the knowledge component is applied, the application is done rapidly and without reference to external representations of the knowledge component (e.g., textbook, friend).
- The student can explain the knowledge component in general terms, and can explain why a particular application (or non-application) was justified.

Even an ITS doesn't have enough information to assess all these characteristics, so it must estimate mastery from the information that it has. Thus, an ITS should calculate only a probability of mastery—given the evidence observed by the ITS, what are the chances that this student has mastered this knowledge component?

It makes sense to adopt a Bayesian approach to assessment of mastery of knowledge components. Many courses build on prior knowledge, so some of the knowledge components used in the course may be mastered by students before they take the course. Of course, the ITS cannot just assume that all students will have mastered all the prerequisites. Some students must learn the prerequisites as they learn everything else. Thus, the ITS must estimate mastery of the prerequisite knowledge components along with the others. Its estimates can converge more rapidly on accurate values if it assumes a fairly high prior probability of mastery for prerequisite knowledge components, and a fairly low prior probability of mastery for knowledge components that are rarely taught in preceding courses. If it has information about a specific student's background (e.g., courses taken), then the student's prior probabilities can perhaps be made more accurate.

At this point, the assessment problem can be stated: Given a set of knowledge components, each with a prior probability of mastery, and given the step attempt history for each step taken by the student while solving a sequence of tasks, calculate the posterior probability of mastery—that is, the probability of mastery of each knowledge component after all the tasks have been completed.

This is clearly not the only kind of assessment that could be computed by an ITS, and it might not even be the most useful one, especially for human decision makers. However, it can be used to calculate several useful kinds of assessments. Some examples follow.

> Suppose an instructor wishes to see a single number that represents "how well the student is doing." Such an assessment can be calculated by simply counting the number of knowledge components that have mastery probabilities greater than .90 (or whatever threshold the instructor chooses).
>
> Suppose an instructor wishes to see what concepts in the current chapter are difficult for students to learn. A nice display would be a bar chart with the chapter's knowledge components on the x-axis, the height of the bars corresponding to the probability of mastery of the component averaged across students in the class, and error whiskers showing the standard error of the mean. Low bars or bars with large whiskers indicate concepts causing students difficulty.
>
> Suppose an instructor (or a student) wants to predict how well the student would do on a certain standardized test (AP Physics B, in the case of Andes). Moreover, suppose the test items have been analyzed in order to determine, for each test item, which knowledge components are relevant. Given the student's posterior probability of mastery of each knowledge component, one can calculate for each test item the probability of a correct answer. This predicts not only the score on the test, but the pattern of correct and incorrect answers. This method has also been used to test the validity of ITS assessments described below (e.g., Corbett, McLaughlin, & Scarpinatto, 2000; VanLehn & Martin, 1998).

A Synthesis of Bayesian Assessments

This section frames the assessment problem as construction and evaluation of a Bayesian network (Russell & Norvig, 2003). Several existing techniques are special cases of this framework, including one of the earliest and arguably the most widely used methods, Knowledge Tracing (Corbett & Anderson, 1995), which is described first. Next, several extensions that overcome the limitations of Knowledge Tracing are described. These extensions synthesize several recent approaches to Bayesian assessment. The resulting system is one view of the "state of the art" in Bayesian assessment.

A Generic Dynamic Bayesian Network Assessor

The assessment problem can be formulated as follows: Given (1) a set of knowledge components each with a prior probability of mastery, and (2) a chronological sequence of M steps along with the student's step attempt history for each, calculate (3) the posterior probabilities of mastery for each of the knowledge components. Put more simply, the assessment problem consists of updating a set of mastery probabilities based on the student's solution process, as revealed in their step attempt histories.

Suppose, for instance, that the problem is so simple that it can be solved in just two steps. If the student did one step successfully on the first attempt but had to be given a bottom-out hint on the other, then some probabilities of mastery would rise (for knowledge components relevant to only the successful step) and some probabilities would fall (for knowledge components relevant to only the unsuccessful step).

A Bayesian network is built from nodes and directed links, where the nodes represent random variables and the links represent conditional dependencies among them. Let us use nodes to represent the mastery of knowledge components, and let each node have two values: mastered or not. A knowledge component's mastery can change over time, so we need to use two subscripts to denote a particular mastery: Let $P(K_{ij})$ denote the probability of mastery of knowledge component i just after step j. Let K_{i0} denote the prior probability of mastery of the knowledge component i before any steps have been done. If we have N knowledge components and the student's solution comprised M steps, then we need $N(M + 1)$ nodes.

We also need a random variable for each step in order to represent how the student accomplished the step. Thus, if there are M steps in the student's solution of the problem, then we need M step nodes. Now we have a representational choice to make. We cannot feasibly represent all possible step attempt histories; there are just too many of them. Thus, the common practice is to define just a few *categories* of step attempt histories, such as (a) entered a correct step on the first try; (b) entered a correct step after seeing the bottom-out hint; (c) all other step attempt histories. With this classification, each step node would have three values. Another popular representation is the binary classification: (a) entered a correct step on the first try; (b) all other step attempt histories.

Next we need assumptions about conditional independence. This establishes the links among the nodes in the Bayesian network. Let us start with the links shown in Figure 5.2. This network topology makes two rather plausible assumptions.

1. The step attempt history depends only on the state of the student's knowledge just prior to the step. Thus, the links *into* a step node (e.g., S2) come only from a subset of the knowledge nodes, namely, those representing the knowledge components' mastery just before the step (e.g., K11, K21, K31, …).
2. Student knowledge just after a step is determined by their knowledge just before the step and what happened during the step, such as whether they got hints on that step. Thus, the links *into* a knowledge component node come from the immediately preceding step and from the node representing its mastery just before the step.

The usual way to update a Bayesian network is to clamp the values of the nodes that are observable, update the network, and read out the posterior probabilities on the nodes of interest. In this case, the step attempt histories are observable, so we clamp each of the M step

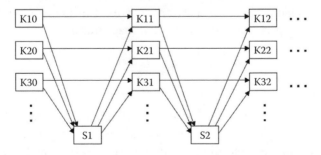

Figure 5.2   A generic approach to assessment, represented as a Bayesian network.

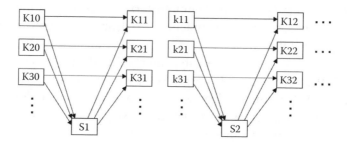

Figure 5.3 Two slices from a generic dynamic Bayesian network for assessment.

node values (e.g., on S1, clamp the value to "Correct on first attempt"; on S2, clamp the value to "Saw bottom-out hint"; etc.). The network is updated, and we read out the posterior probability of mastery on the nodes on the right end, namely, K1M, K2M, K3M, etc.

However, this network would be so large that the computation required to update this network may be intractable. Thus, we use *dynamic* Bayesian networks (Russell & Norvig, 2003). The key idea is to divide the network into time slices, as shown in Figure 5.3. A time slice consists of a step and the knowledge component nodes just before and after it. Slices are updated in chronological order. After a slice has been updated, the *posterior* probabilities on the poststep knowledge component nodes (which represent only the marginal probabilities of those random variables) are copied to the next time slice, where they become the *prior* probabilities on the prestep knowledge component nodes. In Figure 5.3, the posterior probabilities of K11, K21, K31,... become the prior probabilities of k11, k21, k31,.... This method means that only relatively small networks need to be updated. It is somewhat inaccurate, however, because it loses probabilistic dependences among nodes. Dynamic Bayesian networks are used in many applications, and seem to perform well despite their inaccuracies.

Knowledge Tracing

A widely used method of assessment, called Knowledge Tracing (Corbett & Anderson, 1995), is a special case of the generic network discussed in the preceding section (Reye, 2004). It makes several simplifying assumptions that result in networks such as the one shown in Figure 5.4.

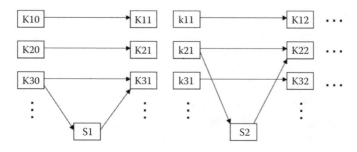

Figure 5.4   Knowledge tracing: Two slices from a dynamic Bayesian network.

First, Knowledge Tracing assumes that each step depends on applying only one knowledge component. That is, the set of knowledge components relevant to a step (as defined in a preceding section) is always a singleton set. To represent this in the network, every step node has just one link coming into it, namely, a link from the one and only knowledge component that should be applied when making that step. In Figure 5.4, step 1 depends only on knowledge component 3, and step 2 depends only on knowledge component 2.

Second, it is assumed that what happens during a step impacts the mastery of only the relevant knowledge component. Thus, there is only one link leaving each node, and it goes to the relevant knowledge component in the time slice just after the step.

Every node in a Bayesian network has a conditional probability table that represents how the value of that node depends on the values of the parent nodes. (When a link comes *into* a node, the node on the other end of the link is called a "parent node.") In knowledge tracing, these conditional probability tables are particularly simple.

For the step nodes, the conditional probability table is shown in Figure 5.5. Knowledge tracing uses a binary categorization of step attempt histories: either the student entered the step correctly on the first try or not. Thus, the P(correct) row represents the probability of a correct response on the first attempt, and the P(other) row represents the probability of any other kind of step attempt history. The columns refer to the values of the parent, which is a knowledge component node. In the "Yes" column, the value .92 represents that if the knowledge

Mastered?	Yes	No
P(correct)	0.92	0.10
P(other)	0.08	0.90

Figure 5.5   Conditional probability table for a step node in Knowledge Tracing.

component is mastered, there is a
high probability that the step will
be answered correctly, but there
is a small probability (.08; called
the "slip parameter") that the
student will answer incorrectly
even though the knowledge is
mastered. In the "No" column,
the value .10 (called the "guess
parameter") represents that there
is a small chance of getting the

Mastered?	Yes	No
P(mastered)	1.00	0
P(not mastered)	0	1.00

Figure 5.6 Conditional probabilities for a knowledge component
node with one parent.

step right on the first try even if the relevant knowledge component
is not mastered, and a large chance (.90) that the step attempt history
will include errors, hints, etc. The columns must each sum to 1.0, so
this table only has two degrees of freedom: the slip parameter and
the guess parameter. Different step nodes can have different values
for these parameters.

Some knowledge components are not relevant to the preceding
step, so they have only one link coming into them, as shown earlier
in Figure 5.4. Knowledge Tracing assumes that such a knowledge
component's probability of mastery is unaffected by the student's step
attempt history. Thus, all knowledge component nodes with just one
parent have the conditional probability table shown in Figure 5.6.

The other knowledge components have two links coming into
them, from the preceding step and from an earlier knowledge component node. This represents the fact that their new probability of
mastery depends on both the step attempt history and their old probability of mastery. For such nodes, the conditional probability table is
shown in Figure 5.7. The top row represents the impact of the knowl-

Was mastered?	Yes		No	
Step response	Correct	Other	Correct	Other
P(mastered)	1.00	1.00	0.56	0.56
P(not mastered)	0	0	0.64	0.64

Figure 5.7 Conditional probabilities for a knowledge component node
with two parents.

P(mastered)	0.21
P(not mastered)	0.79

Figure 5.8 Conditional probabilities for a knowledge component node with no parents.

edge component's prior mastery. The next row represents what happened during the preceding step. The bottom two rows represent the probability of this nodes' mastery given the various combinations of the parent node values. The numbers say that if the knowledge component was mastered, then it certainly (probability 1.0) will still be mastered. On the other hand, if the knowledge component was not mastered, then there is a moderate chance (.56) that it will become mastered regardless of what happened during the step. (As discussed later, this assumption of Knowledge Tracing was modified in subsequent work.) There is only one degree of freedom in this table, namely, the probability that an unmastered knowledge component will become mastered given that the step occurred. This is called the "acquisition parameter" and has the value .56 in Figure 5.7. The acquisition parameter can be different for different knowledge components.

The leftmost knowledge component nodes (Ki0) have no incoming links. Their conditional probability tables represent the prior probability of mastery of the knowledge component. For instance, the table in Figure 5.8 indicates that this knowledge component has a prior probability of .21 of being mastered.

For each knowledge component, we need four numbers: the guess parameter, the slip parameter, the acquisition parameter, and the prior probability of mastery.[3] Thus, calibration of the model requires estimating 4(N) values. This can be done given enough student data. Corbett and Anderson (1995) used a gradient descent algorithm to calibrate their networks from student data, but it appears that Expectation Maximization does an even better job (Chang et al., 2006).

Extensions to Knowledge Tracing

Several projects have explored extensions to Knowledge Tracing that relax some of its less plausible assumptions. This section discusses their basic ideas, but recasts them in terms of the generic dynamic Bayesian network.

The Knowledge Tracing approach ignores considerable information when it categorizes step attempt histories as either correct or other. Intuitively, one would expect a student who makes an error and corrects it with just a mild hint to have a higher probability of mastery than one who makes errors after every hint and only succeeds after seeing the bottom-out hint. Shute (1995) developed an assessment technique that used a larger number of categories. Although it was not compared directly with Knowledge Tracing, its accuracy at predicting posttest scores was quite high. The basic idea of this approach can be easily represented in our dynamic Bayesian network by using multiple categories of step attempt histories instead of the two categories used by Knowledge Tracing. This adds extra rows to the conditional probability tables of the step nodes and extra columns to the conditional probability tables of the knowledge nodes that have multiple incoming links.

It also makes sense to assume that what happens during a step may partially determine whether an unmastered knowledge component becomes mastered. For instance, if a student zooms all the way down to the bottom-out hint without bothering to read the intervening hints, then it seems unlikely that the student will learn the relevant knowledge component. This particular step attempt history is often called help abuse (Aleven & Koedinger, 2000; Aleven, Stahl, Schworm, Fischer, & Wallace, 2003). We can represent this by including help abuse as a step attempt history category, and modifying the relevant knowledge component nodes' conditional probability tables as shown in Figure 5.9. This table assumes that step attempt histories are categorized three ways: correct on the first attempt, help abuse, and other. It assumes that if the knowledge component was not mastered before and help abuse occurs, then the knowledge component

Was mastered?	Yes			No		
Step response	Correct	Help abuse	Other	Correct	Help abuse	Other
P(mastered)	1.00	1.00	1.00	0.56	0	0.56
P(not mastered)	0	0	0	0.64	1.00	0.64

Figure 5.9 Conditional probabilities for a two-parent knowledge component node when step attempt histories have three categories.

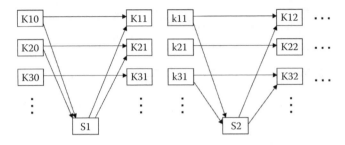

Figure 5.10   A step can have more than one relevant knowledge component.

stays unmastered. Otherwise, it makes the same assumptions as Knowledge Tracing. The point here is only that the formalism allows one to easily represent step → mastery causation that has been uncovered from observation, theory, or intuition.

In the first version of the Andes tutoring system (Conati, Gertner, & VanLehn, 2002), a Bayesian network was used for assessment in a way that extended knowledge tracing. Whereas Knowledge Tracing assumes that there is one and only one knowledge component relevant to each step, this assumption was unwarranted in Andes. Some of the steps in Andes required a student to apply several knowledge components. This can be easily represented by extending the network as shown in Figure 5.10, which shows that knowledge components 1 and 2 are relevant to step 1, whereas knowledge components 1 and 3 are relevant to step 2.

As part of a decision theoretic tutoring system (Murray, VanLehn, & Mostow, 2004), Murray added nodes that represented meta-cognitive strategies and motivation. In particular, observation of students using tutoring systems suggests that some students exhibit a help abuse pattern at every opportunity, whereas others rarely do so (Aleven & Koedinger, 2000). This may be related to a well-known motivation variable (Dweck, 1986), which is whether students are trying to learn the domain (a learning orientation) or merely to get their problems solved correctly and quickly (a performance orientation). Such predilections can be represented by adding a set of nodes to the dynamic network, which we might call M0, M1, M2,… as at the top of Figure 5.11. These nodes might have two values: learning-orientation and performance-orientation. They are linked to the steps because the students' motivation may affect how they respond at the step, e.g., whether they will display the help abuse pattern. On

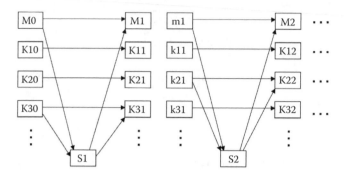

Figure 5.11 Nodes (M0, M1, M2,...) can be added to represent motivation.

the other hand, the way the step plays out may also cause students to change their motivation, so there are links from the steps to the motivation nodes. Zhou and Conati (2003) have explored a similar technique for diagnosing motivation and meta-cognition.

All these extensions to Knowledge Tracing add parameters whose values need to be determined. When a new kind of node is added (e.g., motivation nodes), they have conditional probability tables whose cells need values. When new step attempt history categories are added, they too introduce new cells into the conditional probability tables that need to have values determined for them. Little work has been done on finding calibration techniques that take advantage of the particular topology of these networks. This may be a good topic for future work. Once good calibration algorithms are in use, we can compare these various extensions to Knowledge Tracing and/or other assessment methods in order to see if they actually provide added diagnostic value.

Conclusions

This chapter introduced a particular kind of intelligent tutoring system that helps students solve multistep problems. The key idea is to give feedback and hints at the level of individual steps, instead of on the final answer alone. Although these systems were developed in order to increase student learning rate (and they are demonstrably good at that), they also provide the opportunity to assess student performance. The key assessment idea, as explained in the last section, is to assess individual knowledge components' probability of mastery, and to use the fact that each step requires knowing only a few knowledge components in order to do the step correctly.

An analogy might help. A step is like one item on a multiple-choice diagnostic test, where the test items were designed to tap only a few knowledge components each. When analyzing data from such a test, one assumes that performance on a test item is conditionally independent of the performance on the preceding items given the mastery of the relevant knowledge components, that is, those involved in answering the test item. If one knows the probability of mastery of the relevant knowledge components just before the test item is answered, one's predictions cannot be improved by also knowing their performance on earlier test items. The same Markov assumption is made when interpreting step attempt history data, except that one must allow the knowledge components to change their mastery over time. That is, students are assumed to *learn* as they use the tutoring system, whereas they are assumed *not to learn* during a test. As shown in this paper, learning complicates the data analysis, but not by much.

This sets the stage for increasing the use of assessment embedded in a tutoring system. This may have desirable impacts on schools—it may cause them to teach to a "test" that really deserves to be taught to. It may free up classroom time currently taken up with testing that, by design, does not cause learning. As shown late in the last section, the technique can be used to diagnose motivation and meta-cognitive variables as well as cognitive ones. This technology is so radically different from conventional non-learning testing that it may even have many unanticipated benefits as well, and perhaps some unanticipated drawbacks.

Acknowledgments

This research was supported by the Cognitive Science division of the Office of Naval Research under grant N00014-96-1-0260; and by the Pittsburgh Science of Learning Center (NSF 0354420). I thank Chas Murray for commenting on the manuscript.

References

Aleven, V., & Koedinger, K. R. (2000). Limitations of student control: Do students know when they need help? In G. Gauthier, C. Frasson, & K. VanLehn (Eds.), *Intelligent Tutoring Systems: 5th International Conference, ITS 2000* (pp. 292-303). Berlin: Springer-Verlag.

Aleven, V., Stahl, E., Schworm, S., Fischer, F., & Wallace, R. M. (2003). Help seeking and help design in interactive learning environments. *Review of Educational Research, 73*(2), 277-320.

Anderson, J. R., Corbett, A. T., Koedinger, K. R., & Pelletier, R. (1995). Cognitive tutors: Lessons learned. *Journal of the Learning Sciences, 4*(2), 167-207.

Bloom, B. S. (1984). The 2 sigma problem: The search for methods of group instruction as effective as one-to-one tutoring. *Educational Researcher, 13*(6), 4-16.

Bransford, J. D., & Schwartz, D. L. (1999). Rethinking transfer: A simple proposal with multiple implications. In A. Iran-Nejad & P. D. Pearson (Eds.), *Review of research in education* (Vol. 24, pp. 61-100). Washington, DC: American Educational Research Association.

Chang, K.-m., Beck, J., Mostow, J., & Corbett, A. (2006). A Bayes net toolkit for student modeling in intelligent tutoring systems. In K. Ashley & M. Ikeda (Eds.), *Proceedings of the 8th International Conference on Intelligent Tutoring Systems*. Berlin: Springer-Verlag.

Conati, C., Gertner, A., & VanLehn, K. (2002). Using Bayesian networks to manage uncertainty in student modeling. *User Modeling and User-Adapted Interactions, 12*(4), 371-417.

Corbett, A., & Anderson, J. R. (1995). Knowledge tracing: Modeling the acquisition of procedural knowledge. *User Modeling and User-Adapted Interaction, 4*, 253-278.

Corbett, A., Koedinger, K. R., & Anderson, J. R. (1997). Intelligent tutoring systems. In M. Helander, T. K. Landauer, & P. Prahu (Eds.), *Handbook of human-computer interaction* (2nd ed., pp. 849-874). Amsterdam: Elsevier Science.

Corbett, A., McLaughlin, M., & Scarpinatto, K. C. (2000). Modeling student knowledge: Cognitive tutors in high school and college. *User Modeling and User-Adapted Interactions, 10*, 81-108.

Dick, W., & Carey, S. (1990). *The systematic design of instruction* (3rd ed.). New York: Scott-Foresman.

Douglas, S. A. (1991). Tutoring as interaction: Detecting and repairing tutoring failures. In P. Goodyear (Ed.), *Teaching knowledge and intelligent tutoring* (pp. 123-147). Hillsdale, NJ: Lawrence Erlbaum Associates.

Dweck, C. S. (1986). Motivational processes affecting learning. *American Psychologist, 41*, 1040-1048.

Fox, B. A. (1993). *The human tutorial dialogue project: Issues in the design of instructional systems*. Hillsdale, NJ: Lawrence Erlbaum Associates.

Greer, J., & McCalla, G. (1989). A computational framework for granularity and its application to educational diagnosis. In *International Joint Conference on Artificial Intelligence* (pp. 477-482). Menlo Park, CA: AAAI Press.

Hume, G., Michael, J., Rovick, A., & Evens, M. (1996). Hinting as a tactic in one-on-one tutoring. *Journal of the Learning Sciences, 5*(1), 23-49.

Lepper, M. R., Woolverton, M., Mumme, D. L., & Gurtner, J.-L. (1993). Motivational techniques of expert human tutors: Lessons for the design of computer-based tutors. In S. P. Lajoie & S. J. Derry (Eds.), *Computers as cognitive tools* (pp. 75-105). Hillsdale, NJ: Lawrence Erlbaum Associates.

Litman, D., Rose, C., Forbes-Riley, K., VanLehn, K., Bhembe, D., & Silliman, S. (in press). Spoken versus typed human and computer dialogue. *International Journal of Artificial Intelligence and Education*.

McArthur, D., Stasz, C., & Zmuidzinas, M. (1990). Tutoring techniques in algebra. *Cognition and Instruction, 7*(3), 197-244.

Merrill, D. C., Reiser, B. J., Ranney, M., & Trafton, J. G. (1992). Effective tutoring techniques: A comparison of human tutors and intelligent tutoring systems. *Journal of the Learning Sciences, 2*(3), 277-306.

Messick, S. (1994). The interplay of evidence and consequences in the validation of performance assessments. *Educational Researcher, 23*(2), 13-23.

Mitrovic, A., & Ohlsson, S. (1999). Evaluation of a constraint-based tutor for a database language. *International Journal of Artificial Intelligence and Education, 10*, 238-256.

Murray, C., VanLehn, K., & Mostow, J. (2004). Looking ahead to select tutorial actions: A decision-theoretic approach. *International Journal of Artificial Intelligence and Education, 14*(3-4), 235-278.

Reye, J. (2004). Student modelling based on belief networks. *International Journal of Artificial Intelligence and Education, 14*(1), 63-96.

Rickel, J. (1989). Intelligent computer-aided instruction: A survey organized around system components. *IEEE Transactions on Systems, Man and Cybernetics, 19*(1), 40-57.

Russell, S., & Norvig, P. (2003). *Artificial Intelligence: A modern approach* (2nd ed.). Upper Saddle River, NJ: Prentice Hall.

Schofield, J. W. (1995). *Computers, classroom culture and change.* Cambridge, UK: Cambridge University Press.

Shute, V. J. (1995). SMART: Student modeling approach for responsive tutoring. *User Modeling and User-Adapted Instruction, 5*(1), 1-44.

Shute, V. J., & Psotka, J. (1996). Intelligent tutoring systems: Past, present and future. In D. Jonassen (Ed.), *Handbook of research on educational communications and technology* (pp. 570-600). New York: Macmillan.

VanLehn, K., Lynch, C., Schultz, K., Shapiro, J. A., Shelby, R. H., Taylor, L., et al. (2005). The Andes physics tutoring system: Lessons learned. *International Journal of Artificial Intelligence and Education, 15*(3), 147-204.

VanLehn, K., & Martin, J. (1998). Evaluation of an assessment system based on Bayesian student modeling. *International Journal of Artificial Intelligence in Education, 8*(2), 179-221.

VanLehn, K., Siler, S., Murray, C., Yamauchi, T., & Baggett, W. B. (2003). Human tutoring: Why do only some events cause learning? *Cognition and Instruction, 21*(3), 209-249.

VanLehn, K. (2006). The behavior of tutoring systems. *International Journal of Artificial Intelligence in Education,* 16.

Wood, D. J., & Middleton, D. (1975). A study of assisted problem-solving. *British Journal of Psychology, 66*(2), 181-191.

Zhou, X., & Conati, C. (2003). Inferring user goals from personality and behavior in a causal model of user affect. In *Proceedings of IUI 2003, international conference on intelligent user interfaces* (pp. 211-218). Miami, FL.

Endnotes

1. The assessment technique described later makes the assessment a deterministic function of both the log data and a set of prior probabilities, which describe what is known about the student prior to the problem solving.

2. This definition is deliberately vague, because more precise definitions can only be made in the context of specific tutoring systems. For instance, some tutoring systems require students to enter a step correctly before they can even start working on a new step, whereas others allow students to leave steps incorrect and to change steps that were entered much earlier.

3. In practice, steps that have the same relevant knowledge component are often given the same values for their guess and slip parameters. For the purpose of counting parameters, it is more accurate to count one guess and slip parameter per knowledge component rather than per step.

6

Tensions, Trends, Tools, and Technologies:
Time for an Educational Sea Change

Valerie J. Shute
Educational Testing Service

> Education is not preparation for life; education is life itself.
>
> John Dewey *(1859–1952)*

Introduction

This chapter outlines three educational approaches: (a) *traditional*: the currently dominant approach, a largely lecture-oriented authoritarian style that makes heavy use of "assessments *of* learning," which are useful for accountability purposes but only marginally useful for guiding day-to-day instruction; (b) *progressive*: a highly student-centered approach that relies on "assessments *for* learning," which can be very useful in guiding day-to-day instruction; and (c) *unified*: a new, integrated approach that uses the best of both kinds of assessments—"for" and "of" learning—and that leverages computer technology, educational measurement, and cognitive science to address factors that undermined earlier attempts to implement the Progressive approach. This chapter examines some of the research, trends, and factors that should be considered, understood, and, in some cases, leveraged in order to move toward the unified approach. Further, this chapter presents examples of how Educational Testing

Service (ETS) projects are moving toward the new approach to harness assessment in the service of learning.

Déjà Vu

Think back on your high school years. Whether Elvis, the Beatles, Led Zeppelin, Madonna, Run-DMC, Pearl Jam, or Britney Spears dominated the charts, odds are that you spent your day going from one 50-minute class to another, with a different subject each period. In class, you probably spent most of your time sitting at your desk, listening to lectures from a teacher who was the repository of knowledge to be learned. Your job was to learn the facts and other knowledge that your teacher knew, and you were periodically tested on just how well you absorbed the information and could retrieve the relevant facts. Direct cooperation with other students was a relatively rare event (except perhaps in team sports). This traditional scenario captures the norm for U.S. schools that have underserved too many students for too long (e.g., Barton, 2005).

Now imagine the following: public schools that apply progressive methods—such as individualizing instruction, motivating students by considering their interests, and developing cooperative group projects—to achieve the goal of producing knowledgeable and skilled lifelong learners. The teachers are happy, hard working, and valued by the community. In addition, they hold leadership roles in the school, and work individually and collectively to figure out the best ways to reach and teach their students. These same teachers create new textbooks and conduct research to see whether their methods worked. School days are structured to allow teachers time to meet and discuss their findings with colleagues.

Is this an ideal vision of schools of the future? Yes and no. According to Ravitch (2000), the image above describes several model public schools in the U.S. in the 1920s and 1930s, inspired by John Dewey's vision of education (e.g., the Lincoln School at Teachers College in New York, and the Winnetka, Illinois, public schools). These schools were engaging places for children to learn and were attractive places for teachers to teach; they avoided the monotonous, unfruitful routines of traditional schools.

What happened to these exciting experiments of educational reform, and more importantly, what lessons can we learn from them? First, according to Kliebard (1987), they failed because the techniques and founding ideas were misapplied by so-called experts who believed that mass education could be accomplished cheaply, employing low-paid and poorly trained teachers who would either follow their manuals or stand aside while students pursued their interests. Second, they failed because the reforms rejected traditional subject-matter curricula and substituted vocational training for the 90% of the student population who, at the time, were not expected to seek or hold professional careers (see Bobbitt, 1912, "The Elimination of Waste in Education"). Finally, this period also saw mass IQ testing (e.g., Lemann, 1999) gaining a firm foothold in education, with systematic use of Terman's National Intelligence Test in senior and junior high schools. The testing was aimed specifically at efficiently assigning students into high, middle, or low educational tracks according to their supposedly innate mental abilities (Terman, 1916).

In general, there was a fundamental shift to practical education going on in the country during the early 1900s, countering "wasted time" in schools and abandoning the classics as useless and inefficient for the masses. Bobbitt, along with some other early educational researchers and administrators such as Ellwood and Ayers (Kliebard, 1987, pp. 103–104), inserted into the national educational discourse the metaphor of the school as a "factory." This metaphor has persisted to this day; yet if schools were actual factories, they would have been shut down years ago.

The basic idea I present in this chapter is that serious problems exist in education today, but viable solutions are possible. The particular solution described herein is based on the claims that (1) individual differences among students have powerful effects on learning, (2) these effects can be quantified and predicted, and (3) technology can capitalize on these effects to the benefit of teachers and students (as well as others, such as administrators and parents).

This chapter is organized as follows. First, I describe two distinct educational approaches—traditional and progressive—that have been battling it out in our country for almost a century, although both have valuable contributions to make to education. Second, I summarize factors that are influencing the current state of educational flux, fueling the need for an educational *sea change*.[1] Third, research is presented that seems promising for addressing the particular problem areas that are delineated. I also present specific models and methods that we can use right now to create diagnostic, formative assessments[2] that are woven directly into the fabric of the curriculum, linked to targeted instruction as well as standards, and are likely to make a real difference in the landscape (or seascape) of education. Finally, I sketch out a prototype system currently under development at Educational Testing Service that employs many of the methods and tools cited in the chapter.

The Chasm Between Traditional and Progressive Approaches

The model of school-as-a-factory is inappropriate, particularly in today's rapidly changing and information-rich world. So what is a better model (or models) that we can use to focus educational reform? Very simply: *There are two competing views of education—traditional and progressive—from which we can draw the best features to combine into a new, unified model.* On the one hand, traditional education invokes a more "outside-in" approach whereby teachers provide knowledge to awaiting students. On the other hand, progressive education is more "inside-out," defining the role of the student as an active, creative, and reflective participant in the learning process.

John Dewey believed that the more authoritarian approach of traditional education was too concerned with delivering knowledge, and not enough with understanding students' actual learning or experiences, the cornerstone of progressive education (see Flanagan, 1994). However, he was also highly critical of completely "free, student-driven" education because students often do not know how to structure their own learning experiences for maximum benefit. Fast forward 70 to 80 years and we see the paradigm conflict continuing today.[3]

Traditional Approach

Many educators, administrators, and policy makers support relatively structured, didactic, traditional education. This approach came to the fore with the recession and tax revolt of the 1970s, followed by the publication of the report, *A Nation at Risk* (National Commission of Excellence in Education, 1983), leading to an increased emphasis on basics, national learning standards, and improving results on standardized tests.

Lending credible support for this position, consider the findings from a project called "Follow Through" (e.g., Proper & St. Pierre, 1980; Stebbins, St. Pierre, Proper, Anderson, & Cerva, 1977). This was an enormous, federally funded research project launched in 1967 in response to President Johnson's request to "follow through" on project Head Start. Summaries of the study (e.g., Adams, 1996; Stone & Clements, 1998) describe nine educational Models[4] that were compared in 51 school districts over a 4 to 6 year period. Each of the nine models was yoked to a comparison school. Of the nine, all but two (i.e., Direct Instruction and Behavior Analysis Models; see complete listing in footnote) were, to various degrees, learner centered. Contrary to expectations, the two exceptions significantly outperformed the other Models. Furthermore, Stone and Clements (1998) noted that five of the seven learner-centered models produced worse results than the traditional school programs (i.e., the control groups) to which each Follow Through approach was compared. By far, the most successful of the nine Models was Direct Instruction[5] (Engelmann, Becker, Carnine, & Gersten, 1988), which showed positive scores on all three types of outcome measures—basic skills, cognitive skills, and affective variables (Adams, 1996).

At least three other major re-analyses of the data were independently conducted (see Mac Iver & Kemper, 2002), yet none of these analyses show significant disagreement with respect to achievement data. Results of the national evaluation and all subsequent analyses converge on the finding that the highest achievement scores were attained by students in the Direct Instruction model.

Progressive Approach

There are equally ardent supporters of progressive education,[6] which generally refers to classroom methods that focus on individualized instruction, encourage collaboration among students, provide hands-on learning activities, and stress informality in the classroom (e.g., Brown & Campione, 1990; Darling-Hammond, 1997; Darling-Hammond, Griffin, & Wise, 1992; Pea, 1994; Scardamalia & Bereiter, 1994). Researchers report that intrinsic motivation is enhanced when learning is student-centered, i.e., when students are provided with opportunities to exert control, to determine their fate, or at least have a perception that they are doing so (e.g., Lepper & Chabay, 1985; Ng, Guthrie, Van Meter, McCann, & Alao, 1998). For example, Deci and colleagues (e.g., Deci & Ryan, 1985; Deci, Vallerand, Pelletier, & Ryan, 1991) found that when students have control over their own learning, they achieve more positive learning outcomes, greater interest, more trust, higher self-esteem, and greater persistence. Additional research has reported the increased benefits to students in relation to self-determination (Papert, 1980) and feelings of control (Keller & Kopp, 1987).

Examples from research employing interactive instructional materials report positive outcomes relating student control to improved learning (e.g., Carrier & Williams, 1988). And motivational theory research (Keller, 1979) has similarly demonstrated that when students are given some control over aspects of their learning, they are more likely to have positive feelings toward the task combined with intrinsic motivation. Finally, Laurillard (1984, 1991) reported findings that learning enjoyment increased when students were given control.

Toward a New Approach: A Look at the Interactions

This dichotomy between the two opposing educational philosophies (i.e., traditional and progressive) may also be seen in the implementation of computerized learning environments. Among other variables, such systems can differ in the amount of learner control (one of the main features of the progressive approach) supported during the learning process. The research literature is about evenly mixed in relation to the effectiveness of these two approaches—traditional and progressive (specifically, in this case, less and more learner control)—and the arguments are similar to those described earlier with regard to classroom settings. That is, one approach argues that it is more efficacious to develop straightforward learning environments that do not permit "garden path" digressions (e.g., Koedinger, Anderson, Hadley, & Mark, 1997; Sleeman, Kelly, Martinak, Ward, & Moore, 1989). In contrast, the other approach argues that student learning is enhanced by environments containing assorted tools that allow the learner freedom to explore and learn, unfettered (e.g., Bunt, Conati, Huggett, & Muldner, 2001; de Jong, van Joolingen, Scott, deHoog, Lapied, & Valent, 1994; Shute, Glaser, & Raghavan, 1989).

The disparity between positions becomes more complex because the issue is not just about which approach—traditional or progressive—is the better learning environment; i.e., it is unrealistic to suppose that a statistical "main effect" for "approach" would provide an adequate picture. Instead, a better question may be the following: Which is the better approach for what type(s) of students? In other words, we should examine the data for evidence of classic aptitude-treatment interactions (Cronbach & Snow, 1977), for which the main effect would be an inadequate summary. This may be further extended to include other variables as well, such as outcome and demographic variables. To arrive at recommendations for instructional design, one also needs to consider the *goal* of the instructional environment (Shute, Gawlick, & Gluck, 1998), such as ensuring mastery or efficient topic coverage.

Extreme positions are rarely helpful, and the concept of a single best method of instruction for everyone is overly simplified. On the one hand, traditional education, with its focus on content rather than the learning process, tends to lack a basic understanding of students. On the other hand, progressive education, as Dewey himself noted, can be too reactionary. That is, freedom for the sake of freedom is a weak philosophy of education according to Dewey (1938). Instead, he asserted, experience arises from the interplay of two principles—continuity and interaction. One's current experience is a function of the interaction between one's past experiences and the present situation. Dewey believed, like many educators who followed, that no single experience has preordained value. A rewarding experience for one person could well be a detrimental experience for another.

In short, as with fashion (e.g., Nehru jackets), cars (e.g., the Edsel), and toys (e.g., pet rocks), educational reforms tend to come and go, causing a flurry for some duration, but rarely influencing teaching practices in any lasting or significant way. According to Cuban (2004), and supporting the look-to-the-interactions perspective, there will never be a clear victory for either traditional or progressive education because students differ in their motivations, interests, and backgrounds, and learn at different speeds in different subjects. The bottom line is simply that there is no single best way for teachers to teach, or for children to learn, that optimally fits all situations. Features from both traditional and progressive ways of teaching and learning need to be incorporated into a school's approach.

Bridging the Chasm With Research

The idea of improving teaching through the application of science has been around since the earliest days of organized teacher training. Dewey believed that the scientific study of child development would improve classroom instruction by suggesting ways in which teaching might be fitted to the learner (Dewey, 1916). It was not until the 1960s, however, that government-funded research began expanding toward present-day levels. And it was during this time (1960s and 1970s) that aptitude-treatment interaction (ATI) research flourished. But despite the fact that hundreds of studies were conducted, the jury remained out, and ATI's popularity declined after the 1970s. It is likely that the reason for this decline is that the classroom data were confounded by many extraneous variables (e.g., personality of the teacher, instructional materials, classroom dynamics), making ATIs hard to find and difficult to interpret. During the 1990s, with the emergence of computers and the ability to control extraneous variables, interest renewed (see Shute & Towle, 2003, for more on this topic).

Anderson, Reder, and Simon (1996) provide compelling arguments in support of more research before the adoption of any educational techniques. They point out that new so-called theories of education are introduced into schools every day, solely on the basis of their philosophical or common-sense plausibility, but lacking in empirical support. Substantially more emphasis should be provided for responsible experimentation that explicitly tests such new ideas. In their article, they argue for the equivalent of an "FEA," analogous to the FDA, requiring well-designed clinical trials for every educational "drug" introduced into the market place. Six years later, this idea has materialized in the form of the What Works Clearinghouse, established in 2002 by the U.S. Department of Education's Institute of Education Sciences to provide educators, policy makers, researchers, and the public with a central and trusted source of scientific evidence of what works in education.

From the standpoint of science, experimental studies are far more convincing than descriptive and correlational ones, yet school personnel often ignore the more rigorous studies and adopt innovations suggested by the descriptive ones. For example, during the 1960s and 1970s, correlational studies suggested that enhancing self-esteem was related to improved achievement. This led to substantial changes in teacher training and schooling. Experimental findings to the contrary were ignored. For example, Scheirer and Kraut (1979) showed that self-esteem and achievement are correlated mainly because achievement enhances self-esteem, not because self-esteem enhances achievement.

Educational Needs and the Factors Fostering Flux

Current circumstances make it important and urgent to move to a new way of thinking about and conducting education. Technological advances, growth in research on cognition and learning, and other factors make successful outcomes much more likely. Success depends on what we do. We are in an excellent position to create a sea change, responsive to some of the urgent needs in education.

The basic premise of this chapter is that the seascape of education is unquestionably ready for an extreme makeover, and our goal should be to guide its transformation in the best, most effective direction possible, based on results from research. One salient source of educational discord is the No Child Left Behind (NCLB) Act of 2001, with its requirements for increased assessment and school accountability. Hundreds (if not thousands) of articles appear in the press each day, describing phenomena like a national "grassroots rebellion" against the No Child Left Behind Act, as reported by organizations such as NCLBGrassroots.org.

NCLB Dissatisfaction   In general, dissatisfaction with the NCLB Act is neither a rejection of accountability nor a lack of commitment to narrow the achievement gap. Rather, the shared sentiment among many educators in the field seems to be that the pressure to teach to the test undermines quality education and deepens the adversarial relationship between parents and teachers. More specific complaints raised against NCLB include the following: (a) it is an unprecedented federal intrusion into education, historically an area reserved for states; (b) its one-size-fits-all approach ignores the realities of good teaching and learning; (c) the law devotes too much valuable class time to test preparation; and (d) it is too narrow in its substantive focus, concentrating on reading and mathematics to the exclusion of such basic skills as communication and creative problem solving (see, e.g., Civil Society Institute, 2005; Kahl, 2003).

New 21st-Century Skills   Another factor contributing to the need for a sea change has to do with the aforementioned factory metaphor and its incongruence with our current information age. Students are not acquiring sufficient knowledge and skills to prepare them for careers in mathematics, science, and technology with the traditional approach to schooling, as evidenced by the Program for International Student Assessment (PISA) results (e.g., Lemke et al., 2004), described in more detail later in this chapter. Moreover, students today need new skills (e.g., information communication and technology [ICT] skills: how to define, access, manage, integrate, evaluate, and communicate information) to deal successfully with the deluge of data in the 21st century. The term "lifelong learner" describes this phenomenon and suggests (if not demands) that we change the way we structure learning and the way people access and acquire information and transform it into knowledge. Toward this end, we must figure out what skills we value, and support those for a society producing knowledge workers, not simply service workers. At the same time, we need to be cautious about moving from one extreme to the other, and to be informed by ongoing research-based tests of educational effectiveness, by which procedures, models, and curriculum are rigorously compared. "We need to look to science to give us answers. We need to engage our best researchers in research on how children learn ... and how instruction can be improved" (Paige, 2001).

Major Educational Trends of Today

Over the past 10 years or so, some major educational developments have emerged and gained dominance, as indicated by their increased popularity at educational and psychological research conferences. These trends are characterized by "new" models of teaching and learning, but on closer inspection, many appear very similar to ideas originally envisioned by Dewey. The most salient of these trends relates to curricula characterized by tightly integrated formative assessments that are diagnostic,[7] criterion-referenced, linked to targeted instruction (or instructional prescriptions), and that fit the particular needs of the learner at just the right time (see Appendix for definitions of these terms).

Assessments Tied to Instruction   Bass and Glaser (2004) describe the principles of what they refer to as "informative assessments," to draw attention to the instructional goal of improving student learning. They see the design of such assessments as having a substantial influence on the quality of information provided to teachers and students to support instructional decision making and more meaningful learning. This is, however, conditioned on presenting assessment results in an easy, intelligible, and actionable format—to both teachers and students. Shepard (2000) presents a constructive and comprehensive conceptual framework in which to house many of these new ideas and models. She describes how classroom assessment practices might be structured and implemented to be more effective in enhancing teaching and learning. She outlines the principles of a "social-constructivist" conceptual framework, bringing together cognitive, constructivist,[8] and sociocultural theories as a reformed and nicely blended view of education.

Another good example of this blended approach can be seen in Web-based cognitive tutors called "assistments," the merging together of assessment with instructional assistance into one system (see Razzaq, Feng, Nuzzo-Jones, et al., 2005, for more on the topic).

Black and Wiliam (1998a, 1998b) very clearly establish the importance of formative assessments to both teaching and learning. They conducted a large research review of the relationship(s) between assessment and learning, and their landmark papers have had a major influence on both research and the teaching profession. In addition, they originated the widely used distinction between (a) assessment *for* learning and (b) assessment *of* learning.

Finally, and in line with the "best of both worlds" position of this chapter, Stiggins (2002) argues that both assessment of learning and assessment for learning are essential. Unfortunately, while assessment *of* learning is currently well-entrenched in our educational system (such as through NCLB), assessment *for* learning is not. We need to strike a better, more scientifically informed, balance. For example, if formative assessments (representing assessments *for* learning) were employed throughout the school year, then at the end of the year or marking period, the need for formal summative tests (a common type of assessment *of* learning) would be greatly reduced. To accomplish this goal would require that the student data—collected, analyzed, and recorded by the formative assessments—be valid, reliable, and of a manageable, actionable grain size.

Student-Centered Practices   Another trend appears to be renewed interest in student-centered approaches to teaching (e.g., Pellegrino, 2004), where teacher and student roles are basically redefined. The teacher becomes a facilitator of learning instead of the sole dispenser of knowledge, and students take more responsibility for their own learning. The main idea behind this approach is that learning is most meaningful when topics are relevant to the students' lives, needs, and interests and when the students themselves are actively engaged in creating, understanding, and connecting to knowledge (McCombs & Whistler, 1997). Students will have a higher motivation to learn when they feel they have a real stake in their own learning. In keeping with the idea of bridging the chasm between the traditional and progressive approaches, implementing student-centered practices will require the provision of more freedom than is currently in place, but in a structured way. For example, students can use assessment information to regulate and guide their learning. Sharing assessment information with students is a way to empower them (e.g., Brna, Self, Bull, & Pain, 1999; Zapata-Rivera & Greer, 2004), thus transitioning to a new role for students—from passive assessment recipients to active participants. Furthermore, self-assessments can provide another source of evidence, contributing to a more complete picture of what the student really knows (e.g., Mitrovic & Martin, 2002; Zapata-Rivera, 2003).

Cognitive Modeling   The final big trend being applied to educational research is cognitive modeling, which refers to a set of ideas and procedures that come from cognitive psychology and computer science. Cognitive modeling is generally defined as the representation of what is inside the learner's head: thinking, knowing, and learning. Cognitive models can help predict or control complex human behavior, including skill learning, problem solving, and other types of cognitive activities (e.g., Aleven & Koedinger, 2002; Anderson & Lebiere, 1998; Heffernan & Koedinger, 2002). Computer tutors that have been built using cognitive models have been very successful in improving student learning, especially in mathematics (e.g., Koedinger & Anderson, 1998).   One major advantage we have today compared with even a decade ago, is technology to engender and support many of the reform ideas, some of which were presented nearly a century ago. It has often been said that Dewey was ahead of his time. Perhaps now his time has come, particularly given the confluence of (a) the growing dissatisfaction with NCLB as a vehicle for educational reform (see Hart & Winston, 2005; Phi Delta Kappa, 2005); (b) the presence of the What Works Clearinghouse to evaluate new ideas and interventions; and (c) the collection of available technologies to support innovative ideas that were previously not easy, or even possible, to accomplish in the classrooms and culture of the past.

Issues and Solutions

For the remainder of the chapter, I will define specific educational issues and present concrete solutions, highlighting evidence-centered design (ECD) as a viable tool to design assessment to support learning.[9] This will be followed by a description of the theoretical foundation and implementation of a prototype system we are currently developing at ETS. The system is designed to help struggling middle school students learn mathematics—specifically Algebra I content. The prototype exemplifies the idea of merging assessment and instruction to support learning.

The combination of fields needed to accomplish these objectives includes assessment design, cognitive psychology, educational measurement/psychometrics, artificial intelligence, instructional system design, educational psychology, and others as well. The bottom line, however, is that it's *all about learning*, using informative assessments, tied to good instruction, integrated within the curriculum, and linked to state and/or national standards, in order to maximally support both teachers and learners.

The Problems We Face

In 2004–2005, the United States invested $536 billion in K–12 education, and another $373 billion for higher education (U.S. Department of Education, 2005). But although the U.S. is a world leader in education investment, nations that spend far less regularly achieve much higher levels of student performance (Lemke et al., 2004). The rest of this chapter will focus on assessments within the area of mathematics, but the arguments and findings are applicable to other areas as well, such as reading, science, and cross-cutting skills such as problem solving and reflection.

International Comparison of Mathematics Assessments   America's 15-year-olds performed below the international average in mathematics literacy and problem solving, according to the latest results from PISA. The test, given in the spring of 2003, assesses the ability of 15-year-old students from various countries (including 30 of the most developed) to apply learning to problems with a real-world context (see Lemke et al., 2004). Students in the following countries outperformed the United States in mathematics literacy in 2003: Australia, Austria, Belgium, Canada, the Czech Republic, Denmark, Finland, France, Germany, Hong Kong-China, Iceland, Ireland, Japan, South Korea, Liechtenstein, Luxembourg, Macao-China, Netherlands, New Zealand, Norway, the Slovak Republic, Sweden, and Switzerland. These same 23 countries, plus Hungary and Poland, outperformed the United States in mathematics problem solving. U.S. 15-year-olds scored measurably better than their counterparts[10] in only 3 of 30 nations on the new international test of problem solving in math. Moreover, the U.S. has the poorest outcomes per dollar spent on education. In short, U.S. students are performing poorly on mathematics tasks that involve transfer of learning and problem-solving skills. We need to bolster our students' problem-solving skills to compete effectively internationally in the near future.

Widening Achievement Gaps   Shifting attention from the international to the home front, there are also some disturbing differences in mathematics achievement among U.S. student subpopulations. Despite substantial educational reform efforts directed at poor and minority students across the last two decades, current data show large and growing achievement gaps between ethnic minorities and white students (e.g., Haycock, 2001; Lee, 2002). For example, in 1990, there was a 33-point gap between the scores of black and white students on the National Assessment of Educational Progress (NAEP) mathematics test at the eighth-grade level.[11] By 2000, the gap had grown to 39 points. Latino students were 28 points behind white students in 1990 and 33 points behind a decade later. In California in 2004, fourth- and eighth-grade black and Latino students were found to perform, on average, 3 years behind comparable groups of white students in mathematics. According to Mora (2001a, 2001b), it is reasonable to conclude that for students in California, the achievement gap is most likely due to factors such as language proficiency and its impact on literacy, which relates to accessibility issues, addressed next. And linking PISA findings and the achievement gap, Bracey (2004) analyzed 2003 PISA data, excluding Asian, black, and Hispanic students from the sample. When ranking only white U.S. students in relation to students from the other 30 countries, the U.S. ranked as follows: reading: 2, math: 7, and science: 4.

Accessibility   The third main problem we face concerns the need in K–12 education for better curricula, including embedded diagnostic assessments, that are more "universally designed"—that is, more accessible, effective, and valid for students with greater diversity in terms of disability and English language capability. A committee of the National Research Council recently examined accommodation policies for the NAEP and other large-scale assessments. They reported that, "Overall, existing research does not provide definitive evidence about which procedures will, in general, produce the most valid estimates of performance for students with disabilities and English language learners" (National Research Council, 2004, p. 6).   In addition to the call for universally designed assessments, there are accessibility issues associated with instructional materials. For example, most classroom materials (books, chalkboard, quizzes, etc.) tend to be written in English, and are highly visual in nature. Obviously, this presents obstacles for individuals who are not fluent in English and/or have visual disabilities. *If content is not accessible, it cannot be learned.*

Proaction   So what can we do about these troubling findings? Obviously, many variables contribute to the poor showing by U.S. students relating to students in other countries; and within the U.S., by ethnic minority students. One thing we can do is focus on developing and evaluating, in controlled research studies, valid and reliable tools—technological and methodological—that can expedite the development and implementation of informative assessments that help teachers to teach, students to learn, and learning outcomes to improve. A key component of informative assessments is valid diagnosis; and a key component of valid diagnosis is good evidence, i.e., performance data that form the basis for inferences about proficiencies. Fortunately, technological, educational, and psychological measurement approaches have advanced, and we can now more accurately diagnose student proficiencies. Information, collected and analyzed from the student, can inform both the teacher (for decisions about what to do next, with the student or classroom) and the student (who can use the information to understand what he or she did wrong or right). In addition, proficiencies themselves may be validated through the examination of data. That is, careful inspection of the data provides valuable insights into whether the proficiencies are effective and useful, as defined, or whether they should be modified.

Research, methods, and models will now be described that can be used to design and implement informative assessments. This is followed by a description of a prototype system that is being developed at ETS as a possible solution to some of the major problems facing American education today.

Specific Solutions

This section begins with a brief review of relevant learning research; i.e., timely feedback, tailored content, and multiple representations. Together, these three areas form the research basis for the prototype solution described later in this chapter.

Timely Feedback   Timely feedback in the context of problem solving is generally viewed as important to enhancing student learning (e.g., Corbett & Anderson, 1989; Epstein, Lazarus, Calvano, et al., 2002). In addition to exerting positive effects on achievement, feedback has also been found to be a significant factor in motivating learning (e.g., Narciss & Huth, 2004). However, the story is not quite so simple. According to Cohen (1985), feedback is "one of the more instructionally powerful and least understood features in instructional design" (p. 33). Because of the many differences in types of feedback, results relating to its timing and effects on learning outcomes can conflict. Mathan & Koedinger (2002) review some conflicting results on the timing of feedback, and conclude that the effectiveness of feedback depends on the nature of the task and the capability of the learner. This suggests the need to further explore optimal ways to tailor the type and timing of feedback to learning tasks and to students' individual needs and characteristics (e.g., Schimmel, 1988; Smith & Ragan, 1999).

Tailored Content   Adjusting learning environments and content to suit student needs can substantially improve learning (e.g., Corno & Snow; 1986; Shute, 1993). Computer-based adaptive learning systems are beginning to accommodate differences in learner interests, aptitudes, and background (e.g., Bajraktarevic, Hall, & Fullick, 2003; Conlan & Wade, 2004; De Bra, Aerts, Berden, et al., 2003; Papanikolaou, Grigoriadou, Magoulas, & Kornilakis, 2002; Weber & Brusilovsky, 2001). These systems effectively can act as personal tutors, build models of learners, and intervene with relevant information when needed. Technology has advanced to the point that we can more easily implement adaptive instructional techniques on the Internet (e.g., differential sequencing of content, depending on learners' needs). See Brusilovsky (2003) and Brusilovsky and Vassileva (2003) for more on this topic.

Multiple Representations of Content   Finally, presenting alternative representations of the same concept (in tasks, examples, and so forth) can not only augment comprehension but also accommodate various disabilities, preferences, or learning styles. Research supports the importance of multiple-strategy use and representations in mathematics in terms of skill acquisition, understanding, and transfer (e.g., Katz, Lipps, & Trafton, 2002; Koedinger & Tabachneck, 1994; Tabachneck, Koedinger, & Nathan, 1994). The requirement for integrating different types of response formats, and hence representations, is also consistent with the research-based expectation in state and national standards that students should be flexible in moving across representations (tables, graphs, expressions). Moreover, developing and accessing multiple representations supports deeper understanding (e.g., Shafrir, 1999).   Designing informative assessments with these three research-based features (timely feedback, tailored content, and multiple representations) is a reasonable response to counter some major educational problems. That is, with traditional education, by the time the results of high-stakes accountability tests are disseminated, it is usually too late to effect change in the classroom to address weak areas or misconceptions. We want to develop tasks that have been designed not only to provide feedback about the correctness of the response, but also provide guidance on areas of misconception, and are presented in a timely manner (usually immediately, with our solutions). Examples will be provided later in this section describing a prototype system called MIM (Mathematics Intervention Module).

This kind of educational support system—with immediate diagnostic feedback, multiple and varied tasks, and tailored to a learner's specific and current needs—is expected to significantly help students overcome procedural errors and areas of misconceptions. Furthermore, summary data provided to the teacher can allow her to modify the instructional approach and suggest further activities for a student or class based on targeted problem areas. The feedback can also be used by students to guide self-study and reflection. Over the long term, such an approach should help students understand the material better and improve their performance on high-stakes tests (Mory, 2004).

Methods for Developing a Prototype Solution

The research considerations and methods that we are combining in our prototype solution include (a) individual differences, (b) diagnostic assessments, and (c) instructionally rich learning environments. As part of this process, we are extending the scope of ECD, as originally formulated with its assessment design focus, to embrace learning as well.

Individual Differences   Individual differences are typically defined as persistent and measurable aptitudes or attributes that distinguish people from one another. These variables may be used to predict performance on some learning tasks (see Shute, Lajoie, & Gluck, 2000). Disparities among students that are relevant to education can be cognitive, affective, perceptual, or demographic, or can involve other characteristics. We need to accurately identify variables that affect learning, and then offer appropriate supports, as needed. A key word here is "appropriate," as we need to ensure that accommodation for overcoming accessibility barriers, for example, does not also invalidate assessment results.   The point is that students come to any new learning task with differing profiles. As educators, we want to take what we already know about students and add to that an understanding of what they are doing in real time in the learning environment. We can then combine that information with knowledge about strategies for bringing individuals to a higher level of knowledge, and adapt instruction to carry out those strategies. Valid and reliable cognitive diagnoses, then, are essential to learning environments that adapt to users' needs. According to Bass and Glaser (2004), taking full advantage of informative assessments requires the use of adaptive teaching techniques that yield information about the student's learning process and outcomes. This allows teachers to take appropriate instructional actions and make meaningful modifications to instruction. Two approaches to adaptation are described below.

One way in which content can be customized for a student is through *microadaptation*, the real-time selection of content in response to a learner's inferred knowledge and skill state (Shute & Towle, 2003; Vassileva & Wasson, 1996). Microadaptation occurs during the learning process and is sometimes referred to as domain-dependent adaptation. It can also be thought of as a set of small, ongoing formative assessments. Decisions about content selection are typically based on performance and on subsequent inferences of student knowledge and skill states.

The other approach to adapting content is through *macroadaptation*—the customization of content in line with learner qualities, such as stable cognitive or perceptual abilities. In contrast with microadaptation, macroadaptive decisions are domain-independent and are based on learner information that is usually, but not always, collected before instruction begins (see Shute, Graf, & Hansen, 2005; Snow, 1992, for more on this topic). Macroadaptation relates to decisions about the format and sequence of the content presented to the learner. For a review of some specific macroadaptive examples from the literature, see Shute, Lajoie, and Gluck (2000).

These two forms of adaptation are not necessarily incompatible and may, in fact, improve learning even more when combined. Microadaptation is typically applied to the problem of *what* to present and when to present it, while macroadaptation is applied to the issue of *how* it should be presented. The success of either type of adaptation, however, is a function of the validity and reliability of the underlying assessments.

Assessment Design   Evidence-centered design (e.g., Mislevy, Steinberg, & Almond, 2000, 2003) provides (a) a way of reasoning about assessment design, (b) a way of reasoning about examinee performance, and (c) the means to unify and extend probability-based reasoning to assessment (e.g., to traditional standardized tests, classroom tests/quizzes, simulations, gaming environments, and portfolios). The basic idea of ECD is to specify the structures and supporting rationales for the evidentiary argument of an assessment. By making the evidentiary argument explicit, the argument becomes easier to examine, share, and refine. Argument structures encompass, among other things, the claims (inferences) one wishes to make about a student, the observables (performance data) that provide support for those claims, the task performance situations that elicit the observables from the students, and the rationales for linking it all together. The three main models used in ECD are

- *Proficiency Model*: Establishes claims about a particular piece of knowledge, skill, or ability. The proficiency model describes what is to be measured, conditions under which the ability is demonstrated, and the range and relations of proficiencies in the content area.
- *Evidence Model*: Defines the evidence needed to support the claims. Evidence models describe what is to be scored, how to score it, and how to combine scores to support claims. These models thus establish the boundaries of performance and identify observable actions that are within those boundaries.
- *Task Model*: Identifies tasks that are able to elicit that evidence. Task models specify the inputs required to perform the observable actions as well as the outputs (work products) that result from performing the observable actions.

Cognitive Diagnosis   To determine student strengths and weaknesses, and figure out the nature and extent of difficulties in a student's problem solving efforts, we need to design tasks such that this information can be disentangled and interpreted in valid and reliable ways (see Hunt & Minstrell, 1996; Minstrell, 1992, 2001, for more on this topic). A good diagnostic assessment system should be able to infer proficiency estimates accurately for a student, at various grain sizes.[12] This process begins with the design of a reasonable (i.e., accurate and informative) proficiency model, which provides the basis for task-level (i.e., real-time, formative) and overall (i.e., summative) level diagnoses to occur. This is a very challenging undertaking, and we are currently exploring ways to use cognitive models to integrate evidence of student knowledge gathered from a variety of formative and summative sources.   Information from student interactions with tasks or problems is automatically analyzed based on preestablished scoring rules, to inform and update relevant proficiencies. Task-level diagnoses can provide immediate support to the student via task-specific feedback; estimates of more general proficiencies provide the basis for decisions concerning what to do next, such as selecting a new task or offering other content to the student, providing practice, or some other instructionally helpful activity. This is all accomplished behind-the-scenes, on the computer, via selection rules and/or algorithms. Alternatively, diagnostic results can be handed off to the teacher in the form of instructional prescriptions or suggestions about what to do next, for the student or for the entire class.

Proficiency estimates can assume a variety of forms, from simple percent-correct data to probabilistic estimates of mastery of knowledge/skills using regression equations, to item response theory (IRT), multidimensional IRT models, or Bayesian networks (e.g., Hambleton, Swaminathan, & Rogers, 1991; Lord, 1980; Mislevy, Almond, Yan, & Steinberg, 1999; Reckase, 1997; Shute, 1995). In all these cases, diagnostic assessment requires students to do something (i.e., to produce a "work product") in order to demonstrate knowledge/skill capability on specific tasks. The more student data collected, the more accurate the inference. Thus, it is very important in assessment design to ensure an array of activities with which a learner can interact, receive targeted feedback, and demonstrate his or her level of performance. Interpretation of proficiency is a function of the quality of the evidence collected. In a valid proficiency model, each piece of knowledge, skill, and ability is linked to more than one task so that evidence of a student's performance can be accumulated in a number of different contexts. In a hierarchical proficiency model, evidence of one skill's mastery can also feed into mastery estimations for related skills. An example of a proficiency model is presented later in the context of our prototype system, MIM.

Putting It All Together

To diagnose student status at the task level, and to infer student status at the proficiency level, we employ a variety of technological solutions in our assessments, such as automated scoring of different constructed response types, automatic item generation, adaptive testing, and the capability to present or simulate "authentic" problem-solving contexts. Again, it is important to ensure that each of these are weighed against concerns for construct validity, equity, and access (Bennett & Bejar, 1998; Shute, Graf, & Hansen, 2005).

For implementation of these ideas—which can run the gamut from paper-and-pencil to computer delivery—consider the 4-process model shown in Figure 6.1 (Almond, Steinberg, & Mislevy, 2002). This model specifies the following cycle, shown by the four circles (i.e., main processes) at the corners of the figure: (1) select a task (using a linear, adaptive, or other sequencing algorithm), (2) administer the task, (3) collect evidence and score the response, (4) update the student model,[13] and return to the first step (i.e., select the next task). This process continues until a termination criterion is met (e.g., some preestablished threshold is exceeded, time runs out, or there are no more tasks).

In summary, student responses to assessment tasks, as well as patterns of responses, serve as the primary evidence of proficiencies. This information is culled directly from student behaviors and work products as they interact with and complete items within an assessment task (or task set). Based on exactly what the student produces in response to a given problem-solving task (i.e., the

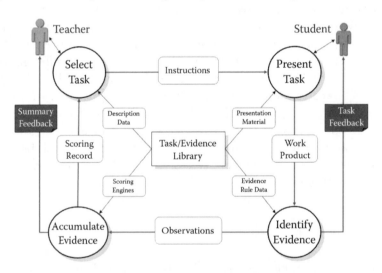

Figure 6.1 Four-process model [modified from "Enhancing the Design and Delivery of Assessment Systems: A Four-Process Architecture" by R. G. Almond, L. S. Steinberg, and R. J. Mislevy, 2002, *Journal of Technology, Learning, and Assessment,* 1(5), 1-63. Copyright 2002 by the Journal of Technology, Learning, and Assessment. Adapted with permission].

evidence), inferences can be made about the source of the problem or strength of a set of skills. Open-ended tasks typically invoke more varied evidence than do multiple-choice responses. ETS has been developing tools to analyze and evaluate various open-ended response types, discussed next.

Mathematics Intervention Module (MIM)

We are currently developing a mathematics intervention prototype, MIM, using ideas and methods described earlier in this chapter. The general topic was selected after consulting with teachers who identified Algebra I as a consistent obstacle for students; and within Algebra I, identified a few particularly difficult learning objectives or standards. We chose one of the most difficult objectives for our initial module: *Translate word expressions to symbolic expressions or equations and then solve and/or graph.*[14]

What Is MIM and How Does It Work?

MIM is an online application designed to help students become proficient in state mathematics standards. The initial focus is on Algebra I, but it may be extended to other subjects in subsequent releases. The module is based on a proficiency model that describes the skills that must be mastered for a student to be judged proficient in that standard. Each module presents students with open-ended questions dealing with the various skills identified in the proficiency model. These questions require the student to respond with a number, an expression or an equation, a graph, or text,[15] all of which are automatically scored.

Diagnostic Feedback   All responses in the intervention module are automatically evaluated, with immediate and helpful feedback provided to the student. Feedback is directed at the error that the student has made, and is not simply, "Wrong. Please try again." Similar to a human tutor, MIM attempts to give some indication of why the student's answer was wrong. The student is given three attempts to answer each question correctly, with progressively more detailed feedback provided along the way if the answers are incorrect. The correct answer, with an associated rationale, is presented if the student answers incorrectly three times. In addition, if the student is judged to be in need, the module presents a short (2–4 minute) instructional video that covers the problematic skill. These "instructional objects" reinforce the learning that is taking place as the student works through the questions and reads the feedback.

Instructional Objects   A specific instructional object (IO) is presented in the case where a student has gone through all three levels of feedback for a given problem. There are about 16 IOs that have been developed for the current MIM prototype. Within an IO, the flow of instruction proceeds as follows: (a) introduce the topic using concrete and engaging context, (b) state a particular problem that needs solving, (c) provide relevant definitions, (d) illustrate the concept within different examples (both prototypical and counter-examples), (e) provide sufficient practice and interactivity, and (f) conclude with summary and reflection screens. Reflection activities can also be used to gather evidence of student knowledge, assuming that these activities are interactive. Figure 6.2 shows a screen capture from an IO on the topic of Use Properties of Equality to Simplify Equations. The IO begins by using a scale as an analogy to "balancing both sides of an equation." A definition is presented, which explains why, mathematically, the scale is balanced. Following screens in the IO show examples of what happens—to the scale and the equation—when weights are added and removed.

Practice Opportunities   Depending on classroom needs and other factors, the teacher has the option of assigning multiple-choice questions for additional practice on each skill. The teacher can (a) require these practice questions of all students who seem not to have mastered the skill, (b) make the practice questions optional, or (c) configure the module so that the practice questions are not delivered.

Integrating Knowledge and Skills   The final section of the intervention module is a set of integrated open-ended questions that deal with a common theme or contextual situation. These questions reflect the standard as a whole. Like the open-ended questions earlier in the module, these integrated questions involve responses

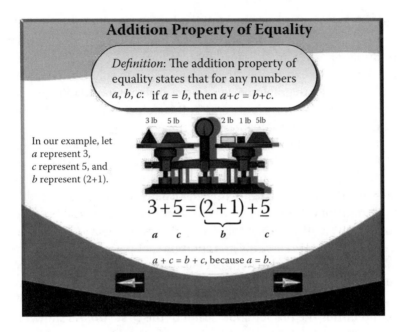

Figure 6.2   Screen capture from a MIM instructional object.

that require the entry of a number, an expression or an equation, a graph, or text.

Information to the Teacher   After the student completes the intervention module, the teacher receives a summary report. In addition, the teacher can review the student's entire session, viewing the student's responses to each question. Classroom summaries are also available, so that teachers can see at a glance how their students are progressing on the target standard.

Proficiency Model   A proficiency model generally describes the skills that must be mastered to be judged "proficient" in relation to a specific standard, and displays the relationships among these skills. The simplified proficiency model shown in Figure 6.3 analyzes the standard: Translate word expressions to symbolic expressions or equations and then solve and/or graph. By working down the model, one can see how the component skills can be isolated.   In this standard, "word expressions" means the information contained in a story, a contextual description, or some other real-life situation. At a high level, this standard can be divided into three parts, each corresponding to a separate skill, and each represented by a node (three white ovals) on the model. The first skill is to translate the information given in the story into an equation or graph or some other symbolic expression. The second skill is to solve the equation, and the third is to graph the equation and obtain useful information from the graph. For the purposes of this model, we assume that the equations and graphs are linear.

The first skill (translate context to equations and/or graphs) can be further divided into several sub-skills. To translate contextual information into an equation or graph, one must first identify the variables, and then translate the operations (addition, multiplication, and so on) that connect the variables, and, finally, put it all together correctly to form the relevant equation. Each of these three skills is represented by a node within the model, and each node is connected to its parent node, *Translate context to equations and/or graphs*. In addition, dotted lines connect the third sub-skill with the first two because the third sub-skill requires the proper application of the first two. As shown in the proficiency model, these nodes are faded. Due to constraints in the current project, we could not fully implement the mathematical content for these skills. Instead, we teased out part of this content area and displayed it as a separate skill—entering contextual information into a table and then translating the table into a linear equation or graph. This skill is displayed as a gray node, indicating that this is one of the skills implemented in the current release of the intervention module.

A similar analysis applies to the second high-level skill (solve linear equations). This skill can be divided into three sub-skills: (1) use the rules of algebra to simplify expressions, (2) use the rules of algebra to simplify equations, and (3) combine the first two skills to solve equations. Again, each of the three skills is connected to the parent skill. In addition, the third skill (*Apply algebraic properties to solve equations*) is connected by dotted lines to the first two skills as it represents a proper application of the first two. All three of these nodes are displayed as gray because all three are implemented in the intervention module.

The third high-level skill (graph linear equations) is subdivided into three component sub-skills: understand intercepts, understand slope, and use knowledge of intercepts and slope to graph equations and determine equations from graphs. In

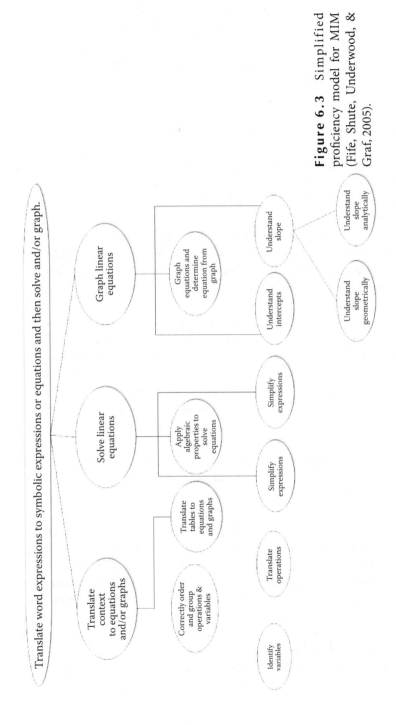

Figure 6.3 Simplified proficiency model for MIM (Fife, Shute, Underwood, & Graf, 2005).

addition, the *Understand slope* skill is further divided into two parts: *Understand slope geometrically* and *Understand slope analytically*. The "leaf nodes" (i.e., nodes with no children, or lower levels) are displayed as gray and are implemented in the intervention module.

Example of an Integrated Task Set in MIM

The following example is an isomorph of a problem from a set of ETS-owned content (Marquez, 2003). This integrated task set, as mentioned earlier, is presented at the end of the module, and its function is to assess the conjoined knowledge and skill elements. Finding a solution to the task requires the student to graph a line, find the equation of the line, identify the *y*-intercept and slope, state their significance in the context of the problem, and extrapolate data.

In the Music World Task, each node in the proficiency model may be linked, via different evidence models, to a number of tasks. As the student interacts with the system and answers questions, evidence is accumulated and the student model is updated. If a student demonstrates that she can calculate the slope using points on a graph and interpret what it means in the context of the problem, the corresponding nodes in the proficiency model will show higher estimates of mastery. Moreover, because of the hierarchical nature of the proficiency model, the parent node, "Understands slope," may also automatically increase slightly. The converse is true for failing to solve the problem correctly. In general, proficiency information in the student model can highlight specific areas that need more instructional support.

Diagnosis   To further facilitate the diagnosis of student performance, the system knows about a number of common misconceptions in relation to the skills in the proficiency model. To illustrate, in relation to the calculation and interpretation of the slope, some of the salient misconceptions and errors include inaccurate symbolic and graphical modeling of data, misunderstanding of slope as a rate of change, misinterpretation of slope and y-intercept in real contexts, and inability to use the equation of a line as a tool to predict linear behavior (i.e., extrapolation). These are used as indicators to help diagnose the problems with the knowledge and skills in the

Music World Task   You found a new Web site that claims to offer the best deal around for buying music CDs. The Web site isn't clear about the cost for each CD or the cost of shipping and handling (except to say shipping is a flat fee), but it does give you the following information:

Number of CDs Ordered	1	2	3
Total Cost (with Shipping & Handling)	$9	$14	$19

1. Plot the data in the table on the graph (provided). Draw the line that contains the data points.
2. Assume that total cost is a linear function of number of CDs ordered.
   a. Write an equation of the line that contains the data points. Show your work.
   b. What is the slope of the line that contains the data points?
   c. What does that slope represent in the context of this problem?
   d. What is the y-intercept of the line that contains the data points?
   e. What does that y-intercept represent in the context of this problem?
3. Your friend says that he can get 15 CDs from the Web site for $64.00. Is your friend correct? Explain.

proficiency model. A teacher or instructional module, armed with this information, can be considerably more effective in providing a targeted intervention.

Scoring   Following are some general requirements for a student to get a maximum score per item element in the Music World example.

1. Graphs points correctly with respect to the axes.
2. a. Writes a correct equation for the line based on an accurate reading of the graph or correct calculations using a linear form.
2. b. Gives the correct slope based on the graph or the equation written in part 2a.

2. c. *Gives clear and correct interpretation of slope in context.*
2. d. Gives the correct *y*-intercept based on the graph or the equation written in part 2a.
2. e. Writes clear and correct interpretation of *y*-intercept in context.
3. Writes an answer and justification that are correct, based on the equation given in question 2 or based on the graph in question 1.

Let's look at requirement 2c in more detail. The learning objective is that the student can give clear and correct interpretation of slope in the context of the problem. The work product is a written (typed) response to an assessment item. The three levels are as follows:

- *Low*: Student describes something that does not relate to the contextual variables related to slope (i.e., something other than CD price and shipping and handling).
- *Medium*: (a) Student describes slope in correct definitional terms (rise/run), but with no link to the context; or (b) student describes the correct contextual variables, but with an incorrect relationship.
- *High*: Student describes the correct contextual variables with the correct relationship (total cost of each CD including shipping and handling).

Now suppose that a student types in the response, "Slope is the rise over the run," which the system recognizes as correct but having no context. The system displays feedback appropriate to the inferred (common) error.[16] For example: *"You've told me the correct definition of slope, but you need to explain it in terms of the problem. For example, what do the rise and run in the graph have to do with the cost of CDs and shipping and handling?"* The student then tries again, and the system uses progressive levels of feedback for scaffolded support of learning.

Updating the Student Model After each response, or some other defined interval, the system updates the relevant nodes in the student model. Thus estimates of relevant proficiencies would be updated according to the evidence model. The example above showcased an ETS tool called C-RATER that can capture and analyze text input. Another ETS tool can "read" points and lines on a graph, and compare values to scoring rules (Bennett, Morley, Quardt, & Rock, 2000). Diagnostic feedback can similarly be embedded in xml files for the task, and linked to different responses. See Figures 6.4 and 6.5 for an example of graph analysis and feedback.

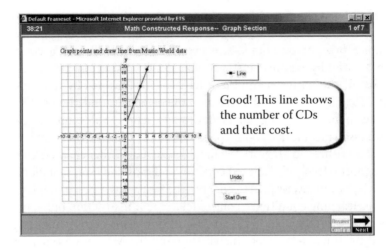

Figure 6.4   Graph analysis with diagnostic feedback shown superimposed on the work product. Additionally, the program evaluates the expressions and equations that a student types (see Figure 6.5) for mathematical accuracy/equivalence. For more information on the various automated scoring methods, see Bennett, Morley, Quardt, and Rock (2000) and Bennett, Morley, and Quardt (2000).

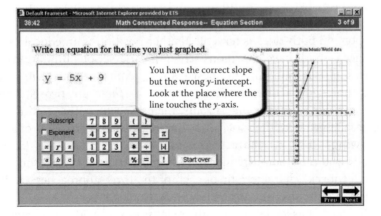

Figure 6.5.   Equation analysis with diagnostic feedback shown on the work product.

Instructional Design   The various elements of an intervention module—the open-ended questions, instructional videos, and multiple-
choice practice questions—are presented to the student according
to a carefully planned instructional design, based on principles of
assessment and instruction that have been developed by researchers
at ETS (Kuntz et al., 2005). We used the principles underlying ECD to
develop the underlying proficiency model, scoring rules, and informative assessment tasks, and incorporated into MIM the three research-
based features to support learning discussed in this chapter: timely
diagnostic feedback, tailored content, and multiple representations of
concepts. Finally, we plan to pilot test the first MIM module, employing
three learning conditions: control (classroom instruction only), practice (classroom instruction and practice problems on relevant topics),
and treatment (classroom instruction and the MIM prototype). This
will be administered to several hundred students in school districts in
southern California. Of interest will be the value-added of MIM over
the other two conditions in relation to student learning.

Summary and Conclusions

> If we take no action to improve teaching and learning, we will just be
> using children as "extras" in a high profile political drama while under-
> mining the social and economic prospects of the nation in the process.
>
> Kurt Landgraf, 2001

The chasm between traditional and progressive educational philosophies, described in the beginning of this chapter, is real. And
support on both sides is fervent. Neither position is an educational
panacea—both have enormous strengths and serious limitations. I
have suggested merging the best features from each into a unified
and more powerful educational approach. *There are two gifts we
can give our students—one is roots, the other wings.* The traditional
approach provides the roots, and the progressive approach provides
the wings. Table 6.1 characterizes four assessment variables (main
role in the classroom, frequency of administration, typical format,
and feedback) characteristic of each of the three approaches: traditional, progressive, and unified.

Evidence-based learning, an extension of evidence-centered
design for assessment, forms the foundation of the unified approach

TABLE 6.1   Assessment Variables Across Three Educational Approaches[a]

	Traditional	Progressive	Unified
Role of Assessment	Assessment of learning, to quantify fixed and measurable aspects of learner knowledge, skills, and abilities. Used for accountability purposes, often with norm-referenced tests. Produces a static/snapshot of the student	Assessment for learning, to characterize important aspects of the learner. Focus is on aspects of student growth, employing criterion-referenced tests, used to help learners learn, and teachers teach better	Both assessments of and for learning have important roles in education. Need to know where the student started, where currently is, where heading, how the journey is progressing, and ultimately degree to which destination is attained
Frequency of Assessment	Infrequent, summative assessments using standardized tests. Focus is on product or outcome (achievement) assessment. Typically conducted at the end of a major event (e.g., unit, marking period, school year)	Intermittent, formative assessment. The focus is more process oriented (but needn't exclude outcomes). Assessments of this type are administered as often as desired and feasible; monthly, weekly, or even daily. Administration is informal	Because assessments are embedded into the curriculum, a constant flow of evidence (student performance data) informs teachers and students. Data include both product (what) and process (how) assessment, as well as collaborative, negotiated, and/or self-assessment
Format of Assessment	Objective assessments, often selected responses. Focus on whether test is valid and reliable more than the degree to which it supports learning, per se	Constructed responses and authentic context, collected from multiple sources (e.g., quizzes, portfolios, self-appraisals, presentations)	Different task types and performance data are acceptable, from selected to constructed responses. Possible to extract data from problem-solving tasks, simulations, and other novel environments. Multiple representations used
Feedback	Correct or incorrect responses to test items and quizzes, or just overall score. Support of learning is not the intention	Global (proficiency) diagnoses attempted, with ways to improve (learning and teaching) suggested. Feedback is crafted to be helpful, rather than judgmental	Task-level and general diagnoses from item to proficiency level; procedural errors and misconceptions addressed and supported with immediate and timely help. Customized feedback is on the horizon

[a] This characterization is intended to convey general aspects of each approach in terms of these assessment variables, and should not be viewed as definitive categorizations.

proposed in this chapter for the design and development of informative assessments that can contribute toward improved teaching and learning. The ETS tools and approaches described herein collect and analyze a variety of evidence from the student across extended periods of time. These data collectively serve as the basis for estimates of proficiency status. This approach for developing informative assessments involves explicitly linking performance data to claims about learner proficiencies via an evidentiary chain, and therefore is more likely to be valid for multiple intended purposes.

Given the range of technology and tools at our disposal, at ETS and elsewhere, assessment tasks can now handle a variety of representations as input and output (e.g., graphics, equations, and text responses). Even more input/output options are on the educational horizon, along with new models and technologies to support learning. Using these tools for assessment *of* and *for* learning, as in the unified approach, can support our teachers and students, and at the same time, satisfy the requirements of NCLB.

Lessons Learned   As noted earlier, Dewey's innovative educational reform ideas did not pan out. What can we learn from that? First, the "school as a factory" metaphor undervalues and undermines teachers. For example, teachers have the very important responsibility of educating future generations of citizens, but their salaries are not nearly commensurate with their responsibilities, leading to a growing shortage of quality teachers. McCoy (2003) surveyed teachers in their first 3 years of teaching, to analyze reasons for teachers leaving the profession. The following categories were identified: societal attitude toward teachers, financial issues, time scarcity, workload, working conditions, and relationships with students and parents. Informative assessments cannot directly help with the first two issues (attitudinal and financial), but they can help with the last four—freeing up more time for teachers to do their jobs, reducing workload, improving working conditions, and fostering better communication and relationships among teachers, students, and parents.   The second reason cited for the failure-to-thrive of Dewey's ideas relates to the zeitgeist of practical education, and the consequent restriction of subject matter that occurred at the time. NCLB is threatening a similar shrinkage with its primary focus on mathematics, reading, and, soon, science. But so many other subject areas (e.g., history and art) comprise a well-rounded education. Another ramification of NCLB is the current trend of teaching to the test. Informative assessments can help reverse that trend by providing ongoing information about the student (to the teacher, student, parent, and so on), thus reducing our currently heavy reliance on formal standardized tests (see Pellegrino, 2004). This, in turn, could re-focus education on its primary mission, which is ensuring that our children learn the things they need to learn to contribute as well-adapted, effective members of society.

The third reason that Dewey's ideas did not become widely implemented concerns the use of measurement in his era. Although student abilities and intelligence were extensively "measured," it was not done to help them learn better or otherwise to progress. Instead, the main purpose of testing was to track students into appropriate paths, with the understanding that their aptitudes were inherently fixed. Thankfully, we have evolved in our thinking since then. We also have considerably more tools and techniques to promote learning, as described in this chapter. Students and teachers are both expected to benefit from (a) a unified approach to education, and more specifically, (b) informative assessments. For students, *tailored content* means that they receive subject matter based on their specific needs. Needs are determined from prior performance data from the student. Content is tailored to individual proficiency levels—not too easy or too hard. Other types of adaptations are possible as well, as discussed earlier. In addition, *diagnostic feedback* is believed to enhance learning by providing immediate diagnosis, assistance, and challenge, in relation to problematic and successful areas. Finally, working with *multiple representations* of concepts promotes flexible and deep comprehension. All these features, and others as well, are expected to increase learning, but must be subjected to rigorously controlled evaluations.

From the teacher's perspective, *timely and flexible reporting* of informative assessments permits the teacher to generate and view reports that show performance of students—as individuals, as groups, and as a whole class, and so on. These reports-on-demand can be used to modify instruction, exactly when it really counts—when students reach an impasse or when they display clear misconceptions. Reports can also show progress over time, as opposed to just a snapshot, for individual students as well as for the class. When coupled with instructional prescriptions or suggestions about what to do next, the reports would be even more valuable to teachers.

As a country, we are poised, with our current collection of research, approaches, and tools, to make a substantial, positive sea change to education. This chapter illustrates the pros and cons of different educational approaches and philosophies and advocated the integration of the "best of both worlds" in a unified approach. This needs to begin with a rational understanding of what we value in terms of proficiencies to be instructed and assessed, now and with an eye toward the future. Knowing what a student knows comes from obtaining quality evidence, which in turn is obtained from carefully designed assessment tasks. The approach described in this chapter is intended to be powerful, for students and teachers, especially when joined with sufficient practice opportunities and targeted feedback. The next step is to systematically test these ideas, and others that follow, in a series of controlled evaluations. The key to accomplishing our sea change goal is to work in a unified manner, toward a shared vision of excellent education for all.

Author Notes

Valerie Shute works at Educational Testing Service, Princeton, New Jersey, in the Center for Assessment Innovation and Technology Transfer.

I'd like to thank my wonderful colleagues for earlier reviews of this chapter: Eric Hansen (who had the tough job of reviewing the first and thus very rough draft), Aurora Graf, Diego Zapata, Jim Fife, Malcolm Bauer, Dave Kuntz, Carol Dwyer, and Evelyn Fisch. I'd like to additionally acknowledge Jim Fife's summary of MIM and analysis of its proficiency model, described in this chapter.

References

Adams, G. (1996). Project follow through: In-depth and beyond. In G. Adams & S. Engelmann (Eds.), *Research on direct instruction*. Retrieved August 25, 2005, from http://darkwing.uoregon.edu/~adiep/ft/adams.htm

Aleven, V. A. & Koedinger, K. R. (2002). An effective metacognitive strategy: Learning by doing and explaining with a computer-based Cognitive Tutor. *Cognitive Science, 26*(2), 147-179.

Almond, R. G., Steinberg, L. S., & Mislevy, R. J. (2002). Enhancing the design and delivery of assessment systems: A four-process architecture. *Journal of Technology, Learning, and Assessment, 1*(5), 1-63. Retrieved August 30, 2005, from http://www.jtla.org

Anderson, J. R., & Lebiere, C. (1998). *The atomic components of thought.* Hillsdale, NJ: Lawrence Erlbaum Associates.

Anderson, J. R., Reder, L. M., & Simon, H. A. (1996). Situated learning and education. *Educational Researcher, 25*(4), 5-11.

Bajraktarevic, N., Hall, W., & Fullick, P. (2003, May). Incorporating learning styles in hypermedia environment: Empirical evaluation. Paper presented at the workshop on Adaptive Hypermedia and Adaptive Web-based Systems, Budapest, Hungary. Retrieved August 26, 2005, from http://wwwis.win.tue.nl/ah2003/proceedings/paper4.pdf

Barton, P. E. (2005). One-third of a nation: Rising dropout rates and declining opportunities (Research Report No. PIC-ONETHIRD). Princeton, NJ: Educational Testing Service. Retrieved August 29, 2005, from http://www.ets.org/Media/Research/pdf/PICONETHIRD.pdf

Bass, K. M., & Glaser, R. (2004). Developing assessments to inform teaching and learning (CSE Report 628). Los Angeles: Graduate School of Education and Information Studies, UCLA. Retrieved April 20, 2007, from http://eric.ed.gov/ERICDocs/data/ericdocs2/content_storage_01/00000006/80/2b/b3/ac.pdf

Bennett, R. E., & Bejar, I. I. (1998). Validity and automated scoring: It's not only the scoring. *Educational Measurement: Issues and Practice, 17*(4), 9-17.

Bennett, R. E., Morley, M., & Quardt, D. (2000). Three response types for broadening the conception of mathematical problem solving in computerized-adaptive tests. *Applied Psychological Measurement, 24,* 294-309.

Bennett, R. E., Morley, M., Quardt, D., & Rock, D. A. (2000). Graphical modeling: A new response type for measuring the qualitative component of mathematical reasoning. *Applied Measurement in Education, 13,* 303–322.

Black, P., & Wiliam, D. (1998a). Assessment and classroom learning. *Assessment in Education: Principles, Policy, and Practice, 5*(1), 7–74.

Black, P., & Wiliam, D. (1998b). *Inside the black box: Raising standards through classroom assessment.* London: School of Education, King's College.

Bobbitt, J. F. (1912). The elimination of waste in education. *The Elementary School Teacher, 12,* 259-271.

Bracey, G. W. (2004). *Setting the record straight: Responses to misconceptions about public education in the U.S.* (2nd ed.). Portsmouth, NH: Heinemann.

Brna, P., Self, J., Bull, S., & Pain, H. (1999). Negotiated collaborative assessment through collaborative student modelling. In R. Morales, H. Pain, S. Bull, & J. Kay (Eds.), *Proceedings of the workshop: Open, interactive, and other overt approaches to learner modelling* (pp. 35-42). Presented at AIED 1999, Le Mans, France.

Brown, A. L., & Campione, J. C. (1990). Communities of learning and thinking, or a context by any other name. *Contributions to Human Development, 21*, 108-126.

Brusilovsky, P. (2003). Adaptive navigation support in educational hypermedia: The role of student knowledge level and the case for meta-adaptation. *British Journal of Educational Technology, 34*(4), 487-497.

Brusilovsky, P., & Vassileva, J. (2003). Course sequencing techniques for large-scale web-based education. *International Journal of Continuing Engineering Education and Lifelong Learning, 13*(1-2), 75-94.

Bunt, A., Conati, C., Huggett, M., & Muldner, K. (2001). On improving the effectiveness of open learning environments through tailored support for exploration. Retrieved August 18, 2005, from http://www.cs.ubc.ca/~conati/my-papers/aied2001.pdf

Carrier, C. A., & Williams, W. D. (1988). A test of one learner control strategy with students of differing levels of task persistence. *American Educational Research Journal, 25*(2), 285-306.

Civil Society Institute. (2005, August). *NCLB left behind: Understanding the growing grassroots rebellion against a controversial law.* Retrieved August 19, 2005, from the NCLBGrassroots.org Web site: http://reliableanswers.com/hs/nclb_open_revolt.asp

Cohen, V. B. (1985). A reexamination of feedback in computer-based instruction: Implications for instructional design. *Educational Technology, 25*(1), 33-37.

Conlan, O., & Wade, V. (2004). Evaluation of APeLS – An adaptive eLearning service based on the multi-model, metadata-driven approach. In P. De Bra & W. Nejdl (Eds.), *Proceedings of Third International Conference on Adaptive Hypermedia and Adaptive Web-based Systems* (pp. 291-295). Eindhoven, Netherlands: Springer LNCS.

Corbett, A. T., & Anderson, J. R. (1989). Feedback timing and student control in the Lisp Intelligent Tutoring System. In D. Bierman, J. Brueker, & J. Sandberg (Eds.), *Proceedings of the Fourth International Conference on Artificial Intelligence and Education* (pp. 64-72). Springfield, VA: IOS.

Corno, L., & Snow, R. E. (1986) Adapting teaching to individual differences among learners. In M. Wittrock (Ed.), *Handbook of research on teaching* (pp. 605-699). New York: Macmillan.

Cronbach, L. J., & Snow, R. E. (1977). *Aptitudes and instructional methods: A handbook for research on interactions.* New York: Irvington.

Cuban, L. (2004). The open classroom. *Education Next.* Retrieved August 28, 2005, from the Hoover Institute Web site: http://www.education-next.org/20042/68.html

Darling-Hammond, L. (1997). *The right to learn: A blueprint for creating schools that work.* San Francisco: Jossey-Bass.

Darling-Hammond, L., Griffin, G., & Wise, A. (1992). *Excellence in teacher education: Helping teachers develop learner-centered schools.* Washington, DC: National Education Association.

De Bra, P., Aerts, A., Berden, B., De Lange, B., Rousseau, B., Santic, T., et al. (2003, August). AHA! The Adaptive Hypermedia Architecture. *Proceedings of the Fourteenth ACM Conference on Hypertext and Hypermedia* (pp. 81-84). Nottingham, UK.

Deci, E. L., & Ryan, R. (1985). *Instrinsic motivation and self-determination in human behavior.* New York: Plenum.

Deci, E. L., Vallerand, R. J., Pelletier, L. G., & Ryan, R. M. (1991). Motivation and education: The self-determination perspective. *The Educational Psychologist, 74*, 852-859.

de Jong, T., van Joolingen, W., Scott, D., deHoog, R., Lapied, L., & Valent, R. (1994). SMILSLE: System for multimedia integrated simulation learning environments. In T. de Jong & L. Sarti (Eds.), *Design and production of multimedia and simulation based learning material.* Dordrecht, Netherlands: Kluwer.

Dewey, J. (1916). *Democracy and education.* New York: Macmillan. Retrieved August 22, 2005, from http://www.ilt.columbia.edu/publications/dewey.html

Dewey, J. (1938). *Experience and education.* New York: Simon & Schuster.

Engelmann, S., Becker, W.C., Carnine, D., & Gersten, R. (1988). The direct instruction follow through model: Design and outcomes. *Education and Treatment of Children, 11*, 303-317.

Epstein, M. L., Lazarus, A. D., Calvano, T. B., Matthews, K. A., Hendel, R. A., Epstein, B. B., et al. (2002). Immediate feedback assessment technique promotes learning and corrects inaccurate first responses. *The Psychological Record, 52*, 187-201.

Fife, J., Shute, V. J., Underwood, J. S., & Graf, E. A. (2005). Proficiency model for Mathematics Intervention Model (MIM). Unpublished manuscript and model. Educational Testing Service, Princeton, NJ.

Flanagan, F. M. (Speaker). (1994, May 9). The great educators, first series. *John Dewey.* [Radio broadcast]. Dublin, Ireland: RTE, Radio 1. Retrieved August 18, 2005, from http://www.ul.ie/~philos/vol1/dewey.html

Hambleton, R. K., Swaminathan, H., & Rogers, H. J. (1991). *MMSS: Fundamentals of item response theory.* Newbury Park, CA: Sage.

Hart, P. D., & Winston, D. (2005). *Ready for the real world? Americans speak on high school reform.* Executive summary. Retrieved August 30, 2005, from http://ftp.ets.org/pub/corp/2005execsum.pdf

Haycock, K. (2001). Closing the achievement gap. *Educational Leadership, 58*(6), 6-11.

Heffernan, N. T., & Koedinger, K. R. (2002). An intelligent tutoring system incorporating a model of an experienced human tutor. *Proceedings of the Sixth International Conference on Intelligent Tutoring Systems,* Biarritz, France.

Hirsch, E. D. (1996). *The schools we need and why we dont have them.* New York, NY: Doubleday.

Hunt, E., & Minstrell, J. (1996). Effective instruction in science and mathematics: Psychological principles and social constraints. *Issues in Education, 2*(2), 123-162.

Kahl, S. (2003, July). Implementing NCLB assessments and accountability requirements into an imperfect world. Paper presented at the Tenth Annual Education Law Conference, Portland, ME. Retrieved April 20, 2007, from http://www.measuredprogress.org/resources/education/nclb.html

Katz, I., Lipps, A., & Trafton, J. (2002). Factors affecting difficulty in the generating examples item type (GRE Board Report No. 97-18P). Princeton, NJ: Educational Testing Service.

Keller, J. M. (1979). Motivation and instructional design: A theoretical perspective. *Journal of Instructional Development, 2,* 26-34.

Keller, J. M., & Kopp, T. W. (1987). An application of the ARCS model of motivational design. In C. M. Reigeluth (Ed.), *Instructional theories in action: Lessons illustrating selected theories and models* (pp. 289-320). Hillsdale, NJ: Lawrence Erlbaum Associates.

Kliebard, H. (1987). *The struggle for the American curriculum, 1893-1958.* New York: Routledge and Kegan Paul.

Koedinger, K. R., & Anderson, J. R. (1998). Illustrating principled design: The early evolution of a cognitive tutor for algebra symbolization. *Interactive Learning Environments, 5,* 161-180.

Koedinger, K. R., Anderson, J. R., Hadley, W. H., & Mark, M. A. (1997). Intelligent tutoring goes to school in the big city. *International Journal of Artificial Intelligence in Education, 8,* 30-43.

Koedinger, K. R., & Tabachneck, H. J. M. (1994, April). *Two strategies are better than one: Multiple strategy use in word problem solving.* Presented at the annual meeting of the American Educational Research Association, New Orleans, LA.

Kuntz, D., Fife, J., Shute, V. J., Graf, E. A., Supernavage, M., Marquez, E., et al. (2005). MIM: Mathematics Intervention Module 1. Unpublished computer program/prototype. Educational Testing Service, Princeton, NJ.

Landgraf, K. (2001, March). *Using assessments and accountability to raise student achievement.* Testimony presented at the Education Reform Subcommittee of the House Committee on Education and the Workforce on Measuring Success, Washington, DC.

Laurillard, D. (1984). Interactive video and the control of learning. *Educational Technology, 23*, 7-15.

Laurillard, D. (1991). Computers and the emancipation of students: Giving control to the learners. In O. Boyd-Barrett & E. Scanlon (Eds.), *Computers and learning* (pp. 64-80). Wokingham, UK: Addison-Wesley.

Lee, J. (2002). Racial and ethnic achievement gap trends: Reversing the progress toward equity? *Educational Researcher, 31*, 3-12.

Lemann, N. (1999, March 9). The IQ meritocracy: Our test-obsessed society has Binet and Terman to thank—or to blame. *Time, 153*, 115-116. Retrieved August 15, 2005, from http://www.time.com/time/time100/scientist/other/iq.html

Lemke, M., Sen, A., Pahlke, E., Partelow, L., Miller, D., Williams, T., et al. (2004). *International outcomes of learning in mathematics literacy and problem solving: PISA 2003 results from the U.S. Perspective* (NCES Publication No. 2005-003). Retrieved July 28, 2005, from http://nces.ed.gov/pubsearch/pubsinfo.asp?pubid=2005003

Lepper, M. R., & Chabay, R. W. (1985). Intrinsic motivation and instruction: Conflicting views on the role of motivational processes in computer-based education. *Educational Psychologist, 20*(4), 417-430.

Lord, F. M. (1980). *Applications of item response theory to practical testing problems.* Hillsdale, NJ: Lawrence Erlbaum Associates.

Mac Iver, M. A., & Kemper, E. (2002). Research on direct instruction in reading [Guest editors' introduction]. *Journal of Education for Students Placed at Risk, 7*(2), 107-116. Retrieved August 23, 2005, from http://www.louisville.edu/edu/jespar/vol_7_no_2_editors.htm

Marquez, E. (2003). *Algebra guide four: Exploring relationships between symbolic expressions and graphs of lines* [Pathwise series: Teacher assistance package]. Princeton, NJ: Educational Testing Service.

Mathan, S. A., & Koedinger, K. R. (2002). An empirical assessment of comprehension fostering features in an intelligent tutoring system. In S. A. Cerri, G. Gouarderes, & F. Paraguacu (Eds.), *Proceedings of the Sixth International Conference on Intelligent Tutoring Systems,* Lecture notes in computer science, Vol. 2363 (pp. 330-343). London: Springer-Verlag.

McCalla, G. I., & Greer, J. E. (1994). Granularity-based reasoning and belief revision in student models. In J. E. Greer & G. I. McCalla (Eds.), *Student modelling: The key to individualized knowledge-based instruction,* NATO ASI Series F: Computer and Systems Sciences, Vol. 125 (pp. 39-62). New York: Springer-Verlag.

McCombs, B., & Whistler, J. S. (1997). *The learner-centered classroom and school: Strategies for increasing student motivation and achievement.* San Francisco: Jossey-Bass.

McCoy, L. P. (2003, March 28). It's a hard job: A study of novice teachers' perspectives on why teachers leave the profession. *Current Issues in Education, 6*(7). Retrieved August 23, 2005, from http://cie.ed.asu.edu/volume6/number7/

McMillan, J. H. (2007). *Classroom assessment: Principles and practice for effective instruction* (2nd ed.). Boston : Allyn & Bacon.

Minstrell, J. (1992). Facets of students' knowledge and relevant instruction. In R. Duit, F. Goldberg, & H. Niedderer (Eds.), *Research in physics learning: Theoretical issues and empirical studies* (pp. 110-128). Kiel, Germany: IPN.

Minstrell, J. (2001). Facets of students' thinking: Designing to cross the gap from research to standards-based practice. In K. Crowley, C. D. Schunn, & T. Okada (Eds.), *Designing for science: Implications for professional, instructional, and everyday science.* Mahwah, NJ: Lawrence Erlbaum Associates.

Mislevy, R. J., Almond, R. G., Yan, D., & Steinberg, L. S. (1999). Bayes nets in educational assessment: Where do the numbers come from? In K.B. Laskey & H. Prade (Eds.), *Proceedings of the Fifteenth Conference on Uncertainty in Artificial Intelligence* (pp. 437-446). San Francisco: Morgan Kaufmann.

Mislevy, R. J., Steinberg, L. S., & Almond, R. G. (2000, January). Evidence-centered assessment design: A submission for the NCME Award for Technical or Scientific Contributions to the Field of Educational Measurement. Retrieved November 12, 2004, from http://www.ncme.org/about/awards/mislevy.html

Mislevy, R. J., Steinberg, L.S., & Almond, R. G. (2003). On the structure of educational assessment. *Measurement: Interdisciplinary Research and Perspective, 1*(1) 3-62.

Mitrovic, A., & Martin, B. (2002). Evaluating the effects of open student models on learning. In P. de Bra, P. Brusilovsky, & R. Conejo (Eds.), *Proceedings of the Second International Conference on Adaptive Hhypermedia and Adaptive Web-based Systems* (pp. 296-305). Malaga, Spain: Springer-Verlag LCNS 2347.

Mora, J. K. (2001a, April 4). Language, literacy and content learning: Being accountable FOR and accountable TO English language learners. Keynote address at the Tenth Annual Administrators Conference, Sonoma County Office of Education, Santa Rosa, CA. Retrieved August 13, 2005, from http://coe.sdsu.edu/people/jmora/Prop227/accountabiliySCOE.htm

Mora, J. K. (2001b). Effective instructional practices and assessment for literacy and biliteracy development. In S. R. Hurley & J. V. Tinajero (Eds.), *Literacy assessment of second language learners* (pp. 149-166). Boston: Allyn & Bacon.

Mory, E. H. (2004). Feedback research review. In D. Jonassen (Ed.), *Handbook of research on educational communications and technology* (pp. 745-783). Mahwah, NJ: Lawrence Erlbaum Associates.

Narciss, S., & Huth, K. (2004). How to design informative tutoring feedback for multimedia learning. In H. M. Niegemann, D. Leutner, & R. Brünken (Eds.), *Instructional design for multimedia learning* (pp. 181-195). New York: Waxmann.

National Commission of Excellence in Education. (1983). *A nation at risk: The imperative for educational reform.* Washington, DC: U.S. Government Printing Office.

National Research Council. (2004). *Keeping score for all: The effects of inclusion and accommodation policies on large-scale educational assessment.* J. A. Koenig & L. F. Bachman (Eds.), Committee on Participation of English Language Learners and Students with Disabilities in NAEP and Other Large-Scale Assessments. Washington, DC: National Academies Press.

Ng, M. M., Guthrie, J. T., Van Meter, P., McCann, A., & Alao, S. (1998). How do classroom characteristics influence intrinsic motivation for literacy? *Reading Psychology, 19,* 319-398.

Paige, R. (2001, October). Math summit speech excerpt. [U.S. Secretary of Education, keynote speaker at the Summit on Math Education]. Retrieved August 30, 2005, from http://www.publishers.org/school/mathsummit.cfm

Papanikolaou K. A., Grigoriadou M., Magoulas G. D., & Kornilakis, H. (2002). Towards new forms of knowledge communication: The adaptive dimension of a Web-based learning environment. *Computers and Education, 39* (4), 333-360.

Papert, S. (1980). *Mindstorms: Children, computers, and powerful ideas.* New York: Basic Books.

Pea, R. D. (1994). Seeing what we build together: Distributed multimedia learning environments for transformative communications. *Journal of the Learning Sciences, 3*(3), 283-298.

Pellegrino, J., Chodowsky, N., & Glaser, R. (2001). *Knowing what students know: The science and design of educational assessment.* Washington, D.C.: National Academy Press.

Pellegrino, J. W. (2004). *The evolution of educational assessment: Considering the past and imagining the future* (Angoff Lecture No. 6, Policy Information Center Research Report). Princeton, NJ: Educational Testing Service.

Phi Beta Kappa. (2005). The 37th annual Phi Delta Kappa/Gallup Poll of the public's attitudes toward the publics schools. Retrieved September 20, 2005, from http://www.pdkintl.org/kappan/k0509pol.htm#exec

Proper, E. C., & St. Pierre, R. G. (1980). *A search for potential new Follow Through approaches: Executive summary.* Cambridge, MA: Abt Associates. (ERIC Document Reproduction Services No. ED 187 809).

Ravitch, D. (2000). *Left back: A century of failed school reforms.* New York: Simon & Schuster.

Razzaq, L., Feng, M., Nuzzo-Jones, G., Heffernan, N. T., Koedinger, K. R., Junker, B., et al. (2005). The ASSISTment project: Blending assessment and assisting. *Proceedings of the Twelfth Annual Conference on Artificial Intelligence in Education* (pp. 555-562). Amsterdam, Netherlands.

Reckase, M. D. (1997). The past and future of multidimensional item response theory. *Applied Psychological Measurement, 21,* 25-36.

Scardamalia, M., & Bereiter, C. (1994). Computer support for knowledge-building communities. *The Journal of the Learning Sciences, 3,* 265–283.

Scheirer, M. A., & Kraut, R. E. (1979). Increasing educational achievement via self-concept change. *Review of Educational Research, 49,* 131-150.

Schimmel, B. (1988). Providing meaningful feedback in courseware. In D. Jonassen (Ed.), *Instructional designs for microcomputer courseware* (pp. 183-195). Hillsdale, NJ: Lawrence Erlbaum Associates.

Shafrir, U. (1999). Representational competence. In I. E. Sigel (Ed.), *The development of mental representation: Theory and applications* (pp. 371-389). Mahwah, NJ: Lawrence Erlbaum Associates.

Shepard, L. A. (2000). The role of assessment in a learning culture. *Educational Researcher, 29*(7), 4-14.

Shute, V. J. (1993). A comparison of learning environments: All that glitters... In S. P. Lajoie & S. J. Derry (Eds.), *Computers as cognitive tools* (pp. 47-74). Hillsdale, NJ: Lawrence Erlbaum Associates.

Shute, V. J. (1995). SMART: Student modeling approach for responsive tutoring. *User Modeling and User-Adapted Interaction, 5,* 1-44.

Shute, V. J., Gawlick, L. A., & Gluck, K. A. (1998). The effects of practice and learner control on short- and long-term gain and efficiency. *Human Factors, 40,* (2), 296-310.

Shute, V. J., Glaser, R., & Raghavan, K. (1989). Inference and discovery in an exploratory laboratory. In P. L. Ackerman, R. J. Sternberg, & R. Glaser (Eds.), *Learning and individual differences* (pp. 279-326). New York: W. H. Freeman.

Shute, V. J., Graf, E. A., & Hansen, E. (2005). Designing adaptive, diagnostic math assessments for sighted and visually-disabled students. In L. Pytlikzillig, R. Bruning, & M. Bodvarsson (Eds.). *Technology-based education: Bringing researchers and practitioners together* (pp. 169-202). Greenwich, CT: Information Age Publishing.

Shute, V. J., Lajoie, S. P., & Gluck, K. A. (2000). Individualized and group approaches to training. In S. Tobias & J. D. Fletcher (Eds.), *Training and retraining: A handbook for business, industry, government, and the military* (pp. 171-207). New York: Macmillan.

Shute, V. J., & Towle, B. (2003). Adaptive e-learning. *Educational Psychologist, 38*(2), 105-114.

Sleeman, D. H., Kelly, A. E., Martinak, R., Ward, R. D., & Moore, J. L. (1989). Studies of diagnosis and remediation with high school algebra students. *Cognitive Science, 13*(4), 551-568.

Smith, P. L., & Ragan, T. J. (1999). *Instructional design* (2nd ed.). Upper Saddle River, NJ: Prentice Hall.

Snow, R. E. (1992). Aptitude theory: Yesterday, today, and tomorrow. *Educational Psychologist, 27*(1), 5-32.

Stebbins, L. B., St. Pierre, R. G., Proper, E. C., Anderson, R. B., & Cerva, T. R. (1977). *Education as experimentation: A planned variation model: Vol. 4.-A. An evaluation of Follow Through.* Cambridge, MA: Abt Associates.

Stiggins, R. J. (2002). Assessment crisis: The absence of assessment FOR learning. *Phi Delta Kappan, 83*(10), 758-765.

Stone, J. E., & Clements, A. (1998). Research and innovation: Let the buyer beware. In R. Spillan & P. Regnier (Eds.), *The superintendent of the future* (pp. 59-97). Gaithersburg, MD: Aspen Publishers.

Tabachneck, H. J. M., Koedinger, K. R., & Nathan, M. J. (1994). Toward a theoretical account of strategy use and sense-making in mathematics problem solving. *Proceedings of the Sixteenth Annual Conference of the Cognitive Science Society.* Hillsdale, NJ: Lawrence Erlbaum Associates.

Terman, L. M. (1916). *The measurement of intelligence.* Cambridge, MA: Riverside Press.

U.S. Department of Education. (2005). *Ten Facts about K-12 education funding.* Retrieved August 25, 2005, from http://www.ed.gov/about/overview/fed/10facts/index.html

Vassileva, J., & Wasson, B. (1996). Instructional planning approaches: From tutoring towards free learning. *Proceedings of EuroAIED '96* (pp. 1-8), Lisbon, Portugal.

Weber, G., & Brusilovsky, P. (2001). ELM-ART: An adaptive versatile system for Web-based instruction. *International Journal of Artificial Intelligence in Education, 12*(4), 351-384.

Zapata-Rivera, J. D. (2003). *Learning environments based on inspectable student models.* Unpublished doctoral dissertation, University of Saskatchewan. Department of Computer Science, Saskatchewan, Canada.

Zapata-Rivera, J. D., & Greer, J. (2004). Interacting with Bayesian student models. *International Journal of Artificial Intelligence in Education, 14*(2), 127-163.

Appendix: Definitions of Different Types of Assessments

Assessment can be conducted at various times throughout the school year or instructional program. Moreover, the format and purpose of the assessment can differ. Following are definitions of different assessments, as used in the context of this chapter.

- *Formative Assessment.* Formative assessment is usually done at the beginning or during a program, providing the opportunity for immediate evidence for student learning in a particular course or at a particular point in a program. The purpose of formative assessment is to improve quality of student learning and should not be evaluative or involve grading students.
- *Summative Assessment.* Summative assessment is comprehensive, provides accountability, and is used to check the level of learning at the end of the program. Program goals and objectives often reflect the cumulative nature of the learning that takes place (or should occur) in a program. Summative assessment is conducted at the end of the program to ensure students have met the program goals and objectives.
- *Diagnostic Assessment.* Although some educators view diagnostic assessment as a component of formative assessment, most consider it a distinct form of measurement (e.g., McMillan, 2001). In practice, the purpose of diagnostic assessment is to determine, prior to instruction or during the course of learning, each student's strengths, weaknesses, knowledge, and skills. Determining this information allows the teacher to remediate students and adjust the curriculum to meet each student's specific needs.
- *Criterion-Referenced Testing.* Criterion-referenced testing (CRT) is based on a well-specified domain with items appropriately sampled, and with the intention of making an inference about the degree of mastery a student attains in relation to the domain. Scores on criterion-referenced tests indicate what individuals *can* do—not how they have scored in relation to the scores of particular groups of persons, as with norm-referenced tests.
- *Norm-Referenced Testing.* Norm-referenced testing (NRT) compares a person's score against the scores of a group of people who have already taken the same exam, called the "norming group." Scores are usually reported as percentile ranks. Most achievement NRTs are multiple-choice tests, although some also include open-ended, short-answer questions. The questions on these tests mainly reflect the content of nationally-used textbooks, not the local curriculum. NRTs are designed to "rank-order" test takers to compare student scores.

Endnotes

1. The expression "sea change" in general refers to a profound change in the nature of something. The phrase appears to have originated in Shakespeare's *The Tempest* (I,ii).
2. See the Appendix for definitions of various types of assessments as used in the context of this chapter.
3. Addressing the basis for this ideological war over the best ways to teach, Cuban (2004) provides this interesting perspective, that the enduring quarrels are "proxies for deeper political divisions between conservatives and liberals on issues ranging from environmental protection to foreign policy. There are, of course, liberals who believe in traditional education and conservatives who embrace progressive ideas, but the lines are fairly well drawn" (p. 71).
4. The nine models are (1) Direct Instruction Model (University of Oregon); (2) Behavior Analysis Model (University of Kansas); (3) Language Development (Bilingual) Model (Southwest Educational Developmental Laboratory); (4) Cognitively-Oriented Curriculum (High Scope Foundation); (5) Florida Parent Education Model (University of Florida); (6) Tucson Early Education Model (University of Arizona); (7) Bank Street College Model (Bank Street College of Education); (8) Open Education Model (Education Development Center); and (9) Responsive Education Model (Far West Laboratory).
5. Briefly, "Direct Instruction" refers to a highly structured instructional approach, designed to accelerate the learning of at-risk students. Curriculum materials and instructional sequences attempt to move students to mastery at the fastest possible pace. Teachers follow scripts and the focus is on basic skills.
6. Some currently-popular terms related to progressive education have been summarized by Hirsch (1996), including lifelong learning, developmentally appropriate instruction, situated learning, cooperative/collaborative learning, multiple intelligences, discovery learning, portfolio assessment, constructivism, hands-on/experiential learning, project method, integrated curriculum, higher-order thinking/learning, and authentic assessment.
7. Diagnoses in this context refer to accurate analyses (measurement and reporting) of what the student knows and does not know, and to what degree.
8. While many ideas in constructivism come from cognitive psychology, it also embodies ideas from developmental psychology and anthropology.
9. ECD adheres to the guidelines for assessment design established by within a recent report by the National Research Council, *Knowing What Students Know* (Pellegrino, Chudowsky, and Gluser, 2001),

which identify three key, interconnected elements for assessments: (1) *cognition*: a theory of what students know and how they develop competence in a subject domain; (2) *observation*: tasks or situations used to collect evidence about student performance; and (3) *interpretation*: a method for drawing inferences from those observations.

10. "Counterpart" refers to similar students, based on age and grade, who reside in different countries. For more on international standing and comparisons among NAEP, TIMSS, and PISA results, see http://nces.ed.gov/timss/pdf/naep_timss_pisa_comp.pdf. The main difference between the two international analyses (TIMSS and PISA) is that TIMSS is the U.S. source for internationally comparative information on mathematics and science achievement in the primary and middle grades, while PISA is the U.S. source for internationally comparative information on the mathematical and scientific literacy of students in the upper grades at an age that, for most countries, is near the end of compulsory schooling.

11. NAEP scores range from 0–500, and are divided into four categories: Below Basic (0–261), Basic (262–298), Proficient (299–332), and Advanced (333–500).

12. In this context, grain size refers to the scope or generality of a proficiency. For instance, a large grain size, and hence general proficiency would correspond to, say, the course level (e.g., Algebra I concepts and skills). A small grain size, thus more specific proficiency may be a particular skill (e.g., can calculate slope from points). Between these extremes are additional levels of aggregation and generality. For more on the topic, see McCalla and Greer (1994).

13. "Student model" refers to a proficiency model that has been instantiated with information (estimations of mastery) in relation to a particular student.

14. This comes from an internal ETS effort to map alignments among state standards, and while it is not a specific state standard, it aligns well with actual state standards, such as Nevada: Translate among verbal descriptions, graphic, tabular, and algebraic representations of mathematical situations; West Virginia: Translate word phrases into algebraic expressions or word sentences into equations and inequalities; and Texas: Translates among and uses algebraic, tabular, graphical, or verbal descriptions of linear functions.

15. An example of a question requiring a textual response is, "Explain in words how you know that...."

16. The common errors, per item, were identified after we reviewed answers to about 500 paper-and-pencil tests covering all eight proficiencies, in each of the four variants (graph, numeric, expression/equation, and text), and with two difficulty levels (easy and hard).

After the tests were scored, incorrect responses, per item, were examined and tallied in a spreadsheet. The more frequent errors were further analyzed to infer misconceptions or procedural bugs underlying them.

Section III

What Policy Makers and Practitioners Need

7

Assessment for Learning—For Teachers as Well as Students

Charlotte Danielson
Princeton, NJ

Introduction

Assessment plays a critical role in education, for both policy makers and practitioners. These roles encompass issues of both accountability (how well students have learned) and instruction (how to promote higher levels of learning). However, assessment can yield more; the potential of assessment for teacher learning, as a result of both designing of student assessments and evaluating of student responses, has been generally overlooked. This paper outlines the uses of assessment *of* learning (summative assessment), and assessment *to guide learning* (formative assessment), and then describes the potential for teacher learning in each of these settings. It argues that at each stage in the process of student assessment—design, calibration, analysis of student responses, and use of assessment results to plan future instruction—opportunities abound for teachers to extend their practice.

The Different Faces of Assessment

Student assessment in the 21st century, in an environment of increased accountability, takes place within a broad political and policy context. In fact, improving schools has become synonymous with improving student scores on external (typically state-developed and mandated) assessments. In some places, these external assessments carry high stakes and serious consequences for students or their schools, or both.

Of course, summative assessment plays an important role inside schools and districts as well; when teachers create tests or other assessments for courses they teach, and use those assessments in awarding grades (and ultimately in deciding passes and failures), they are engaged in high-stakes assessment.

But summative assessment does not encompass everything important about assessment in the school setting. A small chorus of academics and practitioners has protested that there is also an essential role for formative assessment. They use the term not in the sense of "milestones" toward the summative assessments, but as a vehicle to guide student learning, i.e., the use of assessment *for* learning. Thus, assessment takes place in a complex landscape, and takes any number of different forms: summative or formative, high or low stakes, and internal or external. In all of these contexts, as unlikely as it might seem, student assessment has the potential to contribute significantly to enhanced professionalism on the part of teachers.

Issues and Purposes of Summative Assessment of Student Learning

Several features of summative assessments deserve attention. One concerns the purpose of the assessment: Is it to certify individuals, to evaluate the institution, or to evaluate individual teachers? Another issue concerns the locus of development—that is, where have the assessments been created?—at the school or external to the school? Yet another issue concerns the consequences or level of stakes and for whom these consequences exist (students, individual teachers, or entire schools). These issues play out differently in different situations for students and teachers. Finally, it is important to explore the quality of the assessments, and the potential for both student and teacher learning that result from well designed, as compared to poorly designed, summative assessments. Naturally, these issues are not completely independent of one another; they interact in interesting and instructive ways.

Purpose of Summative Assessment—To Certify Individuals

An important, and some would say the original, purpose of summative assessment is to certify individuals; every adult recalls (some with sweaty palms) the high-stakes tests to which one was subjected as a student. The results of these tests are typically used to make the following decisions about individuals.

- Transition from elementary or middle school, or graduation from secondary schooling. These assessments in recent years have become increasingly mandated (typically by state agencies) and the consequences have become increasingly high stakes.
- Completion of a course and the accompanying grade.
- Certification of the completion of advanced courses, e.g., Advanced Placement (AP) or International Baccalaureate (IB) exams. These examinations differ from those developed and used within a school or district in that they are developed and scored by external bodies.
- Admission to postsecondary, e.g., undergraduate and postgraduate and specialty training (SAT, ACT, MCAT). These tests are also external to the institution in which the students are enrolled, and the client in this case is the accepting institution; they use the results to admit or to decline admission to individual students.

The use of tests to make admissions decisions naturally imposes the burden of validity on the tests themselves. In particular, it is essential that they not reflect a gender or cultural bias that would systematically place some individuals at a relative disadvantage.

Purpose of Summative Assessment—To Document Levels of Performance, Both Absolute and Value-Added

Summative assessments are also used to provide evidence of quality, of either an institution or of individual teachers. Schools and colleges are accredited on the basis not only of *inputs* (course offerings, qualifications of faculty, and number of books in the library) but also on *outputs* (what have the students learned). Secondary school reputations are built on the strength of their graduates' admission to selective colleges, which, in turn, is largely based on student scores on tests such as the SAT and the ACT.

In addition, summative assessments can be used to determine the impact of teachers' work on student learning. It is now possible, by analyzing the results of state-administered tests on large numbers of students, to recognize patterns of individual teacher effectiveness on student performance. Whether this *should* be done is a separate, and hotly debated, question.

Locus of Control

An important question about assessment concerns control over both their design and the scoring of student responses. Summative assessments are always external to the students; they are designed by others (their teachers, the school district or state, or an outside examining body) to determine the student level of mastery, with the results used for any of the purposes named above.

Summative assessments may be external or internal to teachers and institutions, depending on who has designed them and for what purpose. As the tool of choice of accountability programs in the United States, assessments developed by or for states have significantly changed the landscape for educators in K–12 settings.

Level of Stakes

The consequences of summative assessments may be high stakes or low stakes for both students and teachers. In some states, failure to pass the third grade reading test can prevent a student from being moved to the fourth grade; poor performance on the high school proficiency test can mean that a student, even if she has accumulated sufficient credits, cannot earn a high school diploma. When the stakes are low for students, teachers and others have been heard to complain that the students are "blowing off" the test, not putting forth their best effort.

As noted above, the results of summative assessments may be used for a variety of purposes (to judge student mastery of a course, for graduation, etc., or to judge the quality of the school or the quality of instruction). They may be designed by teachers for internal school purposes or by external agencies to ascertain the quality of the institution or of individual teachers. These assessments also constitute the foundation for schools to demonstrate that they have met the requirements of "adequate yearly progress" under federal No Child Left Behind (NCLB) legislation. Those schools not meeting such requirements are subjected to increasing sanctions, ultimately resulting, after several years, in closure.

Recent experience has demonstrated that if the assessments are external to teachers and the stakes are high, educators may engage in nonfunctional behavior (from the standpoint of larger purposes of education), e.g., narrowing the curriculum, specifically teaching to the test, offering unethical assistance to students, etc. In many schools and districts, the arts, and even science (if it is not included on the state tests), have virtually vanished from the school day. Many anecdotal reports, and some carefully designed studies (Jacob & Levitt, 2003a, 2003b), have documented teacher practices of allowing students more time than intended, specific coaching during a test, and changing of student responses to correct answers prior to submitting student papers for official scoring.

In some areas, state-mandated assessments result in rank-ordering of school districts and individual schools, and are sometimes published in local newspapers in a type of "league table," to use a British expression. Such rankings have an impact on local property values, as prospective residents shop around for the "best" schools for their children.

Nature of Assessments

Most educators will concede that the emergence of external, high-stakes, summative assessments has had an impact on their practice. They admit to spending more time on those subjects they know will be included on the test, or to analyzing curriculum standards and previous years' tests for clues as to what might be included on the current year's test. While this is not specifically "teaching to the test"—they don't, after, all have access to the actual test—they have altered their behavior in response to the upcoming assessment. And while such practices don't literally constitute "teaching to a test," in a broader definition of the term they do. But then, one must ask, what is so wrong about that, if it is a test worth teaching to? That is, if it is stated in the curriculum standards that fourth graders will demonstrate proficiency in writing a persuasive essay, would policy makers not hope that teachers would teach their students to write a persuasive essay, and thus prepare their students for this test?

The practical and ethical difficulties arise when there is poor alignment between the curriculum standards (for example, writing a persuasive essay) and the methods selected to assess that skill (for example, by selecting from a number of choices on a multiple-choice test the best way to edit a draft essay).

Editing is an important skill, but it is a different skill from that of writing. The only way to assess student writing is to evaluate a sample (or, better, many samples) of writing. Therefore, whether high-stakes assessments will have the desired effect on classroom practice is largely a function of the nature of the assessments themselves, and the extent to which students are evaluated on important curriculum standards.

The same arguments apply to summative assessments designed by teachers and used only internally in the school, for example, to determine which students have passed a course and are eligible for promotion to each grade. It is the fundamental question of validity: Does the assessment assess that which it purports to assess? Thus, students could be receiving a passing or a failing grade for a unit or an entire course based on invalid information. In addition, when teachers uncritically use a test for a course, they are denied one of the most powerful opportunities for professional learning, namely, participating in the design of the test itself. This issue will be explored more fully later in this chapter.

Issues and Purposes of Formative Assessment—
To Guide Student Learning

Recent writings in the academic and practitioner literature have attested to the power of formative assessment to guide student learning (Wiliam, 2004). Formative assessment is no longer regarded as a "nice" thing for teachers to do if they have the time; it is now regarded as integral to teaching itself. It is important to recognize that in this discussion, the term "formative assessment" is used to denote assessment activities conducted in the classroom to shape learning activities, not as "benchmark" assessment intended to predict student performance on later, external, usually high-stakes assessments.

Formative assessment is internal to the classroom, designed by teachers to guide learning. And while it may be informal, it is systematic; teachers use formative assessment to ascertain which of their students understand which of the learning outcomes they hope students will master, and if student understanding is as yet incomplete, in which way it must be strengthened.

These characteristics of formative assessment have several implications.

- Through their use of formative assessment to prepare students for external assessments, teachers can communicate a sense of partnership to students: Our job is to work together to prepare you for the external test, whether it is the state assessment, or an AP or IB exam.

- Formative assessment can be *diagnostic.* That is, not just any question or problem set is equally effective. Through their choice or design of assessment questions, teachers are able to ascertain where each student is in his or her learning, and *which aspect(s)* of the desired learning has not yet occurred. Because well-designed formative assessments are inherently diagnostic, their design is critical to their effectiveness; it is not sufficient to know that a student has answered a question incorrectly. The incorrect response should itself reveal the nature of the lack of understanding.

- It should be noted that multiple-choice test items, if well constructed, can serve this purpose. Distracters, after all, are intended to *distract* students with incomplete or erroneous understanding from the correct answer. But the distracters should, themselves, reveal the source of the misunderstanding or misconception; when students select answer B, for example, rather than the correct C, teachers learn just what it is that they did not understand, and more importantly, what they believe instead.

- Formative assessments are *low-stakes*; they carry no consequences for either the students or the teacher. Therefore, there is no advantage for a student to try to camouflage his or her lack of understanding (as one might do on a high-stakes assessment) since the purpose of the assessment is to guide future learning and that can only happen if the true state of learning is known.

- Formative assessment permits the *individualization* of instruction. Typically, and critically, the results of formative assessments, although they could be aggregated across an entire class or school to reveal patterns of performance, remain in their disaggregated form. This enables teachers to understand the degree of understanding of different aspects of individual students learning so they can make appropriate instructional decisions.

- Formative assessment provides information to teachers as to how
  to proceed. When they understand what it is that students do
  and don't understand, they can engineer further learning activities accordingly. Without this knowledge, teachers are "flying
  blind," and must resort to simple repetition of the material, usually louder.
- Formative assessments are of value not only to teachers, but also
  to students themselves, and can make a material contribution to
  student self-regulation and autonomy in learning. In addition,
  students can be taught to conduct their own formative assessment, using their own work and that of peers. Furthermore, well-
  designed assessment tasks themselves can provide feedback to
  students, as when a problem in mathematics (or physics or chemistry) does not "check out" or when an experiment does not yield
  important information. When used in this way, by students to
  guide their own learning, student self-assessment and monitoring
  of learning become truly embedded in instruction.

An interesting parallel can be found in the perceived value by teachers of the assessment tasks for the National Board for Professional
Teaching Standards (NBPTS).[1] In the NBPTS procedure, teachers
submit a portfolio of their practice (following strict guidelines) and
complete a series of paper-and-pencil tests at an assessment center.
This assessment is external to the teacher in both its design and scoring, and, if real benefits (such as a salary bonus) flow from successful completion, it may be high stakes as well. However, despite what
might be considered unfavorable conditions for learning (externally
controlled and high stakes), many teachers report that, through completing the assessment, they have learned a great deal about good
teaching in general and about *their* teaching specifically. They consistently say that as a result of participating in the NBPTS process, even
when they have not been successful, they have become better teachers. That is, they have learned from the process of assessment itself.

The reasons for this benefit to teachers are instructive as we consider
the role of assessment in the classroom. Several features of the NBPTS
assessments stand out. First, they are organized around very clear
standards of practice. NBPTS publications outline, in unambiguous
terms, the standards of practice for each of the areas (for example, early
childhood or secondary mathematics) in which national certification
is available. That is, teachers are aware of what it is that their submission or test is intended to demonstrate and what the result means.

Second, the procedures for the NBPTS assessment engage teachers in structured reflection on their practice. Teachers are asked, through the questions in the portfolio entries and the questions in the assessment center, to explain their thinking, as they analyze student work or interpret a video of their teaching. Such professional activities are evidently highly effective in promoting learning, and can also be embedded in the formative assessments teachers design for students.

Teacher Learning Through Student Assessment

When teachers develop and use assessments in the classroom, whether for internal summative or for formative purposes, they engage in serious professional work. And although the process of assessment development by state agencies or testing companies must, of necessity, follow a "design down," logical sequence, teachers, when they develop assessments for their own use, tend to weave the various steps together.

The Logical Process

The "logical" steps involved in assessment design and application include the following.

Clarifying the Outcomes   California's curriculum standards require that second grade students will be able to "recognize, name, and compare unit fractions from 1/12 to 1/2"; and that fourth grade students can "recognize that rectangles that have the same area can have different perimeters, and that rectangles that have the same perimeter can have different areas." In order to design learning experiences to enable students to demonstrate such skill, it is important first to determine what sort of statements these are. Do they refer to factual knowledge, or procedural knowledge, or conceptual understanding? The answer to that question carries far-reaching implications for both instruction and assessment.

Determining What Would Count as Evidence, and Aligning the Methodology to the Type of Outcome   For example, if the curriculum outcome is a factual statement, then a selected-response test item could be used. If, however, the outcome involves experimental design or skill in writing, a constructed response format would be more appropriate.

Developing the Actual Assessment Prompts   This step requires formulating the questions, developing "distracters," etc. Preliminary thought will have been given to this matter, but the prompts must be finalized. It is at this stage that issues of gender and cultural bias must be addressed. In addition, if the assessment is to serve a formative purpose, the distracters must reflect typical misunderstandings so they have diagnostic value.

Designing the Scoring Guide or Rubric   The scoring guide identifies the critical assessment criteria and describes student performance that would satisfy the criteria. The rubric can be either holistic or analytic and will reflect the desired level of detail.

Evaluating Student Responses   Lastly, the scoring guide is applied to student responses to determine levels of mastery. Issues of score combining and compensation (Does excellent performance in one area "compensate" for poor performance in another? How is a final score determined? Is it simply a matter of adding the component parts?) come into play at this stage.

When assessments are designed at the state level, valid results can be obtained only if the methods used are suitable to the type of curriculum outcome. As illustrated in Table 7.1, assessments can be categorized as tests (either selecting or supplying answers), products

TABLE 7.1   Forms of Assessment

Test		Product		Performance	
Select	Supply	Written	Physical	Structured	Spontaneous
• True/false test	• Short-answer	• Essay	• Sculpture	• Student	• Group work
• Multiple- choice test	questions	• Term paper	• Model	reading	
	• Essay test	• Lab report		• Speech	
				• Musical performance	
				• French dialogue	

Source: Danielson, C. (1997). *A collection of performance tasks and rubrics: Middle school mathematics* (p. 6). Larchmont, NY: Eye on Education. Reproduced with permission of the publisher.

(either written or physical), and performance (either structured or spontaneous). Naturally, not every assessment methodology is equally suitable to each type of curriculum outcome. For example, for mathematics problem solving, the best, most direct, approach is a constructed response test, where students must explain their thinking.

However, for large-scale state assessments, issues of economics come strongly into play. One of the great advantages of multiple-choice, machine-scorable tests is, after all, the efficiency of scoring them; student answer sheets can be fed into an optical scoring machine and the results tabulated immediately. Computer-delivered testing can make the process even more efficient. But issues of validity remain. If the meaning of a curriculum outcome refers to, for example, conceptual understanding of the relationship between area and perimeter, then a multiple-choice item will not suffice. A constructed-response item is essential, with the consequent need for hand scoring of student responses—an expensive undertaking.

The Practical Process

From the standpoint of teachers, external assessments (whether these are the state's proficiency tests or the AP or IB exams) inevitably arrive from the outside, with teachers typically playing no part in their design. But when teachers, either on their own or with colleagues, want to either certify individual students (for example, to pass a course) or to prepare their students for summative assessments designed by others, they engage in significant cognitive work. And while they must undertake all the steps of the logical assessment design process, they typically do them in a slightly different sequence. Furthermore, it is the analysis of student responses that becomes the linchpin of the effort.

When teachers engage with issues of assessment, they, like those at the policy level, must first clarify curriculum outcomes or standards: What do these statements mean? This is not as simple as it might appear at first glance, and inevitably engages teachers in questions of assessment. Just as at the policy level, when a state's content standard states that second grade students will be able to "recognize, name, and compare unit fractions from 1/12 to 1/2"; or that fourth grade students can "recognize that rectangles that have the same area can have different perimeters, and that rectangles that have the same perimeter can have different areas," educators must determine the meaning of these statements.

But for teachers it is not an academic exercise; when teachers are asked what they mean by a specific curriculum objective, for many the answer is: "the student would be able to solve a problem like *this*" or the student could explain *this concept* in his or her own words. This type of response is, fundamentally, a question of assessment. The assessment provides, in effect, an operational definition of the curriculum objective itself. Thus, for teachers, unlike government officials, the shift from issues of curriculum articulation to assessment is seamless; indeed, they occur virtually simultaneously.

Statements of student performance as written in curriculum outcomes may conceal important differences of meaning and depth. In the case of the fractions for second graders, does understanding the relative size of unit fractions refer only to fractions of a single object, meaning that 1/6 is always smaller than 1/4? This "knowledge" could be taught by a procedural rule, "as the bottom number gets larger the amount becomes smaller." Alternatively, teachers could aim for students who actually *understand the meaning* of the fractional statement, and could explain, in their own words, why it is that 1/6 is smaller than 1/4 or that 1/4 of an object may not be the same size as 1/4 of another object; it would depend on the size of the object.

How one interprets the curriculum statement, as procedural knowledge or conceptual understanding, has different implications for both instructional planning and assessment techniques. Similarly, the fourth grader's "recognition" that shapes of the same area can have different perimeters, and vice versa, could be considered a simple statement of fact, and could be memorized. But if the "recognition" is taken to mean conceptual understanding, then the instructional and assessment implications are different. Furthermore, when teachers design assessments for their own use, they are not restricted by the limitations of machine-scorable, multiple-choice items. Teachers, in other words, have more assessment options than do test developers of large-scale tests.

The following section contains two examples, one for each of the two standards enumerated, at a nonsuperficial level of understanding. The examples also include some samples of student work in response to the prompts.

The Value of Unit Fractions (Second Grade) The following prompt could have been prepared by teachers to assess whether their second grade students understood the concept of a fraction, and the relationship between the unit fraction, in this case 1/2, and the quantity that it refers to.

Pieces of Pizza

Jose ate 1/2 of a pizza. Ella ate 1/2 of another pizza. Jose said that he ate more pizza than Ella did, but she said they both ate the same amount. Who do you think is right? Is it possible that neither Jose nor Ella is correct? Use drawings or pictures and words to explain your answer.

The mathematical principle involved here is that the fraction 1/2 does not, in itself, let one know what quantity is being referred to; 1/2 of a large object is greater than 1/2 of a small object. Therefore, teachers could, with little difficulty, describe what they are hoping student responses would demonstrate, namely that they recognize it is impossible to say, with any certainty, which person ate more pizza without knowing the sizes of the pizzas that each one ate.

Six samples of student responses that illustrate student understanding of this principle follow (Figures 7.1–7.6).

The Relationship Between Area and Perimeter (Sixth Grade)   The following prompt could have been prepared by teachers to assess whether their sixth grade students understood the relationship between area and perimeter of a geometric figure.

Day Care Center

You have been hired by a day care agency to fence in an area to be used for a playground. You have been provided with 60 feet of fencing (in 4-foot sections) and a 4-foot gate. How can you construct a playground using the fencing so the children have the most area in which to play?

Try several shapes that can be made with the fencing and determine their areas. Include pictures of the shapes, drawing them roughly to scale. In addition, write a brief summary that describes which shape you think will have the largest area, and why.

As an additional challenge, imagine that the fencing is flexible, and can be made to bend. What shape would have the greatest area, and why?

This question invites students to explore the relationship between area and perimeter, and can be solved through a process of trial and error. It is also an introduction to the more advanced concept in calculus of maximization; hence, when students encounter that concept later, it will not be completely new.

In student responses, teachers would be interested in seeing that students grasp the fundamental concept that, given the same perimeter, the more closely a shape approximates a circle, the larger will be the area. So, for quadrilaterals, a square would yield the largest area.

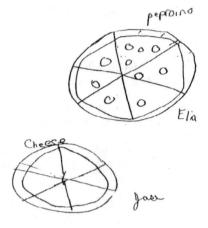

Figure 7.1   Pizza student response #1.

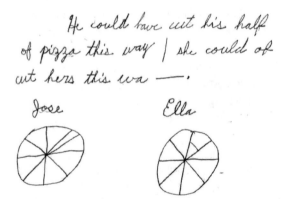

Figure 7.2   Pizza student response #2.

Figure 7.3   Pizza student response #3.

Figure 7.4   Pizza student response #4.

Figure 7.5   Pizza student response #5.

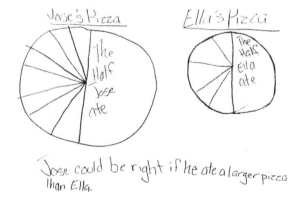

Figure 7.6   Pizza student response #6.

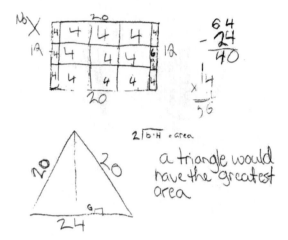

Figure 7.7   Fencing student response #1.

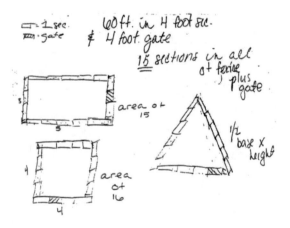

Figure 7.8   Fencing student response #2.

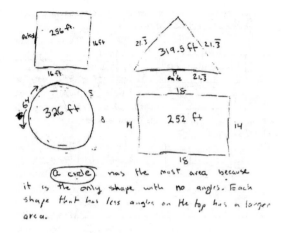

a circle has the most area because it is the only shape with no angles. Each shape that has less angles on the top has a larger area.

Figure 7.9   Fencing student response #3.

Figure 7.10   Fencing student response #4.

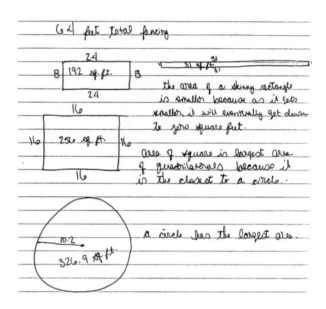

64 feet total fencing

24
8 | 192 sq. ft. | 8

the area of a skinny rectangle
24
16
is smaller because as it gets
smaller, it will eventually get down
16 | 250 sq ft | 16
to zero square feet.

area of square is largest area
16
of quadrilaterals because it
is the closest to a circle.

10.2

a circle has the largest area.
326.9 sq ft.

Figure 7.11   Fencing student response #5.

Five responses that illustrate students' understanding of this principle follow (Figures 7.7–7.11).

It is clear that when teachers examine the student responses, the criteria for understanding emerge. In both cases, it is evident when students understand the question they are being asked. That understanding is not revealed in all the student responses shown in Figures 7.7 to 7.11. Beyond that, the responses reflect different degrees of flexibility with the concepts, and different levels of depth of understanding. Furthermore, as teachers isolate the characteristics of those responses that display high levels of understanding, they can create descriptors that characterize different levels of student command of the concepts, and determine, from those samples of work, the minimum level of student understanding that would constitute mastery; that is, they establish their "cut score."

It should be noted that this process is different than that used by policy makers in developing state-level assessments; they must create the scoring guides before administering the assessments. But such work is at the heart of teacher learning from student assessment; in posing questions to students and analyzing student responses, they clarify their understanding of the curriculum outcomes themselves and determine what student mastery would "look like."

Thus, in the case of the pizza problem for second grade students, teachers might determine that student responses in Figures 7.5 and 7.6 demonstrated adequate understanding, whereas student responses in Figures 7.1, 7.2, and 7.3 did not demonstrate this; the student response in Figure 7.4 is an ambiguous borderline case. Furthermore, in making those decisions, teachers articulate the criteria on which they based those judgments, in this case, the degree to which the student had a stable understanding of 1/2 a pizza, uncontaminated by irrelevant details such as how the pieces were cut, the number of pieces into which the pizza was cut, whether the topping was of cheese or pepperoni, and the like. However, even these conclusions cannot be considered completely valid; a teacher might not be certain, without speaking to the student whose work is shown in Figure 7.3, for example, and hearing the student's reasoning behind a response, whether the student had a firm and flexible understanding of the concept of 1/2. Nevertheless, by examining student work, by studying exemplars of student understanding, it becomes clearer to teachers what the nature of such understanding is.

Based on the student responses, teachers might construct a rubric such as the following.

Level 1—Response is not attempted, or the response is either completely irrelevant to the question or reveals no understanding of the meaning of a fractional part.

Level 2—Response attempted, with some understanding of the meaning of a fractional part. However, response is incomplete, and the drawing does not help illuminate the explanation.

Level 3—Response shows good grasp of the meaning of a fractional part, but with minor inaccuracies or misrepresentations.

Level 4—Response is complete and coherent, demonstrating a clear and complete grasp of the meaning of a fractional part. Drawing helps to illuminate the explanation.

In the case of the fence problem for sixth grade students, teachers might decide that the student whose work was shown in Figure 7.11 understood the interaction between area and perimeter, but students whose responses are shown in Figures 7.7 and 7.8 did not. Student responses shown in Figures 7.9 and 7.10 appear to reflect incomplete understanding. The reasons for these judgments might include such things as the extent to which students seemed to understand the question, the degree of understanding of the concept of the area of a figure, and the fact that figures of the same area can have very different perimeters, and vice versa, the degree to which the student's drawing was a resource to the student in solving the problem, and the clarity and degree of understanding displayed in the student's explanation.

Therefore, the teachers, in examining the student work, extract the essential criteria, create the descriptors related to each of the criteria (the rubric), and set the standard for mastery. In future uses of the assessment task, of course, teachers would be able to build on their initial work, and would not have to begin again.

Hence, a scoring guide for the day care center problem might be:

Level 1—Response is not attempted, or the response is either completely irrelevant to the question or reveals no understanding of the relationship between area and perimeter.

Level 2—Response attempted, with some understanding of the relationship between area and perimeter. However, response is incomplete, or the drawing does not help illuminate the explanation.

Level 3—Response shows good grasp of the relationship between area and perimeter, but may include minor inaccuracies or misrepresentations.

Level 4—Response is complete and coherent, demonstrating a clear and complete grasp of the relationship between area and perimeter, including the reason why the closer a figure approximates a circle, the larger its area will be. Drawing helps to illuminate the explanation.

Unlike the "logical" sequence of assessment design typically used by state policy makers or commercial test developers, the first time an assessment task is used, the practical sequence used by teachers follows a significantly different sequence. In their assessment design, teachers work from samples of student work to determine the assessment criteria, the descriptors, and the cut scores of acceptable performance. This work is highly productive for teachers in clarifying and operationalizing the statements of curriculum outcomes, and in forging professional consensus as to the practical meaning of student understanding.

In addition, as teachers examine the work of their students, they acquire important information about their own practice. First, they learn about the misconceptions of individual students, and can use that information to guide future work with those students. In addition, however, the student responses will no doubt reveal patterns of levels of student understanding across an entire class. Teachers, then, can learn to recognize which aspects of their own practice need to be strengthened, and can devise different approaches to teaching that topic in the future. Moreover, teachers become more aware than previously of common misconceptions regarding the topic at hand; these insights are vital for planning further instruction.

When teachers engage in this work with their colleagues, their reflections and plans are further informed by the perspectives of other teachers, resulting, almost certainly, in additional insights about student learning and how to promote it. As a result, the collective wisdom of the teachers, as a group, the intellectual capital of the school as a whole, is greatly enhanced.

It is significant that when teachers comment on their experience with going through the NBPTS assessment process, many report that the analysis of student work (included as a portfolio entry for every certificate) promotes the most professional learning. Until they engage in this exercise, many teachers regard every incorrect student response as equivalent—the student did not "get it." But when they take the time to actually *look at* and *analyze* the student work, they begin to recognize the information it can yield and the utility of this information.

Teacher Learning Through Large-Scale Student Assessment

As noted above, one of the principal constraints on large-scale, state-mandated assessments is the cost of scoring constructed response items. The consequence of this cost has resulted in the overwhelming use of multiple-choice items in state tests. While it is certainly the case that when experts oversee the process of constructing multiple-choice items, those items can reveal far more about student conceptual understanding than when the work is undertaken by teachers. However, it remains true that the subtleties of student understanding, and the thinking that produces misconceptions, are not revealed easily by students' selection of a wrong answer from among the choices offered.

If it is true that some aspects of student understanding are best revealed through well-designed constructed-response items, if teachers learn from their analysis of student responses, and if a major constraint on states' use of constructed-response items is the expense of scoring student responses, can these factors not be brought together to maximize both teacher learning and the validity of large-scale student assessment?

A modest proposal follows.

- State agencies develop, or contract the development of, their state assessments aligned to their own state content standards.
- State or contractor personnel train teachers to score student responses to the constructed response items, using well-established training techniques and attaining acceptable levels of inter-rater agreement. The number trained could be greater than the number actually needed to score student responses, on the belief that the training itself is of considerable educational value to teachers.
- Teachers score the responses of students (but not those from their own school, to eliminate an obvious source of bias in scoring). The identity of students remains confidential, and discrepancies are moderated by chief scorers. This process would be similar to that currently in use in those states where constructed-response items are used, but with the significant detail that the readers are teachers of the same or similar grade level, rather than other individuals hired by the testing company.
- A small sample of student papers, with their assigned scores, is forwarded to a central location for auditing by experts on the assessment task. Results from this auditing process are reported back to the school-based scoring sessions and are also used to revise the training process used in future years.

Conclusion

Both academics and practitioners have gradually increased their appreciation of the value of student assessment in promoting learning by students. What has been less explored is the potential of student assessment as a vehicle for the professional development of teachers.

This chapter has explored the different purposes of student assessment and some of the issues involved: summative vs. formative, internal vs. external development, and high vs. low stakes. These different settings carry different implications for the use of assessment to support learning, by both students and teachers. It is the argument of this chapter that the potential for learning by teachers derives primarily from teacher development of assessment tasks, and subsequent examination of student responses. It is through these activities that teachers clarify the meaning of the curriculum outcomes, become aware of evidence of student understanding, and incorporate these insights into their planning for future instruction.

References

Danielson, C. (1997). *A collection of performance tasks and rubrics: Middle school mathematics*. Larchmont, NY: Eye on Education.

Jacob, B., & Levitt, S. D. (2003a). Rotten apples: An investigation of the prevalence and predictors of teacher cheating. *Quarterly Journal of Economics, 118*(3), 843-877.

Jacob, B., & Levitt, S. D. (2003b). Catching cheating teachers: The results of an unusual experiment in implementing theory. In W. Gales & J. Rothenberg Pack (Eds.), *Brookings-Wharton papers on urban affairs: 2003* (pp. 185-209). Washington, DC: Brookings Institution Press.

Wiliam, D. (2004, June). Keeping learning on track: Integrating assessment with instruction. Invited address presented at the 30th Annual Conference of the International Association for Educational Assessment, Philadelphia, PA.

Endnotes

1. The National Board for Professional Teaching Standards is an independent, nonprofit, nonpartisan organization governed by a board of directors, the majority of whom are classroom teachers. Other members include school administrators, school board leaders, governors and state legislators, higher education officials, teacher union leaders, and business and community leaders. Web site: www.nbpts.org.

8

Assessment as Instructional Support:
Policies and Practices

Roderick R. Paige
The Chartwell Education Group

Elaine P. Witty
Norfolk State University (Emeritus)

Over the past four years we have visited hundreds of schools in states all across our nation. In fact, there are only four states we did not visit. We can tell you that teachers across America want to be successful with the children they teach. They want to experience the satisfaction of knowing that the work they do is valuable and that it pays off in good returns for student learning. Teachers tell us all the time of the joy they feel when a child who has been struggling with a skill or concept finally grasps it.

Our challenge is that too few teachers are able to experience that joy. Although recent National Assessment of Educational Progress (NAEP) reports indicate that more children are showing greater achievement, not enough children are learning at the rate and level they should (National Center for Education Statistics [NCES], 2005). Because we know what it takes to ensure that all children have good school results, it is unforgivable to have schools that continue to fail in producing the desired educational outcomes for all. It is unacceptable to have teachers working daily in situations that offer inadequate support for effective instruction. Schools should be happy places and they can be.

We should note that there are many teachers who enjoy their daily interactions with students. They find the high level of support needed to do what they know how to do. Yet, there are many teachers whose daily job is a struggle. They want to be successful but they are handicapped by circumstances beyond their control. Because we know that high-quality instruction is crucial to student achievement, supporting instruction must be our first line of defense against schools that fail to educate all children.

The Role of Assessment in Schools

Fortunately, there are technologies, strategies, and materials available to teachers now that can help to ensure their success with children from all types of backgrounds. One of the key resources teachers have is strong assessment programs. We know that improving formative assessment raises student achievement (Black & Wiliam, 1998). Historically, assessment was primarily the domain of the teacher. Today, however, the need for accountability at local, state, and national levels has significantly broadened the concept and uses of assessment. Policy makers now use assessment to set standards, monitor the quality of programs in their states, formulate policies, direct resources, and provide rewards and sanctions. Administrators and school personnel use assessment to designate program priorities, monitor program effectiveness, and plan for improvements. Teachers use assessment to determine the information, skills, and attitudes their students need as a basis for instructional changes.

Even in this expanded vision of assessment, it is the teacher's use of assessment that has the most direct bearing on student achievement. Teachers know that only by carefully assessing what a child has learned can he or she effectively plan the most helpful instructional strategies for that child. For the teacher, assessment is all about getting information that can be used to guide instruction and increase the success rate of students. While the teacher's use of assessment is no longer the only use of assessment, it is still closest to the student and therefore the most critical to learning.

Since 2001 the No Child Left Behind (NCLB) legislation has required states to implement a system that holds schools and districts accountable for the academic achievement of all students.

NCLB is historic in that it requires annual statewide assessment data that are disaggregated by race, income, and other criteria in order to reveal student performance. Recent NAEP trend data show how students are performing. For example, at age 9 years white students showed a gain of 10 points since the first assessment, and black students showed a gain of 30 points. Almost half of that increase came since 1999. Data for Hispanic students were first separately presented in 1975. Their scores followed the same pattern. The gaps between white and black student at age 9, 13, and 17 decreased in reading and in mathematics. Mathematics scores for students at age 9 were 9 points higher in 2004 than in 1999, and for students at age 13, mathematical scores were 15 points higher (NCES, 2005).

The NCLB is a clear reflection of how the world has changed with respect to the need for accountability. Unfortunately, concerns about how to assess learning for accountability purposes have sidetracked some educators who want to improve school results. Considerable energy and time have been lost pointing out the problems associated with NCLB. What is needed now is more discussion of how teachers can build a system of assessment as an integral part of instruction. This would enable teachers to effectively identify the skills, concepts, and knowledge that each student has, and to implement instructional activities designed to fill in the gaps and build on the new level of learning. Many of the teachers who now are responsible for student success completed their teacher preparation programs prior to this widened vision of assessment and accountability. They may thus need targeted professional development to be able to fully utilize assessment programs in today's schools (see, e.g., Stiggins, 2004).

As we look at the evolution that is currently underway in the concept of student assessment, we note four changes in the way we address learning and assessment: Emphases have shifted from single testing to multiple assessments; from cognitive assessment only to assessment of a range of abilities and talents; from assessments of one or two dimensions to multidimensional assessment; and from testing as an isolated event to assessment as an integral part of instruction. These shifts are hopeful signs. School districts are using curriculum-based assessment, progress monitoring, and standards-based assessment as strategies for teachers to use in assessing students and planning instruction. These approaches require specific skills and resources that must be supported in order for teachers to realize their benefits.

Standards-based assessment, now being implemented in states across the nation, serves three important functions: (1) clearly communicating the goals that school systems, schools, teachers, and students are expected to achieve; (2) providing specific targets for teaching and learning; and (3) shaping the performance of educators and students, and, ultimately, schools systems (Linn & Herman, 1997). Business and industry have long relied on standards as a basis for evaluating progress. In some respects, of course, we have also always had standards in schools, as many teachers throughout the years have had very clear ideas about what they were trying to get students to learn. Our current state-level assessments ensure that all teachers are linking their instruction to their state standards. These assessments also provide a uniform standard of performance so that teachers, students, and parents can compare the student's performance with what is expected for that grade level statewide, not just in a particular classroom or school. This is a critical issue in closing achievement gaps.

The current concept of standards-based assessment differs from traditional practice in that the standards-based assessments we see today closely link assessments to curricula. It is important that there be a tight alignment between what is taught and what is tested. Even more importantly, standards-based assessment compares student performance to a clear and specific standard of achievement rather than to the performance level of other students. This type of assessment helps students know specifically what they need to learn in order to meet the desired and agreed-upon standards.

Fears of inappropriate teaching to the test and of inadvertent narrowing the curriculum still generate considerable concern about standards-based testing. If the concept of "teaching to the test" refers to limiting instruction to "test and drill on basic skills," then no support can be given to it. If, on the other hand, teaching to the test means aligning the instruction to the state-approved standards, then it is hard to see how this is a bad thing. Teachers, students, and parents need to know what is expected to be learned. In other words, they need to know the standards. Students should expect to be assessed on how well they perform on these standards. Classroom instruction, then, should be guided by the standards. Reports on how well students perform should be studied by the teachers, students, and parents. All have a role to play in enhancing student performance, with students themselves having a role almost equal to the teacher's role. With respect to breadth of curriculum, standards should not be limited to basic skills, although it is obvious that mastery of basic skills enhances learning of advanced concepts and knowledge. Teachers are right to pay attention to basic skills as the necessary stepping stones to further knowledge and skills, but instruction should not be limited to such skills. Systematic testing of individual student progress on identified curricular goals should be focused on helping teachers adjust instruction to assist the student in attaining the agreed-upon goal and providing a firm foundation for later learning. Teaching to the test, in this sense, is the most effective use of assessment for learning.

There are excellent examples of programs that help teachers use assessment for instructional support, such as the recent work on progress monitoring (National Center on Student Progress Monitoring [NCSPM], 2005). While grounded in work focused on improving special education, progress monitoring provides teachers in general with a system for using assessment results to guide instruction. Progress monitoring, a more recent term than curriculum-based measurement or curriculum-based assessment, is a scientifically based practice used to assess student academic performance and evaluate the effectiveness of instruction. According to NCSPM, implementation of this practice is very straightforward. The teacher assesses the student's current levels of performance and identifies the student's goals for learning by the end of a projected period of time. The student's academic performance on the goals is measured on a regular weekly or monthly basis. Comparisons of the expected and actual rates of learning by the student indicate the progress made. Using these data, the teacher adjusts the instruction as needed. Individual student learning needs are met because the student's academic progress is monitored and instructional strategies are adjusted accordingly.

Using assessment results to determine instructional placement decisions, that is, to determine what the student knows and what to teach next, is only one of the types of decisions teachers make using assessment results. Fuchs (1995) makes an additional distinction between the use of formative and diagnostic assessments.

- Formative evaluation decisions—information to monitor a student's learning while an instructional program is underway—how quickly progress is being made, whether the instructional program is effective, and whether a change in instructional program is needed to promote the student's learning.
- Diagnostic decisions—which specific difficulties account for the student's inadequate progress so the teacher can remediate learning progress and design more effective instructional plans. (p. 1)

Teachers' Use of Assessment

Professional development and teacher involvement in assessment design must be high on our list of policy issues and challenges. Stiggins (2004) points out that the typical teacher will spend one-quarter to one-third of his or her professional time involved in assessment-related activities. In light of this point, we must address teacher comfort and competence with assessment. Tienken and Wilson (2000) describe a program to help teachers improve instruction through a deeper understanding of state standards and test specifications. This may be a model that others can use.

For assessment to be useful as instructional support, we must ensure that teachers have appropriate mastery of the subject matter and the skills necessary to teach it. We have to make sure that teachers know in detail what knowledge and skills students should be learning. There must be a shared understanding of state and district standards for each grade level in each subject area. Teachers must have a deep knowledge of how to select and provide experiences that will ensure that students learn. And, they need to know what evidence will be gathered and used to verify what students have learned. Excellent work in examining assessment-related competencies needed by teachers has been done by Schafer (1991) and McMillan (2000). McMillan suggests that we identify the basic principles, or "big ideas," that when well understood and applied, will effectively guide good assessment practices, regardless of grade level, subject matter, developer, or use of results. The challenge is to help teachers and administrators learn about conceptual and technical assessment concepts, methods, and procedures, for both large-scale and classroom assessment and to apply these fundamentals to instruction. We must help teachers embrace the concept that there can be no effective teaching without assessment. Well-designed and well-executed assessment provides a roadmap for instruction.

We have to be concerned about policies and practices related to how teachers develop the skills needed to utilize standard-based assessments. Are colleges and universities including appropriate courses and experiences for prospective teachers? Are school districts providing the level of effective in-service experiences that teachers need and want? Are accrediting agencies addressing assessment competencies so that new teachers are prepared to use assessment to support instructional decisions? The section "Meeting the Need for High Quality Teaching-Learning Solutions" in the *Secretary's Fourth Annual Report on Teacher Quality* (U.S. Department of Education, 2005, p. 15) noted that teachers, through technology, have more resources available than they have ever had before, but they have not received sufficient training in the effective use of technology to enhance learning. Teachers need access to research, specific and concrete examples, and innovations, as well as staff development, to learn to utilize best practices. The U.S. Department of Education is currently funding research studies to evaluate the effective use of technology for teaching and learning. The National Science Foundation also provides major support for educational research. The Secretary's Fourth Annual Report on Teacher Quality cities the National Education Technology Plan on the following recommendations for states, districts, and individual schools regarding teacher training.

- Improve the preparation of new teachers in the use of technology.
- Ensure that every teacher has the opportunity to take online learning courses.
- Improve the quality and consistency of teacher education through measurement, accountability, and increased technology resources.
- Ensure that every teacher knows how to use data to personalize instruction. This is marked by the ability to interpret data to understand student progress and challenges, drive daily decisions, and design instructional interventions to customize instruction for every student's unique needs. (p. 15)

Impact of Assessment on Students

Despite the many discussions in educational circles about the negative impact of assessment on students, the public strongly believes that the amount of achievement testing in schools is just about right. According to the 37th Annual PDK/Gallup Poll, a majority of respondents support additional testing in three grades at the high school level (Rose & Gallup, 2005, p. 43). It seems that parents and others understand that when teachers assess learning accurately and use results effectively, students prosper. When assessment is used poorly or not at all, students are not helped. It is in the best interest of the student that teachers know what each student knows and is able to do, so that instruction can be appropriately planned.

Students themselves play a major role in this process. A key premise is that for students to be able to improve, they must have the capacity to monitor the quality of their own work during actual production. Chappuis' (2003) summary of Clarke's (2001) research indicates that improving learning through assessment depends on five key factors in which the student is an active participant.

- Adjusting teaching to take account of the results of assessment
- The provision of effective feedback to students
- The active involvement of students in their own learning
- The need for students to be able to assess themselves and understand how to improve
- A recognition of the profound influence assessment has on motivation and self-esteem

It is reported that students feel victimized when test scores are used to make decisions that impact their lives (Bennett, 2002). In our experience, however, it is only when there is a lack of understanding of and experience with using multiple forms of student performance data to inform decisions that this is actually the case. When students and parents understand the importance of collecting, analyzing, and using different data, not only to measure student learning but also to plot an individual's future education, they have a much greater appreciation of the value of assessment. Creating this appreciation is a job for teachers, administrators, and local school boards working together. There is a need for an examination of the policies and practices that guide the way information about assessment is communicated to parents and students. Moreover, as Stiggins (2004) suggests, "We must build classroom environments in which students use assessments to understand what success looks like and how to do better the next time. We must help students use on-going classroom assessment to take responsibility for their own success" (p. 25).

When we engage students in continuous self-assessment over time, we keep them focused on believing that success is within reach if they keep striving. Research by Black, Harrison, Lee, Marshall, and Wiliam (2004) shows us that student self-assessment, along with peer assessment, has an important impact on student learning. Teaching students the skills and attitudes needed for peer and self-assessment will pay off in student success. Assessment provides students the feedback that enables them to improve their own learning process, while at the same time enabling teachers to adapt the instructional process to meet student needs. Assessment helps students understand what is valued and what knowledge and skills are expected of them, and also promotes their self-knowledge about their academic performance.

Technology and Assessment

No one thinks of assessment today without thinking of some use of technology. Technology is changing the learning and teaching environment in schools, just as it is changing the world of work. Granted, the pace is slower in schools than in the workplace, but it is, in fact, occurring. In a review of technology use across the nation, Bennett (2002) indicated that some states and numerous school districts are implementing technology-based tests for low- and high-stakes decisions in elementary and secondary schools and across all key content areas. Most importantly, however, state efforts will need to go beyond the initial achievement of computerizing traditional multiple-choice tests if they are to create assessments that facilitate learning and instruction in ways that paper measures cannot, such as adaptive testing and the use of simulations.

The U.S. Department of Education, in partnership with the U.S. Department of Commerce and NetDay, released *Visions 2020.2: Student Views on Transforming Education and Training Through Advanced Technologies* (U.S. Department of Commerce, 2005). The report points out that there has been explosive growth in the availability of online instruction and virtual schools, complementing traditional instruction with high-quality courses tailored to the needs of individual students. Some tests now can be taken online so that students, teachers, and parents have almost instant feedback. This is a major step forward in tracking progress and identifying needs. New student data management systems will greatly facilitate the collection and use of test, demographic, and other data for more effectively designing and managing instructional programs. The report shows that students are asking for wider and more effective use of technology in schools, and gives examples of how students envision the possibilities of schooling with state-of-the-art technology.

Action steps, recommendations, and examples of effective technology use in schools were presented in the National Education Technology Plan entitled *Toward a New Golden Age in American Education: How the Internet, the Law and Today's Students Are Revolutionizing Expectations* (U.S. Department of Education, 2004). The report points out that integrated, interoperable data systems are the key to better allocation of resources, greater management efficiency, and online and technology-based assessments of student performance. An interoperable system securely connects all information and technologies. For example, connections among systems such as the library, food service, transportation, special education, finance, human resources, and assessment can help teachers and administrators see the big picture. Access to such data systems will empower educators to transform teaching and personalize instruction.

It is important to note some of the recommendations made in the report that relate specifically to assessment and support the views of teaching and learning outlined above.

- Establish a plan to integrate data systems so that administrators and educators have the information they need to increase efficiency and improve student learning.
- Use data from both administrative and instructional systems to understand relationships among policy decisions, allocation of resources, and student achievement.
- Ensure interoperability. For example, consider School Interoperability Framework (SIF) Compliance Certification as a requirement in all RFPs and purchasing decisions.
- Use assessment results to inform and differentiate instruction for every child. (p. 14)

The business world has clearly noted the technology needs of schools and is offering numerous products that may support assessment and instruction. There are companies that provide printed reports and online resources for parents that explain their children's strengths and weaknesses. There are numerous programs that transform assessment results into tools that enhance instruction. As these become more available to teachers and administrators, careful evaluations showing the quality and effectiveness of these tools must be made. For example, Bass and Glaser (2004) pointed out that the KIDMAP software demonstrates how technology can help teachers visualize relationships between assessments and craft individual learning trajectories for their schools by graphing student progress. The program also helps teachers record individual student performance on specific outcomes or standards and create profiles that identify areas for improvement.

Technology has provided opportunities for online assessment to be more learner-centered, in order to promote self-directed learning, and to increase learner autonomy. One of the major challenges for teachers and administrators, however, is how to best communicate assessment results to parents. The Data Use Web site (http://www.ncrel.org/datause/), promoted through the North Central Regional Educational Laboratory, is one example of a resource teachers may access for help in demystifying data. This Web site is designed to give educators and others involved in using data in the classroom, school, or district a variety of places to find resources, tools, and action steps to foster school improvement through data use.

Technology is changing the teaching and learning environment just as it is changing the rest of society. Because of its potential for helping teachers more quickly and efficiently assess specific information about the level of learning of each student, the best technology resources must be made available to all schools, including those with limited funds. Our teachers and children deserve nothing less.

An Example of Assessment as Instructional Support

One of the schools we visited recently gave us a unique opportunity to see how teachers and students use assessment to enhance learning. The J. Erik Jonsson Community School in Dallas, Texas, is a unique community school, created about 10 years ago to demonstrate that children of poverty, living in an urban environment, are capable of high levels of achievement if given an enriched, nurturing, accelerated, and instructionally sophisticated environment. This school is supported by a group of business leaders through an organization called the Salesmanship Club whose members serve on the governing board. The board sets challenging goals and reviews the results of the school; professional educators design the means to achieve the board's goals.

The school includes about 260 students from 3 years old to sixth grade, 98% of whom are Hispanic. Seventy-five percent of the children are eligible for free/reduced lunch, and about 60% of the families speak only Spanish in their homes. There are two other features of this school to highlight: (1) the variety of assessments teachers use, and (2) teacher use of student results to change instruction as well as design interesting interventions, which they call the Red Folder Process.

Frequent assessments are the norm at this school. Teachers use norm-referenced tests such as the Iowa Test of Basic Skills and criterion-referenced exams for Texas Assessment of Knowledge and Skills (TAKS), as well as many teacher-made tests directly tied to daily instruction. During our visit to the school, we was struck by teachers who were constantly pulling individuals and small groups of students to work with them and to check their understanding through observation, checklists, short written assessments, and other practical teacher-made measures. These assessments were then used by the individual teachers and by teams of teachers to continue to plan and rethink their instruction.

The school's Red Folder Process is a process teachers and administrators designed to plan for specific interventions for students who are having academic trouble. The Red Folder Process is a continual, planned, team intervention. Monthly meetings are conducted for every student who is not performing at the expected level. Jonsson teachers initiate the meetings and bring to the meetings results of their assessments of the student, samples of the student's work, and other evidence from the classroom. These Red Folder meetings include the principal, assistant principal, guidance coordinator, reading specialist, and classroom teacher. The team collaborates and develops strategies to assist the student. The teacher returns to the classroom, tries out the strategies, and reports back to the team at the next meeting, which takes place the following month. The teacher brings new samples of the student's work and assessment results. The team considers the progress and makes adjustments. This entire process proceeds until the team and the teacher determine that the student is performing at the expected level and no longer needs the Red Folder Process.

We learned from Mike Murphy, director of the Institute for Excellence in Urban Education and board member, that results of the Red Folder Process meetings are dramatic (personal communication, September 1, 2005). In fall 2001, when the program was started, about 36% of the students in the Red Folder Process read at or above grade level. In spring of the same school year, 65% of Red Folder students were reading at or above grade level. Improvements were dramatic on TAKS as well, with 79% of Red Folder students passing the reading test and 86% passing the math test. Teachers and administrators attribute the success rates to the informal, yet structured, ongoing process totally driven by teacher assessment of individual students.

Here is what the staff at Jonsson Community School tells about what they have learned about their use of assessment. First of all, assessment becomes a way to problem solve and change instruction, not a way to sort, select, and label underachieving students. Secondly, their daily use of assessment allows the teachers to intervene immediately. The Red Folder Process, which really formalizes their focus on intervention, not only quickly helps students feel successful but also adds to the teachers' sense of efficacy. Finally, the teachers' work at the Jonsson Community School highlights teamwork. Teachers work together and problem solve so students can succeed. This is done as a part of their natural and daily use of assessment information. This school's success is a convincing demonstration that when teachers use well-designed and implemented assessment as instructional support, students *will* succeed.

References

Bass, K., & Glaser, R. (2004). *Developing assessments to inform teaching and learning* (CSE Report 628). CRESST/Learning Research and Development Center, University of Pittsburgh; National Center for Research on Evaluation, Standards, and Student Testing, Graduate School of Education and Informative Studies, University of California, Los Angeles.

Bennett, R. E. (2002). Inexorable and inevitable: The continuing story of technology and assessment. *Journal of Technology, Learning, & Assessment, 1*(1). Retrieved August 14, 2005, from http://www.bc.edu/research/intasc/jtla/journal/v1n1.shtml

Black, P., Harrison, C., Lee, C., Marshall, B., & Wiliam, D. (2004). Working inside the black box: Assessment for learning in the classroom. *Phi Delta Kappan, 86*(1), 9-21.

Black, P., & Wiliam, D. (1998). Inside the black box: Raising standards through classroom assessment. *Phi Delta Kappan, 80*(2), 139-148.

Chappuis, J. (2003). *Research on formative assessment: Student-involved assessment strategies.* Portland, OR: Assessment Training Institute.

Clarke, S. (2001). *Unlocking formative assessment: Practical strategies for enhancing pupil's learning in the primary grades.* London: Holder and Stoughton.

Fuchs, L. S. (1995). *Connecting performance assessment to instruction: A comparison of behavioral assessment, mastery learning, curriculum-based measurement, and performance assessment.* Reston, VA: ERIC Clearinghouse on Disabilities and Gifted Education. (ERIC Identifier: ED381984)

Linn, R., & Herman, J. (1997). *A policy-maker's guide to standards-led assessment.* Denver, CO: Educational Commission of the States and the National Center for Research on Evaluation, Standards and Student Testing.

McMillan, J. H. (2000). Fundamental assessment principles for teachers and school administrators. *Practical Assessment, Research and Evaluation, 7*(8). Retrieved July 16, 2005, from http://pareonline.net/getvn.asp?v=7&n=8

National Center for Education Statistics. (2005). Nation's Report Card: Long Term Trend, Trends in Student Groups. Retrieved August 28, 2005, from http://nces.ed.gov/nationsreportcard/ltt/results2004/natsubgroups.asp

National Center on Student Progress Monitoring. (2005). *Common questions for progress monitoring.* Retrieved August 7, 2005, from http://www.studentprogress.org/progresmon.asp

Rose, L. C. & Gallup, A. M. (2005). The 37th annual Phi Delta Kappan/Gallup Poll of the public's attitudes toward the public schools. *Phi Delta Kappan, 87*(1), 41-57.

Schafer, W. D. (1991). Essential assessment skills in professional education of teachers. *Educational Measurement: Issues and Practice, 10*(1), 3-6.

Stiggins, R. (2004). New assessment beliefs for a new school mission. *Phi Delta Kappan, 86*(1), 22-27.

Tienken, C., & Wilson, M. (2000). Using state standards and tests to improve instruction. *Practical Assessment, Research & Evaluation, 7*(13). Retrieved July 20, 2005, from http://PAREonline.net/getvn.asp?v=7&n=13

U.S. Department of Commerce, U.S. Department of Education, & NetDay. (2005). *Visions 2020.2: Student views on transforming education and training through advanced technologies.* Washington, DC: U.S. Department of Education.

U.S. Department of Education, Office of Educational Technology. (2004). *Toward a new golden age in American education: How the Internet, the law and today's students are revolutionizing expectations.* Washington, DC: Author.

U.S. Department of Education, Office of Postsecondary Education. (2005). *The Secretary's fourth annual report on teacher quality: A highly qualified teacher in every classroom.* Washington, DC: Author

9

Correcting "Errors of Measurement" That Sabotage Student Learning

Richard Stiggins
ETS Assessment Training Institute

As we think about what we have accomplished over the past half century of educational measurement in relation to what we might have hoped to accomplish, should we be proud of what we have achieved? Let's take stock.

Without question, we have clearly defined our driving concept: *Assessment* is the process of gathering evidence of student achievement to inform instructional decisions. Further, we know that, if it is done well, sound decisions can contribute to productive student learning. If it is done poorly, unsound decisions can harm student learning. But have we learned to do it well? Clearly, we in the field of educational measurement have

- Spent the past decades devising highly complex and sophisticated mathematical models for documenting, manipulating, and maximizing both the validity and reliability of our assessments
- Devised a wide variety of assessment methods to gather dependable evidence of student achievement
- Learned to interpret results in various ways, from (a) comparing student performance to that of other students in order to produce a dependable rank order to (b) comparing students' performance to preset standards
- Discovered and refined many different kinds of test scores to help us communicate results effectively
- Worked our way into the halls of the highest levels of political power, convincing civic leaders that our methodology rests at the very heart of the process of evaluating the effectiveness of schools

As a result, we have created a commercial success of the highest order. Clearly, we have done well.

But have we helped students learn more? Have we helped to assure that no child of poverty or of any other social context will be left behind, for example? At the end of the day, can we say that we have taken full advantage of the wisdom we have developed about sound assessment practice to benefit students?

As complex and intellectually demanding as our technical concepts and quantitative models have become, we can rely on a surprisingly simple analysis to answer these critical questions. In its simplest terms, we can judge the quality of any assessment based on the five attributes listed below. Violate any of them with any assessment and it is likely to do more harm than good.

1. The assessment must arise from and fulfill the information needs of specific, predetermined decision makers.
2. The assessment must arise from clearly and completely defined, high-quality achievement target(s).
3. The evidence resulting from the assessment must accurately reflect the intended student achievement.
4. Assessment results must be communicated effectively to the intended user(s).
5. The assessment must elicit a productive response (decision) *from the learner.*

The fifth entry is not traditionally included in our quality control frameworks. However, not only will I argue that it belongs here, but I will defend the proposition that it may represent the most important dimension of assessment quality, because this standard of quality will contribute the most to determining if the assessment helps or inhibits student learning.

Further, I will contend that, over the decades, assessment's potential contribution to the development of effective schools has been greatly reduced by routine violations of these five standards of quality, especially the last one. Ultimately, I will argue, we have not begun to tap the full potential of assessment as a school improvement tool because of these violations. In the discussion that follows, I will call the violations "errors of measurement," and I will use them as a basis from which to reaffirm the critical importance of high-quality, day-to-day classroom assessment in assuring the effectiveness of education. According to our measurement traditions, "error of measurement" references the accuracy of a score. But in this presentation I broaden its meaning by using it as a pun connected to the impact of the score.

Attribute 1: Quality Assessments Meet Intended Users' Information Needs

If assessment is the process of gathering evidence to inform instructional decisions, then one must begin the assessment process by asking, what decisions, who's making them, and what information will be helpful to them? We can't build an assessment to provide useful information unless we know precisely what results will be helpful. Our challenge in this regard is to understand that different instructional decision makers need access to different kinds of information in different forms at different times to make the various decisions that will lead to student learning.

For instance, on one hand, policy makers and school leaders need *periodic* access to summaries of *group* achievement of student mastery of state or local achievement *standards* that are *comparable* across classrooms, schools, or districts so as to inform *programmatic, resource allocation and policy* decisions. Obviously, this is the domain of the standardized achievement test.

On the other hand, in order to promote student growth day to day in the classroom, teachers need *immediate and continuous* access to evidence of *individual* student success in mastering the *achievement targets leading up to or that underpin standards* that may be *unique* to an individual student in order to decide *what instruction comes next* for the student. These information needs are fundamentally different from those of the policy maker and school leader. This is not the domain of the standardized test. Rather, in this case, classroom assessment emerges as the only viable data source.

Now for the first "error of measurement": Although our school improvement traditions hold that policy makers, school leaders, teachers, and other adults are the key users of assessment results—that is, the users who make the instructional decisions that contribute the most to the effectiveness of schools—I contend this traditional belief is wrong. In fact, the honor of being the "most important" assessment users must go, not to the adults in the system, but to the students.

Without question, parents, teachers, school leaders, and politicians (adults all) make very important instructional decisions that contribute immensely to school quality. And the more evidence-based the decisions are the better. But, as it turns out, students make data-based instructional decisions that contribute far more to their own ultimate success in school. From day one of their schooling, they continually use evidence of their learning success provided to them by their teacher based on classroom assessment results to decide whether they have hope of meeting their current learning challenges. They decide whether they are capable of mastering the learning target in question or are just too "stupid." They decide whether the learning is worth the effort it will take to attain it, or whether trying is worth the risk of public failure. If they come down on the wrong side of these decisions, it doesn't matter what the adults decide. There will be no learning. Yet, nowhere in our collective assessment traditions or legacy of assessment quality control is there any recognition whatsoever of students as assessment users; that is, as data-based instructional decision makers.

We know how to use the classroom assessment process to encourage and motivate students. We know how to use the assessment process and its results to elicit a productive response from the learner. That kind of response leaves them saying to themselves, "I see and understand these results. I know what to do next. I'm OK with this. I choose to keep trying." In other words, we know how to prevent them from reacting to assessment results in counterproductive ways, such as when they say to themselves, "I see the results, but I have no idea how to do better. I'm not any good at this. I give up." In an environment where educators are to be held accountable for all students meeting standards, obviously, only one of these responses to assessment results is acceptable. We cannot have those who have yet to meet standards giving up along the way. As my chapter unfolds, I will describe how to use the classroom assessment process to meet the information needs of all assessment users—especially students—in productive ways.

Attribute 2: Quality Assessments Arise From Clear and Appropriate Achievement Expectations

We cannot dependably assess achievement expectations that we have not clearly, completely, and appropriately defined. This key to quality forms the foundation of our definition of validity. These days, the starting place for clear targets is state standards, as they define the terms of teaching success, school effectiveness, and, therefore, quality assessment.[1]

It is within this context that we confront our second "error of measurement." Many policy makers and school leaders operate on the faith that merely assessing state standards will lead to learning success. For instance, at strategic times during the school year, statewide and districtwide assessments ask if students have met state standards. More recently, as educators have begun to realize that once a year is not enough, ever more popular interim assessments conducted locally during the school year (short-cycle assessments, benchmark tests, common assessments, quarterly "formative" assessments) strive to predict student performance on end-of-year high-stakes tests by asking which students have met state standards so far. And on top of all of this, very often, teachers are instructed by local school leaders to focus their classroom assessments on state standards in order to inform instruction.

Conducting assessments of each student's mastery of each important state standard more frequently than once a year is a very good idea. The more often we assess, the more informed we become about who needs additional help so we can act more quickly in their best interests. The "error of measurement" obviously is not that we assess state standards—the error is in our constant focus *only* on state standards with high-stakes accountability tests, district assessments, short-cycle assessments, benchmark assessments, common assessments, and even classroom assessments. The problem is that this merely identifies the problem, it doesn't help fix it. To help those found not to be meeting standards, we need to adjust our frame of reference for assessment.

The corrective action needed in this case is to transform each standard into the teachable and learnable sub-elements that form the scaffolding on which students will climb to reach each standard. These are the enabling achievement targets (the building blocks of competence) that must be the focus of day-to-day instruction and classroom assessment for students to succeed. The transformation needed must include the following steps:

1. Assure that the standards that drive instruction and assessment within the state or district represent the best current thinking of the field, are sufficiently well focused for use by teachers, and are

manageable in number to permit universal understanding of their meaning, as well as realistic expectations of student mastery. Only then can they give rise to quality assessments throughout.

2. Make sure that each and every teacher in each and every classroom is a confident, competent master of the achievement standards that their students are expected to master. Only then are they in a position to manage the classroom assessment process in ways beneficial to student learning.

3. Deconstruct each state standard into the knowledge, reasoning, performance skills, or product development proficiencies that students must master over time to achieve ultimate mastery of that standard. The result of this analysis must be appropriate learning progressions (see Shepard's chapter in this volume) articulated both within and across grade levels.

4. Transform the resulting classroom-level achievement targets (the building blocks of competence to be mastered over time) into student-friendly terms that teachers share with students and their families from the very beginning of the learning. Only then can students monitor their own progress and remain confident that success is within reach. In addition, opportunities to self-assess are enhanced when teachers provide both student-friendly targets and models of strong and weak work, so learners can come to understand the performance continuum that maps their path to ultimate success.

5. Transform those classroom assessment targets (the building blocks of competence) into high-quality classroom assessments to be used day to day to help teachers teach and students watch themselves grow.

Only then can assessment be brought to bear in its full force for the good of learners. The problem is that, often, these five foundations for transformation have not been in place—which is one reason, I argue, that assessment has not reached its full potential as a school improvement tool.

Attribute 3: Quality Assessments Yield Accurate Evidence of Achievement

Under Attribute 2 above, clear targets represent an essential foundation for sound assessment. Under this next attribute, the assessment must accurately reflect the intended achievement targets. To do this, the assessment must do the following:

- Rely on an assessment method or format capable of reflecting the achievement in question
- Be built of high-quality ingredients (that is, high-quality test items, for example)
- Include enough exercises to sample student achievement properly
- Minimize the distortion of results due to the state of the examinee, scoring procedures, or distractions within the assessment environment and other sources of bias

Two "errors of measurement" are worthy of discussion in this case, one specific and methodological, and the other more general and overarching.

The first is the long-standing belief on the part of some segments of the measurement community that we can assess the most important outcomes of instruction—that is, our highest priority standards—with multiple-choice tests. In the currently trendy realm of formative assessment, as test publishers across the land sell the idea that more frequent summative assessments of state standards can inform instructional decisions, they rely on test-item banks and standards-referenced multiple-choice tests as their lead methodology—as they have for decades. My point is not that such tests will be of poor quality. Indeed, they can reflect some truly important achievement targets. But to regard this single format as sufficient as a definition of academic proficiency is silly at best and distinctly harmful at worst. It cannot tap complex patterns of reasoning, critically important performance skills, or vital product development capabilities. It is for this reason that we must teach and encourage the classroom use of the full range of assessment methods if we are to bring the full measure of assessment to bear in support of student success.

The second assessment design "error of measurement" arises from the fact that, over the decades, society has come to regard measurement professionals as the only credible source of assessments that meet quality standards. Other potential contributors to the assessment development process, such as classroom teachers, are not trained to do it well and so have not been trusted with this responsibility. The problem is that, in fact, measurement professionals provide only a small fraction of the assessments that inform the instructional decisions that drive student learning. The remaining 99.9% of the assessments that impact a student's academic life are, in fact, developed or selected by their teachers day to day in the classroom. Despite this fact, we have failed to provide teachers with the assessment literacy needed to produce or select good ones. And lest we somehow think that they can turn to their principals for assistance in this regard, let me be clear that assessment training has been and remains nonexistent in leadership training programs across the nation.

The implications of this state of affairs are obvious for instruction, classroom assessment, and the effectiveness of schools. Inept assessment yields inaccurate results that feed into ineffective instructional decisions.

The sequence of actions needed to overcome the effect of decades of neglect of assessment literacy training for teachers and school leaders is to:

- Weave classroom assessment literacy into preservice training (by having teacher education faculty both teach and model sound classroom assessment practice)
- Demand competence in assessment as part of licensure requirements for teachers and administrators (that is, in certification standards and examinations)
- Inspect classroom assessment practices as a key part of ongoing local evaluation and supervision processes, holding teachers accountable for the quality of their work
- Make assessment training available through in-service professional development, both for teachers and administrators, when that training is needed

Typically, practitioners still are not being trained to assess accurately or to use assessments productively at any level. This has been so for decades in the United States. If we assume that others will do the assessment work, then this is not a problem. But in these times when we want to use classroom assessment in direct support of student mastery of standards, lack of assessment training for teachers is a major problem. And we know how to fix it. We know what teachers need to know, we understand how to deliver that wisdom into their hands in a very effective and efficient manner, and we know what the impact will be on their professional practices and student learning. The only remaining question is, will teachers and school leaders actually be given the opportunity to learn about sound assessment practice?

Over the decades, we in the measurement community have contended that this lack of assessment literacy in schools is not our responsibility. We regularly decry this state of affairs in our own professional literature (e.g., Crooks, 1988; Stiggins, 1999). But, we contend, we don't control teacher preparation or day-to-day school management. Our job, as we have defined it, is to assure the quality of the big, policy-level accountability tests.

This view of our role has always been dangerously shortsighted and contributory to this "error of measurement." If we cannot build and present a convincing case to the community around us that the appropriate use of accurate assessment is essential in every learning context, then we fail as shepherds of our accumulated wisdom, in our role as teachers, and in our endeavor to help students learn more.

We in the measurement community must believe that teachers can, in fact, do their assessment jobs well—that is, we should not be trying to teacher-proof assessment. Rather, we must find ways to support them in doing it well. Based on two decades of hands-on experience in transforming complex validity, reliability, and student-involvement assessment concepts and practices into commonsense ideas that can be used by teachers, I promise you it can be done, but only if practitioners are provided with the appropriate opportunity to learn.

Attribute 4: Effective Communication of Assessment Results

The most valid and reliable assessment is wasted if its results are not delivered in a timely, understandable, and credible way into the hands of its intended user(s). Several conditions must be satisfied for communication to be effective.

First, for the message to get through effectively, the assessment results must reflect a vision of the achievement target that is understood by, and is of consistent meaning for, both the assessor and the recipient of those results. If the user of results has no idea what the assessor assessed or what the scores mean, results will obviously be useless. If the definition of achievement differs between the user and assessor, then results are likely to be misinterpreted and misused by the recipient with unfortunate consequences for learning.

Next, again obviously, good communication requires that the assessment results be accurate. We have yet to invent a communication system or process that can convert misinformation into accurate information.

Third, the symbols used to convey assessment results from one person to another must have a common meaning for both. That meaning must be clear and correct in terms of the intended achievement expectations. A report card grade in reading assigned by one teacher based on a composite of evidence of achievement, effort, attitude, attendance, timeliness of homework submission, and compliance with classroom rules will be misunderstood by another teacher or a parent who thinks it reflects only the child's proficiency at reading comprehension.

And finally, the recipient of the information provided by the assessment must be confident and ready to hear and act upon the information provided. For this to be true, the timing must be right to permit focused attention and the assessment must deliver what the student believes to represent credible evidence of achievement. The feedback must come in bite-size pieces that students understand, so as not to overwhelm them. It must also be accompanied by time to respond to it—to put it to profitable use before a final judgment is made of proficiency. Moreover, if the environment surrounding results is not amenable to effective communication, then the message may not get through, be respected as credible, or have the desired impact.

Violations of these standards—that is, more "errors of measurement"—abound. In some cases, deviations of these standards represent accepted routines in the day-to-day practice of schools. Sometimes, miscommunication seems unavoidable.

For example, for decades in the United States, norm-referenced standardized test scores have been being delivered into the hands of practitioners and parents who have no idea what was tested or how to interpret or use the scores. High-stakes standards-referenced test scores derived from complex scaling procedures are provided to educators and to school communities who simply do not understand them.

Then there is the matter of timing in the delivery of high-stakes testing results. Scores that arrive months after the student has departed for the next grade level are hardly timed properly for maximum benefit for learners. Besides, the almost total absence of pre- or in-service assessment training for teachers and school leaders too often leaves them helpless in the face of results.

Our communication problems also carry into the classroom. Teachers often see the assignment of report card grades as the sole purpose for assessment. Often, this is their interpretation of what it means to consider students as assessment users. However, this very limiting, judgmental frame of reference has the effect of denying students access to details about strengths and areas in need of improvement when they are most likely to be useful—while they are still learning. From the student's perspective, when they get their report card grades, it's too late for corrective action. And for low-achieving students, if everything has a grade assigned to it (always low for them), then there is no time to recover, get back on track, and find success. I will say more about the emotional dynamics of this in the next section.

In addition, teachers often implement report card grading procedures that assure miscommunication. Not only might the classroom assessments that feed into grade determination be inaccurate because teachers are not trained to assess accurately, but student characteristics that bear no relationship to achievement often are factored into grades. Such procedures guarantee misinterpretation by students, parents, and the myriad other recipients of the grading message (Brookhart, 2004).

The way to overcome these barriers to effective communication is to assure that the standards of sound practice outlined above are met. High-quality and sharply focused state achievement standards must be deconstructed into classroom targets and then into student-friendly language (accompanied by models of strong and weak work). These must be shared with students from the beginning of the learning to promote universal understanding of achievement expectations. Then professional development can lead to accurate assessment can add another crucial piece to the puzzle. Finally, careful articulation of the meaning of test scores and grades to all intended users can promote effective communication and sound decision-making.

Besides these foundations of communication, we can supplement our reliance on brief summary and judgmental symbols (grades and scores) with communication that incorporates descriptive feedback, actual samples of student work, portfolios of work, and face-to-face conferences. These impart the greater detail and richer meaning about student achievement that is needed for assessment results to support learning. Reliance on these will help us tap the full potential of assessment in the service of student success and truly effective schools.

Attribute 5: Quality Assessments Keep the Learner Optimistic and Striving for Success

The schools of our collective youth were designed to spread us along a continuum of achievement by the end of high school. There were winners and losers. As a result, lots of us were left behind. The winners and losers lived in fundamentally different emotional environments surrounding assessment and grading.

Winners used consistently positive assessment results to become increasingly confident. They were propelled forward by a sense of optimism, always expecting a positive result in the future. This fueled and was fueled by a strong desire to stay on top, to take the risks, and to put forth the effort required to succeed. For them, the emotional dynamics of a demanding assessment environment were decidedly productive. Parents hoped this would be the story for their children.

Although this was the ideal, we all recall that it was not reality for all students. There were those who failed to master the foundations of academic competence in the early grades and who watched the relentless curriculum march on without them. They fell into losing streaks as the grade levels unfolded and thus lived in a completely different emotional environment from that of the winners when it came to assessment and grading. Consistent long-term failure sapped their confidence. A pall of pessimism descended over them and a self-fulfilling prophesy of defeat played out. They came to expect a negative result in the future, effort waned, desire plummeted, and failure came to rule. For them, the emotional dynamics of assessment became distinctly counterproductive. Failure fed on itself.

In the schools of our youth, both scenarios were accepted because the greater the spread in achievement from top to bottom schools could produce, the more dependable would be the rank order. This is why, if a student gave up in hopelessness and stopped trying, it was regarded as that student's problem, not the teacher's or the school's.

However, as society has evolved to greater complexity and ethnic diversity in recent decades and as international comparisons of student achievement have placed our students on the worldwide continuum, we have felt compelled to transform our schools into places where all students meet the essential achievement standards in reading, writing, and math needed to survive and contribute. Given this new social mission of assuring and being held accountable for student mastery of standards, it has become clear that schools can no longer stand by as students give up in hopelessness. The counterproductive emotional state that was the plight of the "losers" in the past no longer has a place in our educational process. If a student has not yet met standards and has stopped trying, we now believe, the school has not done its job.

Thus, we face the potential of an "error of measurement" if we fail to adjust to this fundamental change in mission and use the emotional dynamics of the assessment process to turn all students into winners, at least in terms of the mastery of standards. I address those accommodations in the next and concluding section.

Looking to the Future

We know how to prevent hopelessness and promote hope among all learners. Strategies for doing so were outlined in the previous sections.

- Build assessment environments that accommodate students as assessment users too—as instructional decision makers—along with the adults
- Deconstruct standards into the enabling classroom level achievement targets that form the scaffold leading up to those standards and then transform them into student-friendly terms that are used by students and teachers to guide learning
- Assure the accuracy of all assessments, especially in the classroom, and engage students as partners in the creation and use of practice assessments during the learning so they can clearly see their own improvement over time and respond productively to assessment results
- Communicate assessment results in ways that permit students to respond productively and bring them into the process of communicating about their own achievement, describing both their achievement status at one point in time and their improvement over time

In our work at the ETS Assessment Training Institute, we follow the lead of the Assessment Reform Group in the United Kingdom and others around the world by referring to these practices as our version of "assessment FOR learning" (Black & Wiliam, 1998a, 1998b). We assist teachers and school leaders in learning to apply specific strategies of student-involved classroom assessment, record keeping, and communication (Stiggins, Arter, Chappuis, & Chappuis, 2004). This kind of professional development has proven its worth by promoting profound achievement gains for all learners.

Extensive research evidence gathered around the world consistently reveals effect sizes of half a standard deviation and greater that are directly attributable to the effective use of classroom assessment to support student learning. In his original mastery learning research, Bloom (1984) made extensive use of classroom assessment in support of learning and reported subsequent gains in student test performance. Black and Wiliam's (1998a, 1998b) watershed research review synthesized over 250 studies from around the world on the impact of effective classroom assessment and report gains of a half to a full standard deviation, with the largest gains being realized by low achievers. Meisels, Atkins-Burnett, Xue, and Bickel (2003) involved students in performance assessments and report considerable gains. Further, Hattie & Timberly (2007) synthesize resarch on the effects of feedback on achievement and define attributes of productive classroom communication that profoundly impact learning.

As we take stock of our accomplishments over the past half century, have we tapped the full potential of our technology to help students learn more? Clearly, we have not. Our "errors of measurement" have prevented it. We have made the mistake of believing that our primary concern should be the accuracy of the scores that our tests generate. In fact, we should have been devoting at least as much attention to the impact of those scores on their users. Even when we have attended to the impact of assessment scores we have assumed that we need to focus on adult decision makers. In fact, we should have been giving at least some attention to the impact of the scores on the learners themselves—those who are in charge of the learning.

Looking to the future, we can correct our errors. We understand far more deeply today than ever before how to use the assessment process and its results to benefit all students. The solution is not more frequent summative assessment of student mastery of state standards, although that can help. Instead, it is the effective use of accurate, student-involved classroom assessment used to support learning.

We know what teachers need to know and do to assess effectively day to day. We know what will happen to student learning if they do the right things. We even know how to deliver those proficiencies into their hands in effective and efficient preservice training (Stiggins, 2000) and in-service learning team-based professional development (Stiggins & Chappuis, 2006). The only remaining unanswered question is, will teachers be given the opportunity to learn? Historically, the answer has been, no. But if we give teachers that opportunity, they can do this job.

References

Black, P., & Wiliam, D. (1998a). Assessment and classroom learning. *Educational Assessment: Principles, Policy and Practice, 5*(1), 7-74.

Black, P., & Wiliam, D. (1998b). Inside the black box: Raising standards through classroom assessment. *Phi Delta Kappan, 80*(2), 139-148.

Bloom, B. (1984). The search for methods of group instruction as effective as on-to-one tutoring. *Educational Leadership, 41*(8), 4-17.

Brookhart, S. M. (2004). *Grading.* Columbus, OH: Merrill Prentice Hall.

Crooks, T. J. (1988). The impact of classroom evaluation on students. *Review of Educational Research, 58*(4), 438-481.

Hattie, J. & Timberly, H. (2007) The power of feedback. *Review of Educational Research.* 77(1), 81–122.

Meisels, S., Atkins-Burnett, S., Xue, Y., & Bickel, D. D. (2003). Creating a system of accountability: The impact of instructional assessment on elementary children's achievement scores. *Educational Policy Analysis Archives, 11*(9), 19. Retrieved April 21, 2003, from http://epaa.asu.edu/epaa/vol11.html

Popham, W. J. (2004). *America's failing schools: How parents and teachers can cope with No Child Left Behind.* New York: RoutledgeFalmer.

Stiggins, R. J. (1999). Evaluating classroom assessment training in teacher education. *Educational Measurement: Issues and Practice, 18*(1), 23-27.

Stiggins, R. J. (2000). *Specifications for a performance-based assessment system for teacher preparation.* Washington, DC: National Council for Accreditation in Teacher Education. Retrieved July 20, 2006, from www.ncate.org/documents/articles/stiggins.pdf

Stiggins, R. J., Arter, J., Chappuis, J., & Chappuis, S. (2004). *Classroom assessment for student learning: Doing it right—using it well.* Portland, OR: Assessment Training Institute.

Stiggins, R. J., & Chappuis, J. (2006). What a difference a word makes: Assessment FOR learning rather than assessment OF learning helps students succeed. *Journal of Staff Development, 27*(1), 10-14.

Endnotes

1. Others have questioned the quality of many state standards (see Popham, 2004, for example), contending that often there are too many of them and they fail to reflect the best current thinking of the discipline, are so vague as to be uninterpretable, or are not written in teacher-palatable language. When this is the case, obviously, both the high-stakes and classroom assessment systems are weakened. An evaluation of the quality of state standards is beyond the scope of this paper, however.

10

Assessment and School Reform:
Lessons from 15 Years in the Field

M. Susana Navarro
El Paso Collaborative for Academic Excellence

For almost 15 years, the community of El Paso, Texas, has worked intensively to ensure that all students in our community are academically prepared at the highest levels. This chapter will focus on the work of the El Paso Collaborative for Academic Excellence (http://epcae.org/)— what we've done and what we've tried to do, including some of the lessons learned about that work, particularly related to assessment.

Let me begin with a brief portrait of El Paso. El Paso is a binational community, on the U.S.–Mexican border, with a predominantly Latino population of 700,000 (U.S. Census Bureau, 2003). With the city of Juarez, Chihuahua, Mexico, just across the border, the metropolitan area has a total population of about 2 million (Institute Materno Infantil de Pernambuso, 2001). El Paso is a very low-income community: It is the fifth poorest congressional district in the U.S. It is also predominantly Spanish speaking, with over half of El Pasoans reporting that Spanish is the language of preference in the home. Our 12 school districts (three large and nine rural) enroll over 160,000 students, of which well over 85% are Hispanic. About two thirds of El Paso's students are eligible for free or reduced-cost lunch (Education Service Center, 2005; Texas Education Agency, 2005).

The El Paso Collaborative for Academic Excellence was founded in 1991, motivated by the belief that new approaches to improvement had to bring the entire community together to focus on the essential components of schooling, not only K–12, but K–16 (Shirley, 1997; Stone, Henig, Jones, & Pierannunzi, 2001). The partners who formed the collaborative, and who are still with us today, are:

- The superintendents of the three largest school districts: El Paso, Ysleta, and Socorro
- The presidents of El Paso Community College and the University of Texas at El Paso (UTEP)
- The executive director of the state's Regional Service Center, which serves the rural districts in the area
- The lead organizer of the El Paso Interreligious Sponsoring Organization, a grass-roots interfaith organization affiliated with the Industrial Areas Foundation
- The presidents of the El Paso, Hispanic, and Black Chambers of Commerce
- The Mayor of the City of El Paso and the county judge who heads our County Board of Supervisors

Our goals are straightforward and clear: (1) to ensure academic success among all youngsters in our schools, K–16; (2) to ensure that all students graduate from area high schools prepared to enter, and be successful in, a four-year college or university; and (3) to close the achievement gap between groups of students—those who have traditionally gotten the best and those who need to get the best.

How have we worked to achieve our goals? First, our efforts are standards based. Our own locally developed standards are uniformly high for all students and are based on the best national and state standards (Porter & Smithson, 2001). In the development of our standards, we engaged many in what is the most important step in setting high academic goals, short of implementing them: discussion, debate, and intense and detailed conversations. This discussion was community wide, starting with teams of faculty, from elementary through university levels, who worked for over a year to draft the standards. The process was then expanded to include principals, deans, parents, and business and civic leaders, and gave everyone in the community a clear sense of what K–16 and community-wide engagement looks like and what it means. It continued with a wide set of business and community leaders who came together in 2000 to once again go through the process of discussing and debating education goals for all of our children.

Second, our work focuses on whole schools *and* on the systems within which they operate (O'Day & Smith, 1992). It is not a small or "special" program focused only on a few students, on only one approach, or on only one subject matter area. It is focused instead on the core of what schooling is all about: the relationship between teacher and student; the way knowledge is constructed; the ways in which teachers and students interact with one another around knowledge, problem solving, and learning; and the expectations teachers and students have for themselves and for one another (Elmore, 1990).

Third, we very much believe that this work must be undertaken K–16. Reforming K–12 will only work for the long term if our teacher preparation programs in colleges and universities have themselves improved, if they too are focused on the best national content standards and aggressively working toward fully engaging students in the learning process (Goodlad, 1994). And, given that teacher preparation encompasses the entire university, colleges of education as well as colleges of science and liberal arts, the entire university must work toward improving teacher quality.

We also believe that K–16 partnerships must address the issue of systemic curricular alignment. That is, what to teach, when to teach it, and how to make sure that it is linked across the grades toward ensuring that students are fully prepared for college-level work. Our K–16 Mathematics and Science Alignment work is a good example of that work. It brings together K–12 teachers from the three large school districts with mathematics and science faculty from the El Paso Community College and faculty from UTEP's colleges of science, engineering, and education. A major early goal of the initiative was to develop an Algebra II course outline, along with a curriculum framework, that would be implemented by high school teachers across the three districts. Algebra II was identified as the pivotal course that could provide high school students with preparation for entering and successfully completing a college math course without needing remediation. We have now completed work on Algebra I, Algebra II, and Geometry, as well as K–8 mathematics. In science, we have completed Chemistry and are close to completing Physics. Biology will be the next subject area we address.

These frameworks provide clear and specific information about the critical course content that must be taught to all students and that they must be helped to understand. Importantly, the frameworks also set out the level of cognitive demand—from skills and procedures, at the low end, to conceptual understanding that is transferable, at the high end—at which students must be able to perform in each of those areas in order to prepare for college-level mathematics and science (Blank, Porter, & Smithson, 2001). The outline is mapped to textbooks and to other curriculum programs and materials, and is not limited to any one adopted mathematics program. We have also developed an assessment for Algebra II.

Fifth, we prioritize the development of policies that encourage and monitor the implementation of practices that move forward our K–16 equity agenda. For example, at K–12, we worked closely with area districts to draft, pass, and implement a policy requiring all students to be enrolled in the state's college-preparatory Recommended High School Program. That, by the way, occurred in the mid-1990s, long before the program became the default curriculum across the state of Texas. Our policy was also written so as to limit the number of students that could be waived from the Recommended Program, an important issue that has not yet been addressed in the state's policy.

At the postsecondary level, we have worked closely over the past 2 years with university leaders to revise faculty tenure and promotion policies to ensure that work toward improving K–12 teaching and learning, including teacher preparation and development, is recognized and rewarded in the tenure and promotion process. We have worked most intensively with deans and faculty from the colleges of science and engineering to build buy-in for those policies and have made a great deal of progress. With the university's Provost taking the lead in this effort, we are pleased that the revised policies are now moving to the Faculty Senate for adoption.

A sixth component of our work is the robust set of support and assistance mechanisms aimed at building school capacity, including, most importantly, a focus on improving teacher quality (Desimone, Porter, Garet, Suk Yoon, & Birman, 2002; Porter, Garet, Desimone, & Birman, 2003; Porter, Garet, Desimone, Yoon, & Birman, 2000). In addition to teachers, our professional development work is focused on principals and other site administrators, as well as district leaders, parents, and others (Elmore, 2000). We have, however, made teacher professional development our highest priority.

From the beginning we knew that all of our work—our entire standards-based strategy—rested on the ability of teachers in classrooms across our community to transform teaching and learning. We knew, too, that the ability of many teachers to do just that was, unfortunately, quite limited.

In order to respond to that need, we have moved through several levels of professional development and are now focused on new ways to deepen teacher knowledge and understanding of subject matter content (Garet, Porter, Desimone, Birman, & Yoon, 2001). In particular, we have focused on pedagogical content knowledge, that is, the instructional practices and type and level of content knowledge required to teach specific math, science, and literacy concepts (Ball & Bass, 2000; Elmore, 1996). This deepening of knowledge and practice required a reorganization of where and how we delivered our professional development (McLaughlin, 1998). The majority of that development is now provided in classrooms by resident staff developers, thus bridging the teacher learning and practice gap. Through it all, we continue to raise issues of teacher and administrator beliefs and attitudes about who can learn—and who cannot—and to challenge educators' thinking in ways that make it possible for them to begin to come to terms with their beliefs and the impact of those beliefs on their students' achievement.

Finally, in the last few years we have undertaken an ambitious research agenda to try to determine, more precisely, the impact of the Collaborative's various initiatives. Currently, we are partnering with the Consortium for Policy Research in Education (CPRE) at the University of Pennsylvania to determine the impact of our mathematics and science coaches on teacher knowledge, skills, and classroom practice. CPRE is also examining the extent of usage of our curriculum frameworks and their impact on the enacted curriculum. Our work with principals and other site leaders, as well as district leaders, is the focus of additional research, as is the impact of our work at the postsecondary level, including engagement of postsecondary faculty in K–12 improvement efforts and masters programs for practicing teachers.

The structure of the El Paso Collaborative is a critical part of the success of our work. Although the Collaborative is comprised of key education and community entities, and is based at UTEP, it functions as a free-standing nonprofit organization. As such, we play a role both internal and external to the districts, college, and university. We are able to support, encourage, and work very closely with school and district leaders, college and university deans, and faculty. At the same time, we are also able to provide a different perspective, one from outside of the organization, that can raise a different set of questions, observe classrooms through different lenses, and propose alternate solutions or actions toward addressing problems. The fact that we have a healthy, externally supported budget, with funds available for supporting reform efforts, also enhances our ability to be an active player in the decision making process and to keep partners at the table.

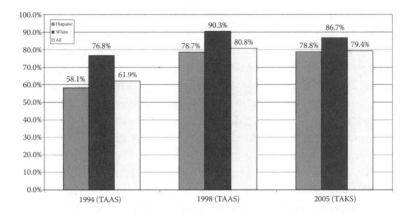

Figure 10.1 Texas Assessment of Academic Skills (TAAS)/Texas Assessment of Knowledge and Skills (TAKS) math results (Grade 03).

A few pieces of student achievement data illustrate what has happened in our community over the past 15 years. Figures 10.1 through 10.3 show what has happened to student achievement on our state accountability assessments. Figure 10.1 shows that performance on mathematics assessments at third grade has risen fairly steadily, even as the assessments have changed and the standards have been increased. Figures 10.2 and 10.3 show similar performance in eighth-grade science and 11th-grade math.

Figures 10.4 through 10.6 show enrollment and completion data for several of the college preparatory courses we track data on. As

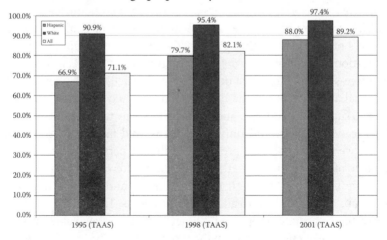

Figure 10.2 TAAS science results (Grade 08).

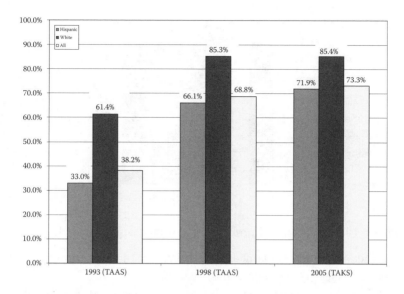

Figure 10.3 TAAS/TAKS math results (Grade 11). Source: TEA AEIS Reports (2005).

you can see in Figure 10.4, Algebra I enrollments have increased greatly, especially among Latino students, as have completion rates. The figures for Algebra II (Figure 10.5) show that in 1993, only 40% of Latino students had enrolled in Algebra II by the end of their junior year in high school. By 2004, that number had increased to 94%, with 88% of students passing the course. Enrollment and completion rates for Chemistry (Figure 10.6) reflect even greater increases in the

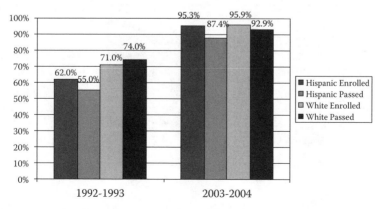

Figure 10.4 Algebra I: Enrollment and completion by Grade 9.

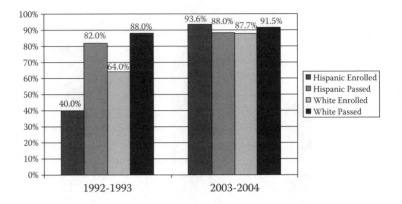

Figure 10.5   Algebra II: Enrollment and completion by Grade 11.

numbers of students, again, especially Latino students, enrolling and passing the course by their junior year.

Figure 10.7 shows that over 90% of all of our students are completing the state's Recommended High School Program, with the college preparatory courses needed for college.

As you can also see in Figure 10.8, we lead other large Texas districts and the state as a whole on this indicator. Finally, graduation rates have continued to increase—from 74% in 1998 to 80% in 2004.

In the 15 years of the Collaborative's existence, we have had our share of things that have worked well and those that haven't, and we have learned lessons from both. I would like to share with you some of the most critical lessons about the most important element

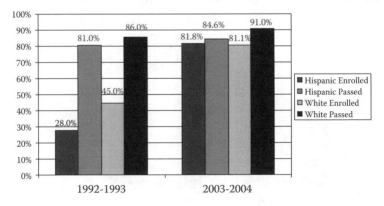

Figure 10.6   Chemistry: Enrollment and completion by Grade 11. Source: TEA AEIS Reports (2005).

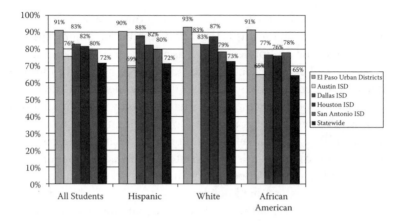

Figure 10.7 Completion of Recommended High School Program or higher for El Paso urban districts and other Texas cities, class of 2004. Source: TEA AEIS Reports (2005).

of our work—improving classroom teaching—especially as it relates to assessment.

The first lesson is that we need a far greater focus on assessment of teacher content knowledge for teaching. If we accept the proposition that teachers matter most, then we have to have a much better understanding of what they know—not just about content, but about how to teach that content (Ball, Hill, & Bass, 2005; Grossman & Schoenfeld, 2005). Across the country, we still face a tremendous challenge in ensuring that all students—especially minority and poor students—

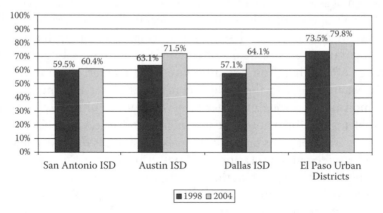

Figure 10.8 Graduation rates for selected Texas school districts. Source: TEA AEIS Reports (2005).

are taught by teachers with deep content knowledge for teaching. A fundamental reason for this is the lack of agreement among specialists in each of the disciplines, as well as among policy makers, about the nature and extent of the teacher knowledge needed to improve student achievement. Thus, district superintendents and their key staff members often do not know what, precisely, they should look for, or help to develop, that is related to content knowledge in teachers. Even if they know about the importance of content knowledge, they may not know what level of content knowledge is required or of what kind, and, very importantly, they have very few instruments helping them to assess that knowledge.

University faculty, within and across departments and colleges, hold widely varying opinions about the level to which teachers need to be prepared and often have only a vague understanding about the crucial difference between content knowledge per se, and *pedagogical* content knowledge. As are many others in the system, they are constrained by their own experiences as students being taught by teachers who "knew their stuff" but who may have had little understanding about how to teach it, especially at the higher conceptual levels (Porter et al., 2003). The persistent disparity in the availability of high-quality teachers in predominantly minority schools will continue until we can provide school leaders with help in assessing teacher content knowledge for teaching, and then help them figure out how to build that capacity among the teachers in their districts.

Second, if we truly want to improve teaching and learning, the design of assessments will have to focus specifically on testing across all levels of cognitive demand. I say specifically because the general framework that guides design and development of both formative and summative assessments often does not address testing the full range of learning, from the procedural and memorization level, all the way through to the highest conceptual understanding that is demonstrated through transfer to new situations or to solving new problems. We all know that if students and teachers believe that testing will not focus on certain topics or concepts or on particular cognitive demand levels, they will not prioritize teaching or learning of those concepts or at those levels. As we have learned through our K–16 Alignment work, this is part of a larger problem. Teachers don't test across all levels of cognitive demand because they don't differentiate clearly among the levels to which students should learn a concept or topic—it just does not stand out as a feature of the goals that they set for teaching or learning. This is so partly because such preparation is almost always absent from the teachers' own preparation programs. Second, if they do differentiate among cognitive levels, they are not prepared to teach well enough at all levels, especially at the highest level of cognitive demand. Finally, even if they do set a range of learning goals for their students and know how to teach at each of those levels, they often have a hard time knowing how to assess at all the levels, again, especially at the highest levels. Through our Alignment work, we are increasingly addressing these teacher skills and abilities, and are beginning to see some promising results.

The third lesson is related to formative assessment. A great deal has been and will be said in this volume about the importance of formative assessment integrally linked to instruction. Clearly, we must help teachers understand the critical importance of assessing and monitoring student learning on a regular basis in their classrooms, as well as help them learn a range of formative assessment approaches that they can readily use (Bransford, Derry, Berliner, & Hammerness, 2005). They need assistance in determining when and how to assess for a variety of purposes in diagnosing student problems in understanding, and in providing feedback often to students that will enhance learning (Shepard, Hammerness, Darling-Hammond, & Rust, 2005).

One of the reasons that teachers have limited skills in doing formative assessments is that it is still the exception for them, in their teacher preparation as students or in their professional development as practicing teachers, to be provided high-quality, extended opportunities to learn how to do quality assessment integrated with instruction. Formative assessment is still not seen as integral to daily lesson planning. And when it is taught in college or in professional development, it is often treated as something separate from content and instruction. Second, truly effective formative assessment should also engage students in becoming more reflective about their understanding of a lesson, thus leading to more productive self-assessment and to learning at a deeper level (National Research Council, 2000). Both teachers and their students need to work to a much greater degree at a metacognitive level. If teachers are assessing meaningfully and frequently, and are providing students with useful feedback that helps them know where they are in the learning process, students are more likely to be engaged and, ultimately, to learn.

Building teacher capacity to assess student learning will not be quick or easy work. It will be time- and resource-intensive, and it will be complicated by the fact that formative assessments are more effective if they are aligned to the curriculum materials that teachers are using. But, if we want to figure out who is learning—particularly at the higher levels of cognitive demand—and how to help those that are not, we will need to address this challenge (Black & Wiliam, 1998). It is this work, too, that can ultimately lead to the recognition by teachers of the changes and improvements that need to be made in their own teaching. We have begun to work on improving teacher understanding about the role of in-class assessment both through our curriculum alignment work as well as through our professional development work. In both of these cases, we are increasingly linking formative assessment to the entire teaching loop, and recognizing that assessment needs to be designed, if not before the lesson, then at least simultaneously with the lesson activities and strategies.

Fourth, we need to do a better job of end-of-course assessment, especially for the most important college preparatory secondary courses. Again, state accountability testing programs do not provide the detailed, course-specific feedback that is required to improve teaching and learning in those courses. End-of-course exams are needed—especially as more states make the college preparatory program the default program for all students—to ensure that the most important course content is being taught with fidelity.

One of the unfortunate outcomes of setting a uniform course of study for secondary students that provides all students access to college-preparatory study is that, too often, the curriculum taught to minority and poor students is much more limited, is watered-down, is focused primarily on procedures and skills, and fails to address some of the most important course topics. End-of-course assessments can provide tools to assist teachers and administrators in focusing on clearly defined course goals, and being accountable for student opportunity to learn key topics across the cognitive demand spectrum. Further, end-of-course assessments can provide critical linkages with formative assessments, allowing teachers to determine the effectiveness of both discrete portions of their enacted curriculum as well as the overall course.

The overarching themes of our work in the El Paso Collaborative for Academic Excellence have been equity, partnerships, and systemic education reform focused on building capacity in people and organizations. We believe that those themes are reflected in all of our work. And yet, the El Paso Collaborative is still very much a work in progress. We have had our share of things that have worked very well and those that have failed. Through it all, we remain committed to continuing to learn what it takes to bring about real and lasting improvements for every single student in our community.

References

Ball, D. L., & Bass, H. (2000). Interweaving content and pedagogy in teaching and learning to teach: Knowing and using mathematics. In J. Boaler (Ed.), *Multiple perspectives on the teaching and learning of mathematics* (pp. 83-104). Westport, CT: Ablex.

Ball, D. L., Hill, H. C., & Bass, H. (2005). Knowing mathematics for teaching: Who knows mathematics well enough to teach third grade, and how can we decide? *American Educator, 29*(3), 14-46.

Black, P., & Wiliam, D. (1998). Inside the black box: Raising standards through classroom assessment. *Phi Delta Kappan, 80*(2), 139-148.

Blank, R. K., Porter, A., & Smithson, J. (2001). *New tools for analyzing teaching, curriculum and standards in mathematics and science.* Results from Survey of Enacted Curriculum Project. (Final Report to the National Science Foundation on Contract No. REC98-03080). Washington, DC: Council of Chief State School Officers.

Bransford, J., Derry, S., Berliner, D., Hammerness, K. (with Beckett, K .L.). (2005). Theories of learning and their roles in teaching. In L. Darling-Hammond & J. Bransford (Eds.) *Preparing teachers for a changing world* (pp. 40-88). San Francisco: Jossey-Bass.

Desimone, L., Porter, A. C., Garet, M., Suk Yoon, K., & Birman, B. (2002). Effects of professional development on teachers' instruction: Results from a three-year longitudinal study. *Educational Evaluation and Policy Analysis, 24*(2), 81-112.

Education Service Center, Region 19. (2005). *PEIMS Data Analysis.* El Paso, TX.

Elmore, R. F. (1990). *Restructuring schools: The next generation of educational reform.* San Francisco: Jossey-Bass.

Elmore, R. F. (1996). Getting to scale with good educational practice. *Harvard Educational Review, 66*(1), 1-26.

Elmore, R. F. (2000). *Building a new structure for school leadership.* Washington, DC: Albert Shanker Institute.

Garet, M. S., Porter, A. C., Desimone, L., Birman, B. F., & Yoon, K. S. (2001). What makes professional development effective? Results from a national sample of teachers. *American Educational Research Journal 38*(4), 915-945.

Goodlad, J. I. (1994). *Educational renewal: Better teachers, better schools.* San Francisco: Jossey-Bass.

Grossman, P., & Schoenfeld, A. (with Lee, C.). (2005). Teaching subject matter. In L. Darling-Hammond & J. Bransford (Eds.), *Preparing teachers for a changing world* (pp. 201-231). San Francisco: Jossey-Bass.

Institute Materno Infantil de Pernambuso. (2001). Plan Director de Desarrollo Urbano. Retrieved September 9, 2005, from http://www.elpaso-texas.gov/quick_facts/default.asp

McLaughlin, M. W. (1998). Listening and learning from the field: Tales of policy implementation and situated practice. In A. Hargreaves, A. Lieberman, M. Fullan, & D. Hopkins (Eds.), *International handbook of educational change* (pp. 70-84). Dorcrecht, Netherlands: Kluwer.

National Research Council. (2000). *How people learn: Brain, mind, experience, and school* (Expanded ed.). Washington, DC: National Academies Press.

O'Day, J. A., & Smith, M. (1992). Systemic reform and educational opportunity. In S. Fuhrman (Ed.), *Designing coherent education policy: Improving the system* (pp. 250-312). San Francisco: Jossey-Bass.

Porter, A. C., Garet, M. S., Desimone, L. M., & Birman, B. F. (2003). Providing effective professional development: Lessons from the Eisenhower Program. *Science Educator 12*(1), 23-40.

Porter, A. C., Garet, M. S., Desimone, L., Yoon, K. S., & Birman, B. F. (2000, October). *Does professional development change teaching practice? Results from a three-year study.* (Report to the U.S. Department of Education, Office of the Under Secretary on Contract No. EA97001001 to the American Institutes for Research). Washington, DC: Pelavin Research Center.

Porter, A. C., & Smithson, J. L. (2001). Are content standards being implemented in the classroom? A methodology and some tentative answers. In S. H. Fuhrman (Ed.), *From the capitol to the classroom: Standards-based reform in the states – One hundredth yearbook of the National Society for the Study of Education, Part II* (pp. 60-80). Chicago: University of Chicago Press.

Shepard, L., Hammerness, K., Darling-Hammond, L., Rust, F. (with Baratz Snowden, J., Gordon, E., Gutierrez, C., & Pacheco, A.). (2005). Assessment. In L. Darling-Hammond & J. Bransford (Eds.) *Preparing teachers for a changing world* (pp. 275-327). San Francisco: Jossey-Bass.

Shirley, D. (1997). *Community organizations for urban school reform.* Austin: University of Texas Press.

Stone, C. N., Henig, J. R., Jones, B. D., & Pierannunzi, C. (2001). *Building civic capacity: The politics of reforming urban schools.* Lawrence: University Press of Kansas.

Texas Education Agency (2005). *Adhoc Reports.* Retrieved September 9, 2005, from http://www.tea.state.tx.us/adhocrpt/index.html

U.S. Census Bureau (2003). State and county quick facts. Retrieved September 9, 2005, from http://www.census.gov/qfd/index.html

Section IV

*Values and Prospects
for Assessment in the
Age of Accountability*

11

Classroom Assessment:
Staying Instructionally Afloat in an Ocean of Accountability

W. James Popham
University of California, Los Angeles

Once upon a time, I was a teacher in our nation's public schools. I taught in a small eastern Oregon high school—and I loved it. Because I tested my students back then, and because that testing took place in a classroom, it is reasonable to conclude that I was engaging in classroom assessment. But, at the time, I definitely didn't know it.

Back then, my fellow teachers and I routinely tested our students to see how much those students knew. That was really all there was to testing. We didn't think of it as "classroom" testing, that is, as a distinctive genre of testing. For us, testing in the classroom was the only kind of testing we knew anything about. I understand now, having dipped into the history of American educational measurement, that when I taught high school there were a number of published standardized aptitude and achievement tests available in the United States. But back then, my colleagues and I never paid any attention to such tests. Educational testing was what went on in our classrooms when we handed out our final exams, midterm exams, unit tests, and pop quizzes. In retrospect, I now understand we were doing classroom assessment, but we surely didn't realize it at the time.

Early Uses of Classroom Assessment

Grading Students

Classroom assessment in those days, and "those days" were literally over a half century ago, had one mission and one mission
only. Classroom assessment took place so we could give grades
to students. Thinking back to my years as a high school teacher,
I really can't remember a single second when I ever conceived
of my tests as anything other than devices to help me grade my
students.

I'm not suggesting that teachers in that era had never been
exposed to any information about educational testing during their
teacher education days. We had been given some tips about the care
and feeding of certain item-types. But these tips were intended to
help us (1) construct better tests so that (2) we'd more accurately
determine what our students had learned in order that (3) we could
decide on more defensible grades for those students. Never, during
my teacher education experiences, did I ever hear one professor
suggest that I could use my students' test performances to help me
evaluate the effectiveness of my own instruction. Never, during my
teacher education experiences, did I ever hear one professor suggest that classroom tests could help me instructionally. But that
was then, and this is now. What's happened to classroom assessment during the last 50 years—other than my belated recognition
that, at one time, I did it?

Evaluating Instruction

The nature of classroom assessment in our nation, interest-
ingly, has been most directly influenced by the increasing use of
large-scale achievement tests that took place after passage of the
Elementary and Secondary Education Act (ESEA) in 1965. That
law, a key component of President Lyndon B. Johnson's "great
society," was, of course, the initial version of an oft-reauthorized
law whose most recent incarnation is the No Child Left Behind
(NCLB) Act. ESEA had an enormous impact on U.S. education
because that law dispensed an unprecedented number of dollars to local public schools. And, as any Skinnerian can tell you,

potent reinforcers are likely to modify behavior. ESEA of 1965 did just that.

During the Congressional debates preceding the enactment of ESEA, a number of lawmakers expressed serious misgivings about providing huge levels of federal support to U.S. public schools. Led by Robert F. Kennedy, then the junior senator from New York, a series of safeguards were incorporated in the law to guarantee that ESEA's dollars would be well spent. Chief among those safeguards was the provision that a large number of ESEA-supported educational programs were required to supply evaluative *evidence* demonstrating that students' achievement had been increased because of those programs. In particular, evidence had to be provided by recipients of ESEA funds to show that historically underserved student groups had benefited from this brand new form of federal largesse. In essence, ESEA called for student test performances to serve as the chief evaluative indicator of instructional effectiveness. And, thus, tests were—by federal law—instantly transformed into the tools to tell us whether instruction was any good. Forty years later, we are still experiencing the impact of that transformation.

Choosing the most expedient way to comply with ESEA's call for evidence of program effectiveness, many recipients of that law's federal dollars began evaluating their ESEA-funded programs by using one of the several off-the-shelf nationally standardized achievement tests then available. These tests were accompanied by reams of supportive psychometric data, and were generally regarded with favor by educators and citizens alike. Moreover, they were *nationally* standardized achievement tests and, therefore, were surrounded by an aura of acceptability. Unfortunately, these carefully developed achievement tests, although well suited for the comparative assessment mission they were intended to serve, were not designed for, nor were they appropriate for, a program evaluation function. But that is another story altogether.

As the 1960s ran down, student scores on large-scale tests were widely regarded as the key evaluative data for judging an instructional intervention's worth. For the most part, test-based evaluations associated with ESEA-funding took place at the district level. But the basic idea of using student test scores to evaluate instruction slowly seeped into the consciousness of more and more American teachers. Tests, they concluded, *should* be used to evaluate teaching.

So, not too many years after ESEA had triggered the use of achievement tests as evaluative tools, many U.S. teachers perceived that classroom tests could not only be used to award grades, but could also be used as tools to appraise instructional effectiveness. Although classroom assessments were not widely *used* by many teachers to evaluate their own instructional success, increasing numbers of teachers began to recognize that classroom assessment *could* play a role in judging instructional effectiveness.

I joined the UCLA faculty in 1962. My chief instructional responsibility was to teach large-enrollment courses in instructional procedures for prospective teachers. Every academic year, I was charged with the task of supplying almost 1,000 prospective teachers with the rudiments of how to plan and deliver effective classroom instruction. The first 2 years I taught the course, I used as my textbook a skinny booklet that Ralph Tyler had authored when he taught a similar class early in his career at the University of Chicago. The no-frills pedagogical approach that Tyler had advocated in his own classes really appealed to me, for it was rooted in a classic ends-means approach to instruction. That is, teachers first identified the curricular aims (ends) they wanted their students to attain, devised what they believed would be suitable instructional procedures (means) to promote student mastery of those ends, then collected test-based evidence of whether students had, in fact, achieved the hoped-for ends.

Because, without getting an accurate fix on student entry behavior, it is impossible to use student postinstruction performances to draw defensible conclusions regarding the effectiveness of an instructional sequence, I pushed my UCLA prospective teachers not only to employ postassessments, but also to use preassessments as a way of determining the caliber of their own instruction. If I were teaching that same course tomorrow, I'd still base it on a Tylerian ends-means model.

My impression is that, although there were sporadic instances in the 1960s and 1970s wherein U.S. teachers used student posttest results as indicators of their instructional effectiveness, most classroom assessments of that era were still being employed chiefly as grade-giving instruments. Any views that classroom assessments could play a prominent *instructional* role were rarely heard or seen in print. Classroom tests, it was recognized, could be used for grade-giving or for assessing instructional effectiveness, but few assessment specialists really pushed for much more.

Instruction Ambles Onto the Scene

In the mid-1980s, Rick Stiggins, then working on assessment issues as a staff member of the Northwest Regional Educational Laboratory, began dealing with classroom assessment not from a grade-giving perspective or from an evaluative perspective, but from an instructional point of view. He developed a variety of print and video materials designed for professional development activities, many of which dealt with ways that classroom tests could contribute to the quality of teachers' *instructional* decisions. In 1992, when Stiggins established his own organization, the Assessment Training Institute, he continued, sometimes almost single-handedly, to champion the instructional applications of classroom assessment. Stiggins stressed, for example, a series of important instructional payoffs that could ensue when students were made active participants in the classroom assessment process. Stiggins deserves considerable credit for keeping classroom assessment at least on the back-burner rather than off the stove entirely during those years.

Most observers regard the *Phi Delta Kappan* article by Paul Black and Dylan Wiliam (1998) as a powerful spur to American educators' interest in the instructional dividends of classroom assessments. Drawing on their work at Kings College in England, Black and Wiliam presented a persuasive meta-analysis of research indicating that when classroom assessment was used deliberately to enhance student learning, there were also meaningful increases in student performances on external examinations. Black, Wiliam, and their colleagues drew a key distinction between "assessment *of* learning" and "assessment *for* learning." Assessment *of* learning, in their view, represents a more traditional role of testing in which we test students to see how much they know. In contrast, assessment *for* learning represents a role for classroom testing that focuses more specifically on the ways that assessment can engender more and better learning by students.

More recently, Shepard, Hammerness, Darling-Hammond, and Rust (2005) have presented an array of ways that classroom assessments, if used *formatively*, can benefit student learning. Shepard and colleagues regard classroom assessments as formative when teachers not only use test results to indicate whether student answers are correct, but also link such feedback to clear performance standards while providing strategies for improved learning.

Formative classroom assessment, as conceptualized by Shepard et al., is altogether consonant with the instructionally oriented role for classroom assessment seen in the work of Stiggins and Black and Wiliam. To illustrate, Shepard and colleagues argue that if classroom assessments are genuine *embodiments* of the curricular aims being sought, then the clarity available from such assessments-as-exemplifications can lead to the teacher's delineation of more appropriate "learning progressions." A learning progression (referred to in earlier years as a task analysis) sets forth a progress map that identifies the enabling subskills and/or bodies of knowledge that students must master en route to their attainment of a more distant curricular aim being sought. By relying on learning progressions, teachers can more accurately ascertain where (in a particular progression) a student is having difficulties, what comes next, and so on. A teacher can then use along-the-way assessments dealing with key stages of a learning progression to determine whether to proceed with instruction as planned or, instead, to alter it.

Other formative uses of classroom assessment recommended by Shepard and her colleagues include assessing students' prior knowledge and skills before actually commencing instruction so that those entry behaviors can be taken into account instructionally. Also advocated are (1) the frequent provision of feedback to students so they'll know how they are progressing and (2) fostering the habit of self-assessment on the part of students so that they can critique their own growth based on the results of classroom assessment.

In the remainder of this analysis I shall use the descriptor *instructionally oriented classroom assessment* to refer to what other writers refer to as formative assessment or as assessment *for* learning. The essence of all such assessment approaches is to enhance student learning by the deft *instructional* utilization of classroom assessments.

Clearly, then, a number of thoughtful educators have, for more than a decade, enthusiastically urged that teachers not only use classroom assessment for its formerly accepted functions but now, as never before, use classroom assessment to bolster the caliber of student learning. This instructionally focused approach to classroom assessment, in my view, constitutes a powerful way to enhance educational quality for our nation's students. Happily, I frequently find myself attending a number of conferences these days in which teachers are becoming genuinely excited about the instructional payoffs of classroom assessment. Unhappily, I think that most of this excitement about classroom assessment's instructional dividends will soon wither away.

Fervor Quashed by Failure

Here is the essence of my discontent regarding today's classroom assessment. I have seen teachers' perceptions regarding the role of classroom testing change dramatically over the last half century. Currently, we find a number of prominent advocates urging teachers to test their students in ways that will contribute to improved learning by those students. I think that's great. Moreover, we see increasing numbers of teachers embracing the idea of assessment *for* learning and regarding classroom assessment from a formative perspective. I think that's also great.

However, the current indicator of a school's success—the indicator regarded by the world as the definitive reflection of instructional effectiveness—is the performance of a school's students on its state's NCLB tests. If a school's students do not earn high enough scores on those NCLB tests, then the school will fail to achieve the *adequate yearly progress* (AYP) targets that NCLB requires. And schools that fail to make their AYP targets are generally viewed as "failing," that is, as ineffective schools.

Regrettably, in all but a few states, the NCLB tests that have been chosen by state officials are *instructionally insensitive*, that is, they are incapable of detecting improved instruction even if such improved instruction were present. The dominant determinator of NCLB test scores in almost all states, unfortunately, is not what students were *taught* in school, but what those students *brought* to school based on their socioeconomic status (SES). I'll try to defend this contention later in this analysis.

So, if a school's teachers enthusiastically adopt instructionally oriented classroom assessment and thus do a superb job of enhancing student learning, the odds are that student NCLB test scores won't reflect it. Teachers' fervent adoption of instructionally sensible, classroom assessment approaches will, to those teachers, seem ineffectual. A few years of big-time effort coupled with no NCLB payoff will soon lead to the abandonment of instructionally oriented classroom assessment—a measurement approach that benefits children.

In the past few years I have seen scads of teachers gleefully adopting instructionally oriented, classroom assessment strategies. I am sure that those teachers' students will be advantaged by this sort of assessment. But I am just as sure that many of those teachers will scurry from such an assessment approach if the state's NCLB tests indicate, year after year, that instructionally oriented classroom assessment does little good on the tests that *really* count.

With mixed feelings, I observe these plucky proponents of instructionally oriented classroom assessment preparing to adopt such an assessment strategy even though their state's upcoming NCLB tests will almost certainly shower them with AYP-based failure. It's like watching Florida homeowners, in the direct path of a Force-5 hurricane, carefully mowing and edging their lawns. There's part of me that wants to yell, at the top of my voice, "Teachers, what you're up to is not going to do any good!"

Why is it that most teachers who now are beginning to embrace instructionally sensible approaches to classroom assessment probably won't continue doing so for more than a year or two? Although those teachers' students will probably learn lots more than will students whose teachers aren't using instructionally oriented classroom assessment, the nature of what is being learned is not apt to mesh well with what's being measured on state NCLB tests. That sort of mismatch is predictable, in large part, because of the sprawling array of content standards (curricular aims) that almost all 50 states have adopted. Not only are there far too many curricular aims for teachers to teach effectively in the available instructional time, but there are also far too many curricular aims to accurately measure in the available assessment time.

Let's say a teacher is forced to consider an overwhelming collection of curricular aims that are eligible for NCLB assessment. Such aims are often subsumed under more global content standards, and are referred to as "benchmarks," "indicators," or some similar labels. If the teacher realizes that only a portion of those curricular aims can ever be meaningfully taught during the school year, then it is likely the teacher will be obliged to pursue those curricular aims that seem (1) worthwhile and (2) are probable contenders for inclusion in the state's NCLB tests. But what if this well-meaning teacher selects certain curricular aims, yet that year's NCLB tests are based exclusively on *other* curricular aims? The teacher's students may have been well taught, but on NCLB-unmeasured content. And, of course, the teacher's students will not have been taught, or certainly not well taught, on what the state's NCLB tests actually measure. When that teacher's students take the NCLB test, they're apt to perform poorly. And their poor performance might just be the straw that breaks the AYP-back of that school's evaluation camel.

To get genuine instructional mileage out of classroom assessment, teachers need to (1) preassess their students' entry skills and knowledge in order to make appropriate adjustments in instructional plans, (2) develop appropriate learning progressions so that student progress toward a more ultimate curricular aim can be monitored, (3) provide en route feedback and instructional suggestions to students, and (4) nurture self-assessment dispositions on the part of students. This sort of assessment-catalyzed instructional approach will almost always promote solid student learning. But, obviously, it takes time! And if a teacher chooses to emphasize a set of state-approved curricular aims that don't coincide with what's measured on the state's NCLB tests, then that teacher and, quite possibly, that teacher's school will be seen as "failing." How many years do you think teachers will persevere in using instructionally oriented classroom assessment if, on the tests that are regarded as the true indicators of instructional success, those teachers look like losers?

Two Culpable Culprits

There are two reasons why many of the teachers who employ instructionally oriented classroom assessment today won't be doing so in a few years. Both reasons flow from the way almost all states have implemented the assessment provisions of NCLB. That law's accountability strategy rests squarely on the extent to which student scores, over time, improve on the NCLB tests that measure student mastery of a state's officially approved curricular aims. Schools that don't promote sufficient improvements in student NCLB test scores have thereby failed their federal litmus test and, as a consequence, can be placed on a sanction-laden improvement track that can improve the school into nonexistence.

Chaotic Content Standards

The first collection of culprits in this situation is, clearly, the content standards that most states have approved as the curricular aims for their educational systems. In a nutshell, there are simply too many of those content standards. I recently heard a colleague aptly say that, "Most states have never seen a content standard that they didn't love." In many instances, these state-sanctioned content standards were spawned well before NCLB's enactment, and were frequently formulated in an attempt to carve out truly "world-class, challenging" curricular aims. Accordingly, most of our 50 states' official content standards currently resemble curricular wish lists rather than realistic descriptions of the skills and knowledge that can be taught to children during a school year.

Moreover, the "chunk size" of content standards in one subject area is often quite different from that of content standards in another subject. To illustrate, in subject X, there may be a medley of small-scope curricular aims, but in subject Z there might be broader, but often ambiguously phrased, curricular aims. Most states' official content standards are too numerous, too inconsistent, and too vague to be of much help in guiding the creation of a state's NCLB tests. Those content standards were rarely created to be suitable curricular targets for accountability-focused assessments. It is small wonder, then, that the NCLB tests allegedly aligned with those content standards invariably fail to provide a state's teachers with a clear set of assessment targets around which to create instructionally oriented classroom assessments.

Nasty NCLB Tests

The second set of culprits that tend to dissuade teachers from using instructionally astute classroom assessments is the NCLB tests themselves. In the main, there are two versions of these NCLB tests, both of which are instructionally insensitive, that is, unable to detect the very instructional improvements that represent the accountability cornerstone of NCLB's game plan.

Many states have attempted to satisfy the need for standards-aligned NCLB tests by selecting off-the-shelf nationally standardized achievement tests, then salting those tests with additional items intended to address content standards not satisfactorily measured in the original version of the test. Such lick-and-a-promise "augmented" NCLB tests, however, because of the underlying comparative measurement mission of nationally standardized achievement tests, are so directly tied to students' socioeconomic status (SES) that the resultant NCLB "customized" tests tend to measure the SES composition of a school's students rather than the effectiveness of the school's instructional efforts. This is because the items in oft-revised standardized achievement tests that do the best job of promoting the score-spread needed for comparative measurement turn out to be those items linked to SES, a nicely spread-out variable that doesn't change all that rapidly.

Eschewing nationally standardized tests, about the same number of states have created their own "standards-based" NCLB tests to measure student mastery of their state's official content standards. Unfortunately, because the framework for such standards-based tests are the state's anarchical and too numerous content standards, the state's teachers must often guess about which standards will actually be assessed in a given year. And, of course, those teachers often guess wrong. Consequently, much classroom instructional time is often "wasted" because it is unrelated to the items that actually won out in the annual NCLB test's item-selection lottery. Even more dismaying, from an evaluative perspective, the content of numerous NCLB test items will simply not have been treated in many classrooms. The almost certain mismatch between what's tested and what's been taught will obviously lead to NCLB test scores that aren't indicative of a teacher's true instructional skill.

And because there are so many content standards to assess, and too few items to assess them, it is clearly impossible to provide teachers with any sort of meaningful test-based reports regarding which content standards have actually been mastered by a teacher's students. Test results from almost all of the nation's current standards-based NCLB tests are, from an instructional perspective, consummately dysfunctional.

Thus, because a twice-burned or thrice-burned teacher will soon tire of trying to make sense out of NCLB assessment targets or NCLB results, we will find increasing numbers of such teachers abandoning any genuine reliance on NCLB tests, that is, what those tests supposedly measure and what those test results signify. Then, not surprisingly, what determines student scores on these instructionally flawed standards-based NCLB tests, just as was true in the case of nationally standardized achievement tests, turns out to be students' SES.

Teachers who work in states where instructionally insensitive NCLB tests are being used to evaluate schools and districts, and this represents the vast majority of our nation's teachers, thus find themselves required to play a no-win accountability game where even the most adroit application of instructionally oriented classroom assessment will be unable to overcome the barriers erected by the instructionally insensitive, SES-determined NCLB tests now being used to decide whether teachers are successful or unsuccessful.

What Next?

The issue I've been describing thus far is nontrivial. Schoolsful of children will be less well educated if their teachers do not employ instructionally oriented classroom assessment. And even if there were not a dollop of empirical research to support the virtues of instructionally oriented classroom assessment (and there is more than a dollop), teachers' reliance on assessments closely linked to ongoing classroom instruction is so consummately commonsensical. We need more of this sort of assessment in classrooms, not less of it.

And yet, I have been arguing that the nature of today's NCLB tests will tend to extinguish most teachers' continued use of instructionally oriented classroom assessment. Those NCLB tests, because they are instructionally insensitive, tend to provide a distorted underestimate of a teacher's instructional effectiveness. Although many teachers may be doing first-rate instructional and/ or assessment jobs in their classrooms, those teachers are certain to seem so-so based on their students' performances on instructionally insensitive NCLB tests.

My fear, in a nutshell, is that inappropriate NCLB tests will extinguish teachers' adoption and continued use of instructionally oriented classroom assessment. What can today's educators, that is, U.S. teachers and administrators, do to prevent such a calamity? An incorrect answer to the foregoing question is, "Do nothing." We are facing a situation in which a stance of *assessment acquiescence* will harm children. If teachers are currently playing in a no-win accountability game that's destined to erode instructional quality, then it will obviously be necessary to alter the game's rules.

More specifically, I recommend the three-step strategy identified below for those who wish to use instructionally oriented classroom assessment, yet realize that such a classroom assessment approach is not apt to win any NCLB medals.

A Three-Step Strategy to Promote Wider Use of Instructionally Oriented Classroom Assessment.

Step 1. Use of instructionally sensible classroom tests. Organize the bulk of classroom assessments around a modest number of truly important state-sanctioned curricular aims that, abetted by instructionally focused measurement, students can master in genuine depth.

Step 2. Learn why certain accountability tests are instructionally insensitive. Understand enough about large-scale assessments to be able to explain to colleagues, educational policy makers, parents, and everyday citizens why it is that particular kinds of educational accountability tests are actually unable to detect the impact of excellent instruction.

Step 3. Become an advocate for instructionally sensitive accountability tests. Drawing on your insights about instructionally sensitive and insensitive accountability tests, initiate a serious advocacy effort so that instructionally oriented classroom assessment can be accurately recognized as a key factor in enhancing student learning.

Briefly, then, let me elaborate on each of these three steps.

Sensible Classroom Tests

As Step 1, I suggest that a teacher try to engage in classroom assessment practices that, in the teacher's opinion, can best benefit students. I suggest this even if this means a teacher's classroom assessments are basically uninfluenced by what happens to be measured by a given year's NCLB tests. To do so, a teacher should select from the full array of state-approved content standards a set of the most important curricular aims that—abetted by the appropriate infusion of instructionally oriented classroom assessment—can be effectively taught in the available instructional time. In contrast, teachers who attempt to "cover" an interminable list of state-sanctioned content standards, but superficially, do a disservice to their students.

In other words, in order to engage in instructionally oriented classroom assessment—the kind of testing that will help kids learn, and learn well, the most important things they ought to be learning—I recommend that a teacher's curricular targets be judiciously selected. There should be no pretense made that *all* of a state's too numerous content standards will have been taught or tested. Teachers who currently make such claims are either naïve, hypocritical, or disingenuous. (In days of yore, being disingenuous was known as *lying*.)

If the more limited focus for classroom assessment I'm recommending in Step 1 does not seem to mesh well with the assessment folly currently represented in a state's NCLB tests, well, that's tough. After all, given the instructional insensitivity of most of today's NCLB tests, it usually makes little difference what goes on in the classroom. Thus, why not give students the best education that the teacher can provide?

A Deeper Understanding of Instructional Insensitivity

It is important for today's educators to know why it is that certain kinds of accountability tests, often created with the best of intentions, are incapable of accurately discerning whether instruction was great or ghastly. To understand about accountability tests' instructional sensitivity does not require statistical sophistication or psychometric suave. Actually, the reason that some accountability tests are instructionally sensitive and some are not can be explained using very simple, common-sense concepts. Step 2, therefore, calls for educators to dig into the nuts and bolts of large-scale accountability tests as those bolts and nuts pertain to a test's instructional sensitivity.

There are several sources of information regarding this topic, most of which present the content in a noncomplicated fashion. A few years ago, I wrote a short book on these issues (Popham, 2001), and last year a new set of assessment-related booklets were published that deal with similar concepts (Popham, 2006). If educators are more interested in a discussion of accountability tests in the context of NCLB, there's a book out on that topic as well (Popham, 2005). Although, bristling with bias, I regard my own books dealing with this topic as altogether boffo, many other writers effectively address the question of whether large-scale accountability tests are really appropriate for judging educational quality (e.g., Kohn, 2000; Linn, 2000). It is imperative for educators to take Step 2, that is, become more knowledgeable about the nature of educational accountability tests, because without such knowledge it would be impossible to undertake Step 3.

Assertive Advocacy

The final step in this three-step strategy calls for educators to try to either change the nature of their state's NCLB tests or alter their state's official curricular aims. Ideally, both alterations should take place. Until one or both of those transformations transpires, then instructionally oriented classroom assessment really can't prosper. The particular ways in which an educator attempts to influence the nature of a state's NCLB tests or its content standards, of course, depends completely on the specifics of the educator's setting. For example, teachers may find it most effective to channel their advocacy efforts through one or more of the professional associations to which they belong. This is also true for school-site or district-level administrators. Solo efforts to influence policy makers, such as legislators, while often feckless, can also be effective (especially if someone knows an appropriate, clear-thinking policy maker).

Personally, I have always believed that because educators of any stripe will often be regarded as self-serving partisans in such debates, it makes sense to educate *parents* to the perils of having their schools evaluated on the basis of instructionally insensitive tests. I'd then encourage those parents, if they choose to do so, to exercise whatever political muscle they have at their disposal to change their state's NCLB tests or content standards. Parents, although obviously concerned with the schools, are nonpartisans in any accountability-related debates. Educators are not. And, because parents clearly care about their children's well being, parental advocacy groups can have substantial influence.

Step 3 is crucial because, unless there are instructionally sensible modifications made in a state's content standards or in its NCLB tests, I fear that the negative evaluative impact of student NCLB performances is apt to drive instructionally oriented classroom assessment from many of our schools.

Staying Afloat

If a three-step strategy such as that outlined above were energetically implemented, there's a chance that instructionally oriented classroom assessment could stay afloat in today's ocean of accountability. The trick, of course, is to remove whatever is contaminating that ocean. Currently, those contaminants consist of excessively numerous content standards and instructionally insensitive NCLB tests. Unless we take care of those two pollutants, then instructionally oriented classroom assessment will soon sink all the way to the bottom of the sea.

References

Black, P., & Wiliam, D. (1998). Inside the black box: Raising standards through classroom assessment. *Phi Delta Kappan, 80*(2), 139-148.

Kohn, A. (2000). *The case against standardized testing: Raising the scores, ruining the schools.* Westport, CT: Heinemann.

Linn, R. L. (2000). Assessments and accountability. *Educational Researcher, 29*(2), 4-16.

Popham, W. J. (2001). *The truth about testing: An educator's call to action.* Alexandria, VA: Association for Supervision and Curriculum Development.

Popham, W. J. (2005). *America's failing schools: How parents and teachers can cope with No Child Left Behind.* New York: RoutledgeFalmer.

Popham, W. J. (2006). *Mastering assessment: A self-service system for educators.* New York: RoutledgeFalmer.

Shepard, L., Hammerness, K., Darling-Hammond, L., & Rust, F. Assessment. (2005). In L. Darling-Hammond & J. Bransford (Eds.), *Preparing teachers for a changing world: What teachers should learn and be able to do* (pp. 275-326). New York: Wiley.

12

Formative Assessment:
Caveat Emptor

Lorrie A. Shepard
University of Colorado at Boulder

Formative assessment as a part of good teaching has been around for a long time. In the past two decades, however, formal theory about this type of assessment—used to further students' developing understandings and to engage students in taking responsibility for their own learning—was developed in other countries (Black & Wiliam, 1998; Cowie & Bell, 1999; Sadler, 1989), in part to counter the negative effects of external accountability tests exported by the United States. Recently, this robust and well-researched knowledge base has made its way back across the oceans, offering great promise for shifting classroom practices toward a culture of learning (Shepard, 2000; Stiggins, 2002).

Unfortunately, the arrival of formative assessment in America was ill timed. This potentially powerful classroom-based learning and teaching innovation was overshadowed almost immediately by the No Child Left Behind Act (January 2002) with its intense pressure to raise scores on external accountability tests. The title of my chapter is prompted by the recent burgeoning of so-called formative assessments offered by commercial test publishers to help raise test scores for NCLB. 'Everyone knows that formative assessment improves learning,' said one anonymous test maker, hence the rush to provide and advertise "formative assessment" products. But are these claims genuine? Dylan Wiliam (personal communication, 2005) has suggested that prevalent interim and benchmark assessments are better thought of as "early-warning summative" assessments rather than as true formative assessments. Commercial item banks may come closer to meeting the timing requirements for effective formative assessment, but they typically lack sufficient ties to curriculum and instruction to make it possible to provide feedback that leads to improvement. The misappropriation of the formative assessment label has become so pervasive that one assessment CEO invested in a series of essay-length ads in *Education Week* (Kahl, 2005a, 2005b, 2006a, 2006b, 2006c) to warn educators that what vendors are selling are not truly formative assessments.

Because of the widespread confusion in terminology, I begin this chapter with a definition of formative assessment and contrast it with formative program evaluation and with testing for remedial placement. I argue that benchmark and interim assessments are better suited for making instructional program decisions and gross remedial placement decisions rather than day-to-day, individual student adjustments in instruction. Although I do not have any individual authority to insist that the definition of formative assessment that I propose is the correct one, my argument is that the official definition of formative assessment should be the one that best fits the research base from which its claims of effectiveness are derived. One might think of this as a "truth in labeling" definition of test validity (Shepard, 1993). Following the discussion of definitions, I provide a brief overview of the research base for formative assessment focusing on those features that directly link to learning theory and thereby help to explain how formative assessment works to improve learning. Then I turn to a quite different research literature. While the effects of benchmark and interim assessments do not have a foundation in research, it is plausible that findings from the implementation of other external summative tests would generalize to this new application. Therefore, I review the teaching-the-test research as a lens for thinking about the possible effects of administering standardized tests more frequently.

In the concluding sections of the chapter, I offer criteria that help to clarify further the distinction between formative assessment and formative program evaluation. If met, these criteria also ensure that each type of formative inquiry is effective. Finally, I propose solutions for test makers interested in ensuring the integrity and efficacy of their products and for state and district policymakers interested in enhancing teachers' formative assessment skills.

Distinguishing Formative Assessment From Formative
Program Evaluation and Remedial Placement Tests

The terms *assessment* and *evaluation* are used interchangeably in
many contexts. Here, however, we want to distinguish the type of
formative assessment that helps students learn during the course of
instruction from other types of testing or data gathering. I find it
useful, therefore, to adopt the clear distinction made by the Office
of Economic Co-operation and Development (OECD) in a study of
formative assessment in eight countries: "For purposes of this study,
assessment refers to judgments of student performance, while evaluation refers to judgements of programme or organizational effectiveness" (OECD, 2005, p. 25).

Similarly, in a review of the formative assessment literature from
French-speaking countries, Allal and Lopez (2005) traced the history of formative assessment from Scriven's (1967) original definition of "formative evaluation" of educational programs, noting that
the term "assessment" had "progressively replaced 'evaluation' when
the object is student learning in the classroom" (p. 241).

Formative assessment is defined as assessment carried out during the instructional process for the purpose of improving teaching or learning (Shepard, Hammerness, Darling-Hammond, & Rust,
2005). Similarly, OECD authors (2005) said that "Formative assessment refers to frequent, interactive assessments of student progress
and understanding to identify learning needs and adjust teaching
appropriately" (p. 21). When Kahl (2005a) argued against misuse of
the term by test vendors, he emphasized that formative assessment
is a "midstream" tool that teachers use "to measure student grasp of
the specific topics and skills they are teaching" (p. 38). What makes
formative assessment *formative* is that it is immediately used to make
adjustments so as *to form* new learning. As Sadler (1989) explained
in his early contribution to the theory of formative assessment, feedback is a critical element, requiring that teachers (and ultimately students) have a clear vision of the skills to be learned, appraise current
student progress, and make clear to students how to improve.

Benchmark and interim assessments have been adopted by many
school districts to help monitor progress during the school year
toward meeting state standards and NCLB performance goals. Typically these assessments are formal, machine-scored instruments
administered at the end of every quarter, or sometimes as frequently

as once per month. They serve as formative program evaluation tools by providing teachers with information about which content standards have been mastered well and which will require additional instructional attention. In addition, benchmark and interim assessments may report the specific content standards mastered by each student, thereby identifying individual student strengths and weaknesses. The individual profile data from these assessments are not directly formative, however, for two reasons: the data available are at too gross a level of generality and feedback for improvement is not part of the process.

Benchmark and interim assessments function much more as remedial placement tests rather than as substantive formative assessments. For example, if a fourth grade student is low on the "number, operation, and quantitative reasoning" standard, a teacher would have to work with that student further and do additional assessment to find out whether this meant that the student was having problems with understanding place value, representing fractions, or understanding multiplication and division. For most teachers, scores on benchmark tests simply signal which students are most at risk and therefore require the most attention rather than indicating the specific learning area that is in need of improvement. Such focusing of effort may indeed be one of the primary purposes for using these assessments, but the scores do not provide substantive insights about how to intervene.

Because of the grossness of the information from reliable subtest scores, interim assessment results can only be used to make relatively gross, instructional program-level decisions. For example, if class results show a relative weakness on the math subtest Statistics and Probability and the teacher notices that many of the items on the test involved bar graphs using objects, bars, and tally marks, then the teacher might plan a review lesson on bar graphs. One might think that responses to individual test items would provide more insight for specific students, but the item-level information is unreliable and only loosely coupled with instructional lessons and units of study. This is what I call the "1,000 mini-lessons problem." Over the course of a year it would take a thousand mini-lessons to respond item by item and student by student to all the missed items on interim assessments. And resulting lessons would be incoherent and decontextualized for the students as well as impractical for the teacher. The truth is that teachers do not have time to go back and reteach lessons, after the fact, for all the topics missed on interim assessments, without jeopardizing the curriculum for the next months of the school year. In contrast, true formative assessment, which involves natural questioning and follow-up as teachers interact with students during the course of instruction, is both more targeted to specific student needs in the context of meaningful lessons and more time efficient because it occurs as a part of normal teaching.

Research Base for Formative Assessment

Formative assessment has an extensive research base that draws on both cognitive and motivational research. An early review provided by Crooks (1988) from the University of Otago in New Zealand, for example, was noteworthy because it brought together findings from the literatures in educational measurement, motivational psychology, learning theory (both behaviorist and cognitive), and research on teaching—literatures that at the time rarely acknowledged one another. The recommendations Crooks offered for educational practice already contained most of the important features of more comprehensive present-day research syntheses. For example, classroom assessments guide student judgments about what is important to learn and affect students' self-perceptions of competence. Greater learning occurs when assessments focus on deep learning rather than surface or memorization approaches to learning. Useful feedback is much more important for learning than is maximizing the reliability of summative evaluations. Cooperative learning contributes to students' active engagement and helps to develop valuable peer and self-assessment skills.

The landmark review by Black and Wiliam (1998) is the most widely cited reference on formative assessment and stands behind the common knowledge that "Everyone knows that formative assessment improves learning." Black and Wiliam examined 250 studies from research literatures addressing current classroom practices; student motivation and student participation in assessment practices; learning theory; specific classroom strategies such as discourse and questioning; and the properties of effective feedback. They concluded that formative assessment has a more profound effect on learning than do other typical educational interventions, producing effect sizes of between .4 and .7. Moreover, formative assessment practices tend to help low-achieving students more than they help high-achieving students. One way to think about this latter finding is that formative assessment helps to develop metacognitive skills and enhance motivation differentially for low-achieving students because high-achieving students already have these resources intuitively or through other supports.

Close examination of the research literature helps us identify the features of formative assessment, or causal mechanisms, that make it work to improve learning. For example, we know from cognitive research that having students become self-aware in monitoring their own learning, also referred to as *metacognition*, improves achievement. In the case of Palincsar and Brown's (1984) *reciprocal teaching*, for example, teaching reading comprehension strategies—such as thinking about the story and making predictions about what comes next—dramatically improved the reading proficiency of low-performing middle school students. Similarly in the formative assessment literature, teaching students to self-assess so they can internalize and use criteria as they carry out their work increases both the quality of student projects and conceptual understanding (White & Frederickson, 2000). Other bodies of work in the cognitive literature demonstrate the importance of engaging students' *prior knowledge* to support new learning and the effectiveness of focusing on principled understanding to enable *transfer* and knowledge generalization. Formative assessment processes connect directly to these learning strategies when they address Sadler's questions (Where are you now? and where do you want to go?). In addition, transfer is supported when a rich array of tasks is used both for assessment and for instruction (Shepard, 1997).

Understanding the cognitive and motivational theories underlying formative assessment is essential because these theories explain why formative assessment works when it works. Feedback is the most obvious feature of formative assessment and the one with the strongest research base (i.e., the largest number of studies). Surprisingly, however, feedback is not always or even usually successful. Kluger and DeNisi's (1996) meta-analysis cautions that in one third of studies feedback worsens performance, when evaluation focuses on the person rather than the task. In one third of comparisons there is no difference in outcomes with and without feedback. Only in the one third of studies where the feedback focused on substantive elements of the task, giving specific guidance about how to improve, did feedback consistently improve performance. Thus, merely telling students their score or proficiency category is not the type of feedback endorsed by the formative assessment literature.

Understanding the theoretical basis of formative assessment is also important because it provides coherence, thus helping to ensure that separate elements of effective practice make sense and work together. If we think of teachers as learners, then our goal should be a deeper and more coherent understanding of learning theory as a means to tie together not only formative assessment strategies but also to aid in seeing how formative assessment relates to discourse reforms in mathematics, comprehension strategies in reading, inquiry methods in science, and so forth. Although teachers and teacher education students often have little patience with theory, big-picture understandings are especially important when we are trying to change our teaching practices. Theory helps us think about what to do when we can't rely on past experience.

Findings from the research on motivation provide additional insights, especially regarding the relationship between classroom summative and formative assessments. Research on motivation might also have significant implications for the increased frequency of external testing. We know that extrinsically motivated students work toward "performance goals," i.e., to get good grades, please the teacher, and appear competent to others. In the literature this is termed a "performance orientation." Performance-oriented students pick easy tasks and are less likely to persist once they encounter difficulty. In contrast, intrinsically motivated students, or students with a learning orientation, work toward "learning goals," i.e., to feel an increasing sense of mastery and become competent (in contrast to appearing competent). Learning-oriented students are more engaged in schoolwork, use more self-regulation, and develop deeper understanding of subject matter. The most alarming finding from this literature is that students can learn to be extrinsically motivated, or to become extrinsically motivated in some contexts and not in others. Normative grading practices and extrinsic rewards produce performance-oriented students (Stipek, 1996). Obviously, not all mastery-oriented students will give up their love of learning because of a teacher's comparative grading practices, but the evidence is substantial that many students learn to focus on grades because grades have been used so pervasively as rewards to control behavior and direct student effort.

A goal in developing a formative assessment classroom culture is to counteract students' obsession with grades and to redirect interest and effort toward learning. Motivation research on self-efficacy and children's beliefs about ability also teaches us valuable lessons about how day-to-day uses of feedback and praise can shape children's confidence about their abilities as learners. Praising children for "being smart" when they perform well on tasks can have negative consequences for learning because such praise fosters students' implicit beliefs that intelligence and ability are fixed. In studies over the course of three decades, Carol Dweck (2002) has found that students who believe that intelligence is an unchangeable characteristic they were born with, what she calls an "entity" theory of self, are flummoxed by difficult problems and tend to avoid academic challenges. In contrast, students who have been taught that ability can be increased by effort, who hold an "incremental" theory of self, are more likely to seek academic challenges and to persist when faced with difficult problems. Feedback that focuses on a student's level of effort, evidence of alternative reasoning strategies used, and the specifics of work products fosters incremental beliefs about ability and results in more constructive behavior in the face of learning obstacles. Similar to Claude Steele's (Steele & Aronson, 1995) research on stereotype threat, Dweck and other attribution researchers find that female and minority students are more likely to hold entity theories of intelligence and to lack confidence in their ability to perform difficult tasks. Importantly, praise focused on effort and strategies can change children's adherence to "entity" beliefs, which in turn increases their resilience and learning.

Insights from the cognitive and motivation literatures can be drawn together in the more encompassing sociocultural theory of learning. According to this theory, children develop cognitive abilities through social interactions that let them try out language and practice their reasoning. Instead of being born with a fixed level of intelligence, children become "smart" through what Barbara Rogoff (1990) calls an "apprenticeship in thinking." In various learning contexts—talking at the dinner table, helping in the kitchen, doing math in classrooms—learners have both expert models and supports from adults or peers to enable them to participate in that activity. This process of providing support to help the learner attempt and then master increasingly complex tasks on their own is called *scaffolding*. When Ed Gordon talks about the idea of creating an environment or a culture where we support student learning and their ability to participate in demanding academic contexts, he is talking about this theory. Sociocultural theory folds together an understanding of how children learn and at the same time how they develop identities as capable learners. When implemented by master teachers, formative assessment practices further cognitive goals and at the same time draw students into participation in learning for its own sake.

Research on Teaching the Test

A well-known finding from the cognitive literature is that principled learning and transfer are aided when learning takes place across multiple contexts (Brown, Collins, & Duguid, 1989). In a sense, transfer is made possible when it is built into instructional routines, thereby allowing students to gain experience with tasks that look different (superficially) but that tap the same underlying principles. By contrast, to permit their frequent use at reasonable cost, benchmark and interim assessments are typically multiple-choice, machine-scoreable instruments and thus are quite limited in the knowledge representations they offer. There is reason, therefore, to be concerned that the increased frequency of standardized test administrations will narrow conceptions of subject matter and thereby harm student learning. A brief review of the literature on teaching the test helps to document how this narrowing works and what impacts it has.

After the first decade of high-stakes testing in the 1980s, the U.S. Congressional Office of Technology Assessment (1992) produced a report on *Testing in American Schools*, which concluded that test-driven reforms produce "test-score inflation" and "curriculum distortion." Test-score inflation is a useful term that reminds us that it is possible for test scores to go up without a commensurate increase in learning. Curriculum distortion occurs when teachers teach what is on the test and ignore other content. Recent declines in science test scores, for example, have been attributed to neglect of science because of increased pressure to raise test scores in reading and mathematics. Another, potentially more serious meaning of curriculum distortion is to distort even the way that reading and mathematics are taught, conceiving of knowledge in these subject areas only in the ways they are represented on the test. It is this type of fundamental curriculum distortion that explains how test-score inflation happens. Unhappily,

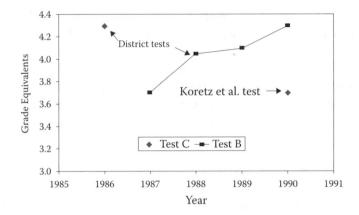

Figure 12.1 Performance on familiar and unfamiliar standardized tests with very similar content and format.

another significant finding from the teaching-the-test literature is that these negative impacts are greatest for poor and minority children because the poorer the school, the more time is devoted to instruction that imitates the test (Madaus, West, Harmon, Lomax, & Viator, 1992).

Figure 12.1 illustrates the phenomenon of test-score inflation. These data are from third graders in a very large urban district in a high-stakes testing environment. Prior to 1987, the district had been administering Test C, a well-known standardized achievement measure. In 1987 a new standardized test was adopted and scores dropped dramatically. The two standardized tests looked very much alike. Subtest names were nearly identical and items on both tests were all multiple-choice. Almost immediately after the first administration of the new tests, test scores went up and continued to rise until they reached the same high level of the previous test. In 1990, as an additional check, Koretz, Linn, Dunbar, and Shepard (1991) administered the old test to a random subsample of district third graders. Now that the old test had become unfamiliar to the current third graders, performance fell off dramatically. We believe that these comparisons illustrate the nongeneralizability of test-score gains in this high-stakes context. Students had become more proficient on the exact test formats, without the conceptual understanding that good test performance should signify.

This idea of being able to do well on a test without really understanding the concepts is difficult to grasp. Indeed, many educational

DIRECTIONS: Write the Arabic numerals for the following Roman numerals.

1. XXI   _____   4. DCLXXXIX _____

2. LXVIII   _____   5. DCCLIX   _____

3. XIV   _____   6. MCMLI   _____

DIRECTIONS: Write the Roman numerals for the following Arabic numerals.

1. 11   _____   4. 546   _____

2. 20   _____   5. 417   _____

3. 89   _____   6. 1608   _____

Figure 12.2 Examples of items used in both teaching materials and in testing materials in the study by Koczor (1984).

reformers believe that teaching the test might not be all bad: "At least they'll know what's on the test." The two sets of questions in Figure 12.2 are examples from a much larger set of items used in a study by Koczor (1984). Koczor's findings illustrate sharply how it is possible to look as if you understand Roman numerals without understanding them at all. In the Koczor study, students were randomly assigned to one of two conditions. One group learned and practiced translating Roman to Arabic numerals. The other group learned and practiced Arabic to Roman translations. At the end of the study each group was randomly subdivided again (now there were four groups). Half of the subjects in each original group got assessments in the same format as they had practiced. The other half got the reverse. Within each instructional group, the drop-off in performance, when participants got the assessment that was not what they had practiced, was dramatic. Moreover, the amount of drop-off depended on whether participants were low, middle, or high achieving. For low-achieving students, the loss was more than a standard deviation. Students who were drilled on one way of translation appeared to know the material, but only so long as they were not asked to translate in the other direction. Koczor's findings show clearly the harm of teaching content using only a narrow range of problem types.

In principle, multiple-choice test questions can be written to elicit higher-order cognitive processes. However, it is more difficult to write such items and even more difficult to have them survive pilot testing because high-inference items are often found to be ambiguous

Cats are fun animals to have as pets. Read the following passage and fill in the missing words.

Cats make great pets. They are soft and cuddly. They play with toys. Sometimes they get tired and need to rest. They ___{1}___. There are many kinds of cats. Cats have four legs.

Cats like to play outside. Dogs chase them. Cats have to climb trees to get away. They get ___{2}___.

{1} ○ bite   {2} ○ scared
     ○ sleep   ○ hurry
     ○ ski   ○ cold
     ○ close   ○ hungry

Note: These reading passages resemble a cloze technique but, in fact, are based on unnatural paragraphs. Instead of inference, they invite learning the strategy that the answer is nearly always in the sentence before.

Figure 12.3   An example constructed to imitate items on a "Formative Assessment" Web site.

by reviewers and examinees. These difficulties are multiplied a hundred-fold by the sheer quantity of test items being generated for item banks and high-frequency testing. For example, the prompt and questions in Figure 12.3 were written to imitate as closely as possible the type of items displayed on a current "formative assessment" Web site. Although these reading passages resemble sophisticated cloze techniques, in fact, they are based on unnatural paragraphs. Instead of emphasizing comprehension of the overall meaning of the passage, repeated use of the same format invites students to learn the strategy that the answer is nearly always in the sentence before the blank. Given the large volume of items currently being generated by test publishers, it is not surprising that interim tests are disproportionately low-level, fact-type questions. Use of such questions increases the likelihood that students will correspondingly adjust their learning strategies to conform to what the tests tell them are the goals for learning.

The motivation literature cited previously also warns us that teaching to the test is likely to have negative motivational consequences as well as negative cognitive outcomes. The Fall Conference Sheet and Student "Self-Assessment" in Figure 12.4 illustrates how well-intentioned efforts to raise test scores can, perversely, lead to a performance orientation and to an emphasis on evaluation, which we know reduces students' intrinsic motivation and interest in material

Fall Conference Sheet and Self-Assessment

Student Name:_____   Date:_____

Math

My fall RIT score is _____.

In the spring, my target goal will be _____.

Here is how I rate myself.

1. Paying attention in class   excellent/good/okay/need to improve
2. Effort on homework   excellent/good/okay/need to improve
3. Effort on tests   excellent/good/okay/need to improve
4. Class participation   excellent/good/okay/need to improve
5. Behavior   excellent/good/okay/need to improve
6. Attendance   excellent/good/okay/need to improve

Figure 12.4   A recent example of materials used to motivate students to raise their test scores.

for its own sake (Stipek, 1996). The claim of self-assessment in this example is thus a distortion of key principles from the research on self-assessment, because the rating form does not engage students in thinking about the substantive features of their work. Indeed the only inference that could be drawn from the rating task about how to improve would be to try harder (good advice if you were not making much effort before, but frustratingly unhelpful if you were already trying hard). Learning that the purpose of learning is to perform on examinations exacerbates what Lave and Wenger (1991) pointed to as the commoditization of learning, which often occurs in school when knowledge and skills to be learned are entirely removed from any context of use. When this is the case, students have no compelling reason to participate except to produce for the test.

There are no definitive studies demonstrating either the harm or the benefit of benchmark or interim assessments. The widespread use of these instruments is too new to have been studied systematically. Indeed, these instruments are for the most part being sold without even the minimum validity evidence required for standardized tests (American Educational Research Association, American Psychological Association, & National Council on Measurement in Education, 1999). It is not unreasonable, however, to generalize from the findings from research on high-stakes accountability tests, noting in particular that negative impacts on learning will be greatest when assessments based on limited item formats are administered at frequent intervals.

Criteria for Effective Interim Assessments and Formative Assessment

Knowing What Students Know (Pellegrino, Chudowsky, & Glaser), the landmark report on assessment issued by a National Research Council committee in 2001, called for "balanced assessment systems" to redress the balance of resources between classroom and external forms of assessment. Key features recommended for a balanced assessment system were comprehensiveness, coherence, and continuity. *Comprehensiveness* refers to the need for multiple sources of evidence to draw inferences about an individual student's proficiency. The property of *coherence* refers to the need for a shared model of learning linking curriculum, instruction, and assessment within the classroom and also linking classroom assessments and external, large-scale assessments. *Continuity* extends the underlying model of learning to allow for a longitudinal assessment of learning progress over time. As recently as 2001, in *Knowing What Students Know,* there was no mention of interim assessments as necessary components of a balanced assessment system.

Recently, at the 2006 Council of Chief State School Officers Large-Scale Assessment Conference, for example, a new use of the term "comprehensive assessment system" has been adopted to try to bring coherence to a landscape that now includes three levels of assessments: state accountability tests, district interim tests, and classroom formative and summative assessments. Superintendents, school board members, and other policy leaders at the state and local level should be cautioned that interim assessments are not essential to an effective assessment system and, as stated previously, they lack a research base. Benchmark and interim assessments are an invention of the testing industry that has been welcomed by policy makers as a way to "do something" immediately in response to NCLB. The decision to invest in interim assessments should be weighed against other potentially more effective uses of the same resources.

If the decision is made to purchase benchmark or interim assessments, then meeting the criteria detailed below will help to increase the likelihood that interim tests will provide useful information and avoid negative side effects for students. Criteria are also offered for effective formative assessment in classrooms. Comparing the two sets of criteria, as illustrated in Table 12.1, shows how the two types of assessment can be coherent while at the same time emphasizing what each should do uniquely.

TABLE 12.1 Criteria for Effective Interim Assessments and Formative Assessment

Criteria for Effective Interim Assessments	Criteria for Effective Formative Assessment
• More than simplistic alignment, they must "embody" learning goals.	• More than simplistic alignment, tasks must "embody" learning goals.
• They should be timed to be instructionally linked.	• It should be curriculum-embedded (both in timing and substance). Tasks should be instructional tasks to provide insights about learning as it is occurring.
• They should meet a cost/benefit test, i.e., instructional insights must be greater than instructional time lost and negative side effects. (At a minimum they must yield new insights beyond NCLB accountability test.)	• By definition, it must enable the supportive learning processes invoked in the formative assessment literature.
• Instructional insights should lead to coherent, theoretically sound improvements in teaching.	• Instructional insights should lead to coherent, theoretically sound improvements in teaching.

Assessments Must Embody Learning Goals

The first criterion, desired of both interim assessments and day-to-day formative assessment, is that they "embody learning goals" and fully represent what it is that we want students to master. The term *authentic assessment* is often used to convey this idea that students be engaged in demonstrating their skills and "know-how" in the context of realistic tasks that reflect the "core challenges of the field of study, not the easily scored" (Wiggins, 1998, p. 23). In classrooms, formative assessment can readily be done in the context of mathematics problems, history papers, and science experiments, focusing on the key concepts and competencies that are the aims of a given instructional unit. Interim tests could similarly present mastery tasks calling on students to apply the knowledge and skills developed during a quarter or semester's time and would therefore be coherent with the preceding instruction and with classroom assessment. For example, the Center for Research on Evaluation, Standards, and Student Testing is developing POWERSOURCE assessments to tap powerful principles, such as representation, equivalence, and transformation that underlie mathematical understanding across problem types (Niemi, Vallone, & Vendlinski, 2006).

By contrast, typical interim tests being sold today do not provide rich conceptual tasks, primarily because of the cost of scoring more open-ended problem types. The cost of developing and field testing more challenging items is also a limiting factor. Choosing an interim test that is "aligned" with a district's curriculum should ensure adequate content coverage. Unfortunately, the meaning of the term *alignment* has been debased so that items on the test can be mapped to the list of content standards, but they do not necessarily reflect the full range of cognitive competencies implied by the standards. Districts and teachers are advised to conduct their own evaluations of interim tests and item pools to determine whether test content goes beyond rote-level knowledge and formulaic problem types.

Assessments Should Be Timed to Be Instructionally Linked or Instructionally Embedded

As noted earlier, timing is one of the key dimensions on which formative program evaluation instruments and formative assessments differ. To be formative, assessment insights must be used immediately as part of the instructional process. For example, a teacher sees that several students are confused and intervenes immediately, or a student receives feedback in a writing conference and works to rewrite his essay accordingly. Formative assessment is effective, then, when it is timed so that the information can be used. Comments on a term paper, for example, are not formative if students do not have the opportunity to use feedback to improve the particular piece of work or a subsequent assignment.

Interim assessments are not a part of on-going instruction but they can be effective as program evaluation tools if they are instructionally linked. In other words, the objectives tested should match those taught in the preceding weeks and months. Although this may seem obvious, some interim tests are merely parallel forms of the end-of-year accountability test, and cover the same content whether they are administered in October or January. Repeat administrations of the end-of-year test is the least effective and most incoherent form of interim testing because it means that students are being tested on content that has not yet been taught. Benchmark or interim tests are more effective if they are substantively linked to instructional units and timed to be an external summative check on student mastery of a particular unit of study. This criterion is a reasonable *Consumer Reports* type of requirement for this new type of test product, but just like the switch from maximum horsepower to energy efficiency for automobiles, the desire for better instructional links will require some retooling by the industry.

Assessments Must Satisfy Their Respective Definitions by Providing Program Insights or Supporting Learning Processes

By definition, program evaluation tools and formative assessments have different purposes and their effectiveness can be judged by how well they accomplish those respective purposes. Given the extensive amount of testing that takes place in schools today, it is reasonable to require that new benchmark and interim assessments meet a cost/benefit test, i.e., the program evaluation insights gained about objectives that need to be retaught, for example, should be greater than the instructional time lost and other potential negative side effects. At a minimum, interim tests must yield new insights beyond what has been learned from the state assessment administered as part of NCLB. It is surprising that in many districts currently adopting interim assessment instruments there has not been a systematic effort to first learn as much as possible from state assessment results at the individual student level or by content strand. Similarly, formative assessments are to be judged by how well they accomplish their intended purpose and work to enhance student learning. Claims from the research literature can be used to evaluate whether formative assessment practices are working as intended. For example, is feedback provided that helps students to see how to improve performance over time? Is self-assessment used as a means to support internalization of criteria and personal ownership of the learning process?

Assessments Should Produce Coherent Improvements in Teaching and Learning

Ultimately the effectiveness of both program evaluation tools and formative assessment will be determined by how well they guide efforts to improve teaching. Knowing that a student performs poorly on an interim test is hardly a new insight because teachers almost always know who their low-performing students are. For an interim test to be effective, it has to provide new information that is coherent and can feasibly be acted upon by the teacher. Most significantly, it must avoid the 1,000-mini-lessons problem. Many publishers produce a class roster for teachers showing objectives mastered; and their advertisements display deceptively simple examples where only one or two students have significant gaps or the class as a whole missed only one or two objectives. For many teachers, however, these grids are actually a checkerboard of checks and zeros, and even veteran teachers may find it difficult to plan engaging lessons that will address multiple objectives. They may be tempted, instead, to gather groups of students for drill on the items missed. As suggested by both the embodiment and timing criteria above, interim assessments are likely to be the most effective as formative evaluation tools, if they are tied in a coherent way (aligned in the original sense of the term) to the district curriculum. Then using the curriculum as a guide, teachers can use interim test results formatively to see which parts of the curriculum are not working or which subgroup of students needs special help to catch up.

Because formative assessments are embedded in instruction, they should more naturally lead to coherent, theoretically sound improvements in teaching. Unlike more formal assessments intended to produce a score, formative assessment, grounded in specific instructional activities, provides much more detail as well as *qualitative* insights about student understandings and misconceptions. For example, a typical interim assessment might report that a student had or had not mastered the following algebra objective.

> Develop an understanding of function. Translate among verbal, tabular, graphic, and algebraic representations of functions. Identify relations and functions as linear or nonlinear. Find, identify, and interpret the slope (rate of change) and intercepts of a linear relation. Interpret and compare properties of linear functions from tables, graphs, or equations.

By contrast, formative assessment in an algebra class might occur as students are working in groups to solve problems. In conversation with one student, the teacher notes that the student is thinking about the steepness of a line in terms of its angle above the x-axis, but she is not thinking about the change in y related to the change in x. The student can also give a memorized definition of slope, but has not learned what it means until the teacher asks her to show on the graph how change in y and change in x relate to the steepness of the slope. Then to make sure the student is understanding, the teacher asks a follow-up question, "So what would the change in x need to be, in order to make the slope flatter?"

Conclusion: Potential Solutions for Test Publishers and for States and School Districts

Although formative assessment and interim assessments could peacefully coexist with each serving its respective purpose, in the current NCLB context, the risk is great that interim assessments will prevent implementation of real formative assessment. Interim assessments are easier to install than classroom-based formative assessment practices. More significantly, when labeled as formative assessment, purchasing interim assessment data systems diverts attention and resources that might otherwise be directed toward professional development needed to implement formative assessment reforms.

Ideally, testing companies would stop using the term "formative assessment" to market interim and benchmark tests. Occasionally in the past, when confronted by ethical rather than technical challenges, test publishers have taken very public ethical stands. For example, when Mehrens and Kaminski (1989) showed that using test preparation materials such as *Scoring High* was tantamount to practicing on a parallel form of the actual test, the parent company for test-maker CTB/McGraw-Hill divested its ownership of *Scoring High*. Gregory Anrig, president of ETS, refused to sell the National Teacher Examination (NTE) to states or school boards that used the test inappropriately to determine the futures of practicing teachers (Owen, 1984). Benchmark and interim assessments are immensely popular with local school boards because, in theory, they provide an early indication of what test results will be at the end of the year in time for teachers and students to do something about them. It is unlikely that this enthusiasm would abate if test publishers stopped using the term *formative assessment,* but truth in advertising would improve. Publishers can get equal mileage from concepts such as data-driven decision making or program evaluation, without falsely promising results (Black & Wiliam, 1998).

In the midst of the flurry of assessment activity related to NCLB, states and districts want to know how best to help teachers target and improve instruction. The choice between investing in interim data systems or formative assessment is not a 50/50 proposition, whether to buy product A or buy product B. This asymmetry, in fact, makes it particularly difficult to further the use of real formative assessment. On the one hand, purchasing an interim assessment system is relatively straightforward. A school board agrees to the cost of the product plus the additional costs for technical support and for a limited amount of teacher professional development. In contrast, because real formative assessment is so entwined with instruction and pedagogical processes, much more sustained professional development and support are needed to help teachers make more fundamental—and more effective—changes in their teaching practices. In more recent work, based on their famous review, Black and Wiliam (2004) and Black, Harrison, Lee, Marshall, and Wiliam (2003) have demonstrated directly the positive impact of using formative assessment as an instructional intervention, with an average gain in achievement across classrooms of .32 standard deviations (equivalent to an extra half grade level of growth). In contrast, as noted earlier, research on the impact of interim assessments on student achievement is not yet available.

Black and Wiliam's (2004) teacher professional development focuses on specific formative assessment strategies: questioning, feedback, sharing criteria, and student self-assessment, all of which lead to significant changes in teaching repertoires and in subsequent student learning. States and districts may not have considered investing in professional development to introduce teachers to formative assessment because they are already heavily vested in teacher professional development that is focused on implementation of new, standards-based literacy, mathematics, or science curricula. Rather than imagining that learning about formative assessment would need to be a new, entirely separate initiative, states and districts might consider building formative assessment ideas and processes into their subject-specific professional development offerings. In this way, both the theory of the reforms and the specific instructional strategies would be more coherently tied together for teachers attempting to try out these reforms for the first time. Literacy, mathematics, and science curriculum experts in each state are often deeply knowledgeable about formative assessment strategies that are uniquely tailored to the pedagogical demands of their respective disciplines. Running records, author's chair, and conferencing are all examples of formative assessment strategies specific to literacy instruction. In mathematics, showing your solution on a white board or coming to the overhead to explain your reasoning are assessment strategies that also fit with the reform goal of developing student abilities to communicate mathematically.

To date, districts have had the lion's share of responsibility for purchasing interim assessment data systems, and occasionally for investing in subject-specific curricular reforms with formative assessment components. This makes sense because both interim and formative assessment reforms should be implemented at the organizational level that has curricular authority. Not only can districts choose the most effective interim assessment system and formative assessment reform using the criteria developed in this chapter, they can also engage in the follow-on strategies that ensure maximum effectiveness. For example, consider the effectiveness criteria in Table 12.1 requiring that interim assessments should be "timed to be instructionally linked" and that formative assessment should be "curriculum-embedded (both in timing and substance)." In addition to picking an interim assessment product that has the capacity to be tailored to specific instructional units, districts can also foster instructional linkage and effective use of interim assessment results by convening professional development workshops focused on what to do in response to specific patterns of results. Because districts have control over curriculum, they can also support the curriculum-embedded power of formative assessment either by picking rich curricular materials in the first place or by providing rich conceptual tasks to supplement more procedurally oriented traditional textbooks.

States also have a key role to play by providing leadership to help local school boards and educators understand what is at stake in choosing among myriad assessment products all promising to boost student test scores. The argument about whether benchmark and interim assessments can legitimately be called formative assessment is more than a debate among pointy-headed academicians. Understanding the difference is essential for understanding what each type of assessment can do, for investing in either type, and for making effective use of assessment results and practices once the investment has been made.

The research on formative assessment is compelling and shows us explicitly how formative assessment works to improve learning—by helping students internalize the features of good work, showing them specifically how to improve, developing habits of thinking and a sense of competency, and so forth. An understanding of how these formative assessment processes are tied to standards-based reform in each of the disciplines makes it possible to coordinate and integrate reform efforts so that they need not be assembled as a laundry list of new approaches. Benchmark and interim assessments can also be very helpful to teachers as program evaluation tools and as a means to identify students who need special help, but professional development may be needed to avoid interpreting the results to mean reteach everything. States should also be alert to the ways that interim and benchmark systems may exacerbate the problems of teaching the test. The literature on test-score inflation has taught us not to celebrate dramatic test score gains until their credibility has been assured by demonstrations of student competencies beyond overly practiced, multiple-choice formats.

Acknowledgment

I wish to thank Sara Y. Bryant for her assistance in collecting examples of products advertised as formative assessments, for constructing the sample item in Figure 12.3, and for thoughtful comments in response to earlier versions of the paper.

References

Allal, L., & Lopez, L. M. (2005). Formative assessment of learning: A review of publications in French. In Office of Economic Co-operation and Development, *Formative assessment: Improving learning in secondary classrooms*. Paris: OECD Publishing.

American Educational Research Association, American Psychological Association, & National Council on Measurement in Education. (1999). *Standards for educational and psychological testing.* Washington, DC: American Educational Research Association.

Black, P., Harrison, C., Lee, C., Marshall, B., & Wiliam, D. (2003). *Assessment for learning: Putting it into practice.* Maidenhead, Berkshire, UK: Open University Press.

Black, P., & Wiliam, D. (1998). Assessment and classroom living. *Assessment in Education: Principles, Policy, and Practice, 5*(1), 7-74.

Black, P., & Wiliam, D. (2004). The formative purpose: Assessment must first promote learning. In M. Wilson (Ed.), *Towards coherence between classroom assessment and accountability: 103rd yearbook of the National Society for the Study of Education*, Part II (pp. 20-50). Chicago: University of Chicago Press.

Brown, J. S., Collins, A., & Duguid, P. (1989). Situated cognition and the culture of learning. *Educational Researcher, 18*(1), 32-42.

Cowie, B., & Bell, B. (1999). A model of formative assessment in science education. *Assessment in Education, 6*(1), 101-116.

Crooks, T. J. (1988). The impact of classroom evaluation practices on students. *Review of Educational Research, 58*(4), 438-481.

Dweck, C. S. (2002). Messages that motivate: How praise molds students' beliefs, motivation, and performance (in surprising ways). In J. Aronson (Ed.), *Improving academic achievement: Classic and contemporary lessons from psychology.* New York: Academic Press.

Kahl, S. (2005a, October 26). Where in the world are formative tests? Right under your nose! *Education Week, 25*(9), 38.

Kahl, S. (2005b, November 30). Coming to terms with assessment. *Education Week, 25*(13), 26.

Kahl, S. (2006a, January 25). Helping teachers make the connection between assessment and instruction. *Education Week, 25*(30), 27.

Kahl, S. (2006b, February 22). Beware of quick-fix tests and prescriptions. *Education Week, 25*(24), 31.

Kahl, S. (2006c, April 26). Self-directed learning *plus* formative assessment *equals* individualized instruction. *Education Week, 25*(33), 29.

Kluger, A. N., & DeNisi, A. (1996). The effect of feedback interventions on performance: A historical review, a meta-analysis, and a preliminary feedback intervention theory. *Psychological Bulletin, 119*, 254-284.

Koczor, M.L. (1984). *Effects of varying degrees of instructional alignment in posttreatment tests on mastery learning tasks of fourth grade children.* Unpublished doctoral dissertation, University of San Francisco, California.

Koretz, D., Linn, R. L., Dunbar, S. B., & Shepard, L. A. (1991, April). *The effects of high-stakes test: Preliminary evidence about generalization across tests.* Presented at the annual meeting of the American Educational Research Association and the National Council on Measurement in Education, Chicago.

Lave, J., & Wenger, E. (1991). *Situated learning: Legitimate peripheral participation.* Cambridge, UK: Cambridge University Press.

Madaus, G. F., West, M. M., Harmon, M. C., Lomax, R. G., & Viator, K. A. (1992). *The influence of testing on teaching math and science in Grades 4-12: Executive summary.* Chestnut Hill, MA: Center for the Study of Testing, Evaluation, and Educational Policy, Boston College.

Mehrens, W. A., & Kaminski, J. (1989). Methods for improving standardized test scores: Fruitful, fruitless, or fraudulent? *Educational Measurement: Issues and Practice, 8*(1), 14-22.

Niemi, D., Vallone, J., & Vendlinski, T. (2006). The power of big ideas in mathematics education: Development and pilot testing of POWER-SOURCE assessments (CSE Report 697). Los Angeles: National Center for Research on Evaluation, Standards, and Student Testing.

Office of Economic Co-operation and Development. (2005). *Formative assessment: Improving learning in secondary classrooms*. Paris: OECD Publishing.

Owen, D. (1984). Testing teachers. *APF Reporter, 7*(3), 1-5.

Palincsar, A. S., & Brown, A. L. (1984). Reciprocal teaching of comprehension-fostering and comprehension-monitoring activities. *Cognition and Instruction, 1*(2), 117-175.

Pellegrino, J. W., Chudowsky, N., & Glaser, R. (Eds). (2001). *Knowing what students know: The science and design of educational assessment*. Washington, DC: National Academy Press.

Rogoff, B. (1990). *Apprenticeship in thinking: Cognitive development in social context*. New York: Oxford University Press.

Sadler, R. (1989). Formative assessment and the design of instructional assessments. *Instructional Science, 18*, 119-144.

Scriven, M. (1967). The methodology of evaluation. *AERA Monograph Series on Evaluation, 1*, 39-83.

Shepard, L. A. (1993). Evaluating test validity. In L. Darling-Hammond (Ed.), *Review of research in education* (Vol. 19, pp. 405-450). Washington, DC: American Educational Research Association.

Shepard, L. A. (1997). *Measuring achievement: What does it mean to test for robust understanding?* William H. Angoff Memorial Lecture Series. Princeton, NJ: Educational Testing Service.

Shepard, L. A. (2000). The role of assessment in a learning culture. *Educational Researcher, 29*(7), 4-14.

Shepard, L., Hammerness, K., Darling-Hammond, L., Rust, F. (2005). Assessment. In L. Darling-Hammond & J. Bransford (Eds.), *Preparing teachers for a changing world: What teachers should learn and be able to do* (pp. 275-326). San Francisco: Jossey-Bass.

Steele, C. M., & Aronson, J. (1995). Stereotype threat and the intellectual test performance of African Americans. *Journal of Personality and Social Psychology, 69*(5), 797-811.

Stiggins, R. J. (2002). Assessment crisis: The absence of assessment FOR learning. *Phi Delta Kappan, 83*, 758-765.

Stipek, D. J. (1996). Motivation and instruction. In D. C. Berliner & R. C. Calfee (Eds.), *Handbook of Educational Psychology* (pp. 85-113). New York: Simon & Schuster Macmillan.

U.S. Congress, Office of Technology Assessment. (1992). *Testing in American schools: Asking the right questions* (OTA-SET-519). Washington, DC: U.S. Government Printing Office.

White, B. Y., & Frederiksen, J. R. (2000). Metacognitive facilitation: An approach to making scientific inquiry accessible to all. In J. Minstrell & E. van Zee (Eds.), *Inquiring into inquiry learning and teaching in science* (pp. 33-370). Washington, DC: American Association for the Advancement of Science.

Wiggins, G. (1998). *Educative assessment: Designing assessments to inform and improve student performance.* San Francisco: Jossey-Bass.

13

Improving Achievement and Closing Gaps Between Groups:
The Role of Assessment in Helping Us Move Further, Faster

Kati Haycock
The Education Trust

The portraits painted by certain researchers can be compelling: fabulous teachers, doing fabulous classroom assessment, thwarted by evil NCLB[1]-required tests, and fleeing the profession in response. Perhaps I live in some alternate universe, but that is not what I see and not what data tell me. Not only do survey data from teachers point to higher job satisfaction today than at any time during the last decade, but teachers' leaving rates are about the same as they have been in the last decade. Furthermore, teaching is still among the most stable of all professions—perhaps more stable than it should be, given teaching's rate of pay, working conditions, and general level of prestige.

But whether we are looking at data or spending time in classrooms in schools around the country, I don't see the dismal picture of NCLB impact that some others apparently see. On a recent Saturday, for example, I spent some time with Jason Kamras, the 2005 National Teacher of the Year. The two of us spend most of our time traveling, talking with teachers and principals and superintendents all around the country. Jason said, "You know, my teacher audiences don't often like to hear this, but from what I see, this law has made a huge positive difference for poor kids and kids of color." He said, "Every single day, for example, I'm coming across school principals who tell me, 'You know, I used to not care much about who taught those Special Ed kids, but I have to care today, and I've moved some of my strongest teachers into teaching those kids.'" And he said, "I hear teachers tell me, 'You know, I didn't used to care much about the kids who were struggling in my classroom, but let me show you what I'm doing now to provide them with the extra instruction that they need.'" Frankly, I see much the same thing as Jason did.

As I will make clear a little later on, I don't want to give the impression that I am so naïve as to suggest that more focus on students necessarily leads to good educational practice. I believe that there are worrisome signs that, at least in some cases, such a focus can yield bad practice. And I do want to make clear that I agree very much with Jim Popham when he argued that we must soon—not a long time from now—work toward better assessments that are more instructionally sensitive. But let me start with a reminder of the basic reason for doing all this. I want to put students right back at the front of this conversation.

In the mid-1960s, there was a very strong message to educators across this country that they needed to take poor children and children of color more seriously. Some of that was, of course, related to the *Brown v. Board of Education* decision. Some of that message was implicit in the creation of Title I. Some of it was about other anti-poverty programs. But the important point is that, for the first time, there was a very clear message sent to schools that we needed to do better by these students.

Over the next decade, tests signaled to us that some combination of things that were going on was yielding some progress for poor and minority children. In the 1970s and early 1980s, there were real gains in achievement among low income children and children of color. On the National Assessment of Educational Progress (NAEP), for example, reading was improving among low-income and minority 17-year-olds. Mathematic skills were improving among eighth graders. In fact, no matter what subject matter and grade combination you consider during this era, there are very strong improvements in the achievement for both poor children and children of color. During the 1970s and 1980s, achievement gaps between black and white students nationally were cut in half. The gap between white and Latino students declined by about one third.

There were, of course, improvements not only on NAEP, but other indicators of student attainment as well. And in those years, the reports of those increases in performance among minority students were trumpeted from every rooftop in the country. Looking at SAT

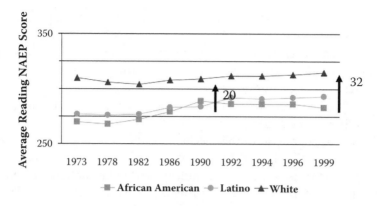

Figure 13.1   NAEP mathematic scores, 17-year-olds, 1973–1999. Source: National Center for Educational Statistics, 2000a, p. 108.

results, NAEP results, state test results, or other indicators, governors, educators, and others clearly agreed that things were getting better.

Unfortunately, much of that progress came to a halt between 1988 and 1990. Since that time, achievement gaps actually started widening again.

As indicated in Figure 13.1, in NAEP 12th grade mathematics, the gap between African American and white students, and between Latino and white had shrunk to 20 points by 1990. But by 1999 this gap had widened again by about 50%. The same patterns can be observed in the NAEP 12th grade reading results (Figure 13.2). The black/white gap had narrowed to about 21 points by 1988; but, again, by 1999 this gap had widened by about 50%.

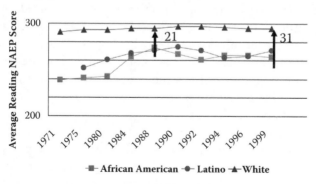

Figure 13.2   NAEP reading, 17-year-olds, 1971–1999. Source: National Center for Educational Statistics, 2000a, p. 108.

At first nobody really seemed to notice that we had stopped making progress. One reason for that, of course, is because while education leaders were trumpeting the earlier progress, nobody was trumpeting the current stagnation. Eventually, however, it became quite clear that the upward trajectory we had been on in the 1970s and 1980s was over, and that we were no longer making progress in delivering on the American promise.

Tests, of course, were the mechanism that signaled that lack of progress and that brought us to attention. Indeed it was concern about the results of both state and, in particular, national assessments that led in 1994 to the Improving America's Schools Act. This act sought to refocus attention on closing gaps between groups, but left much of the decision making to states. Unfortunately, most states didn't step up to their new responsibilities, so the new law—NCLB—took some of that state flexibility away.

The signaling function of assessment is hugely important, both for educators and the public, in reminding us who needs more attention. Let's start with grade 4 reading. I doubt that there is anyone who doesn't believe it is really important to get students off to a strong start in reading. If they reach the end of grade 4 without having mastered the fundamentals of reading, the rest of their education is certainly going to be a struggle. When you look at national data, however, you see immediately that there is a very serious problem in this respect. Although there have been many technical concerns through the years about the precise nature of NAEP's Proficient, Advanced, and Basic levels, few would argue the students *below* the Basic level are in good shape. NAEP data show that almost 4 in 10 of our fourth graders are trapped at the end of fourth grade without having mastered the basics of reading (Figure 13.3). But the numbers are much worse for minority and low-income students.

Figures 13.4 and 13.5 show that, compared with white students, nearly twice as many black, Latino, and Native American students were performing below the Basic level, as were Poor students compared to Not Poor students.

Let me turn now to eighth grade mathematics. Again, I don't believe that there is anyone who would argue with the proposition that if students hit the end of grade 8 without having mastered at least the basics in mathematics, the rest of that math sequence in high school is going to be torture. But what do NAEP data show us? One in three of our eighth graders is still trapped below the Basic

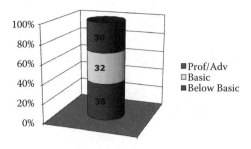

Figure 13.3 NAEP fourth grade reading levels for all students, 2003. Source: National Center for Educational Statistics, 2000b.

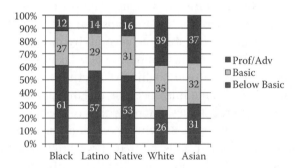

Figure 13.4 NAEP fourth grade reading, 2003, by race, ethnicity. Source: National Center for Educational Statistics, 2000b.

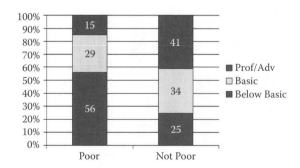

Figure 13.5 NAEP fourth grade reading, 2003, by family income. Source: National Center for Educational Statistics, 2000b.

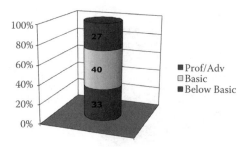

Figure 13.6 NAEP eighth grade mathematics, 2003. Source: National Center for Educational Statistics, 2000b.

level (Figure 13.6), and, again, black, Latino, Native American, and poor students are two to three times as likely to be below the Basic level as are white and Not Poor students (Figures 13.7 and 13.8).

Most of us are well aware that the gaps that you see in the NAEP data actually begin before students even arrive at the schoolhouse door. Every single year in this country, a significant number of students arrive at school already behind. Sometimes they are behind because of poverty, sometimes because of language issues, sometimes because of family issues. But regardless of the reason, a significant number of students are arriving at our doors seriously behind.

Common sense alone tells us that if we only give these students who arrive with less an education that is of exactly the same quality and duration that other students get, the chances are that they will leave school behind as well. That is, if they come in behind, and get a treatment of the same kind as everyone else, they will leave behind as well. What is important for all of us to

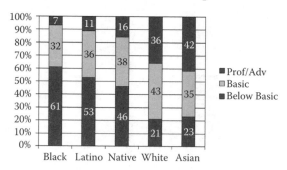

Figure 13.7 NAEP eighth grade mathematics, 2003, by race, ethnicity. Source: National Center for Educational Statistics, 2000b.

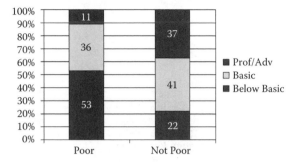

Figure 13.8 NAEP eighth grade mathematics, 2003, by family income. Source: National Center for Educational Statistics, 2000b.

acknowledge, however, is *we don't even do that*. We have basically organized the American educational system to take students who come to us with less and give them less in school. In fact, we give these students less of all the things that both research and experience tell us make a difference.

Some of those inequities are, of course, a function of choices that policy makers make, including the choice that most state legislatures have made to actually spend less on schools serving poor students than they do on schools serving other students. It is equally important, however, for us to acknowledge that some of those inequities flow not from the choices that policy makers make, but from the choices that we as educators make. These include the choices we make about what to expect of whom, what to teach to whom, and perhaps the most devastating choice of all—the choice of who teaches whom. As a result of the inequities that flow from the choices of policy makers and educators, the students who are entering our schools somewhat behind are actually leaving us much more behind. In other words, the gaps that separate different groups of students grow wider and wider, the longer they remain with us in school.

Figure 13.9 shows what this situation looks like at the end of high school. This figure shows the full distribution of mathematics achievement. The students described here are white eighth graders and African American and Latino 12th graders. As you can see, their attainments are identical. This tells us, quite simply, that Latino and African American students at the end of high school have skills in mathematics that are indistinguishable from those of white youngsters at the end of middle school.

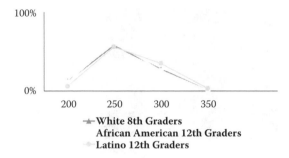

Figure 13.9   African American and Latino 17-year-olds compared with white 13-year-olds on NAEP mathematics. Source: National Center for Educational Statistics, 2000b.

And unfortunately, as you can see in Figure 13.10, which also compares white eighth graders to African American and Latino 12th graders, the same thing is true in reading. In reading and mathematics, the two core skills fundamental for accessing any other kind of learning, this is where we are now in the country as a whole. These gaps have enormous significance to the students themselves in terms of what they are prepared to do when they leave school. These gaps also have enormous significance to a community, to a state, or in fact to a country that is home to differences among groups of that magnitude. If, as people so often say, schools are what create our community and our country's future, we must ask ourselves what kind of future we are creating.

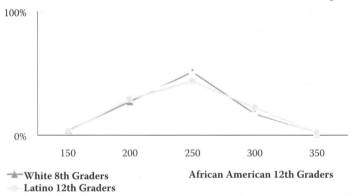

Figure 13.10   African American and Latino 17-year-olds compared with white 13-year-olds on NAEP reading. Source: National Center for Educational Statistics, 2000b.

Rather than acknowledging our part in this tragedy, most educators today, when shown the national achievement gaps in math and reading, have exactly the same answer about why those gaps exist. The children are poor, their parents don't care, they come to school without an adequate breakfast, they don't have enough books in their homes, they don't have a quiet place to study in the home, they live in difficult neighborhoods. This whole list of reasons is always and only about the children and their families. My question in reply is a very simple one: If you're right, that things like poverty and difficult home circumstances make low achievement inevitable, how then can it be that very poor children and children of color are performing so high in some places? Let me provide some examples.

Central Elementary School in Kentucky is a school that serves rural white students. About 71% of its students are low income with most of them very low income. A few years ago this school was one of the lowest performing schools in all of Kentucky. Through a very focused effort led by its principal and teachers, however, this school is now one of the highest performing elementary schools in Kentucky, despite demographics that would make people project that it would be in the bottom 20% of Kentucky's schools. Central Elementary is not an isolated example. Consider Lapwai Elementary School in northern Idaho. Lapwai is a school that serves Native American students, most of whom are poor. Its teachers attended a meeting at which they heard Willard Daggett talk about the future, and they realized that they were not preparing Lapwai's kids for that future. Figure 13.11 shows enormous gains in mathematics and reading

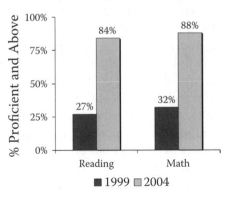

Figure 13.11   Grade 4 reading and mathematic gains at Lapwai Elementary School, 1999–2004. Source: Idaho Department of Education, 2004.

achievement at grade 4 over a 5-year period. These results are not just better than other Native American schools in this state, but well above the state average for all students.

Next, consider Centennial Elementary School in Atlanta, Georgia. This school is 92% African American. About two thirds of its students are low income. It is a neighborhood elementary school. Again, however, despite demographics that would make many people predict that it would probably be in the bottom 10% of Georgia's schools, it is in the top 2% of all Georgia elementary schools in reading and the top 7% in mathematics. In Elmont Memorial Junior-Senior High School in New York, the students are 75% African American and 12% Latino. Again, despite demographics that would make many people guess this school would perform in perhaps the bottom third of schools in this state, this school performs near the top on the Regents Exams in both mathematics and English. And finally, University Park High School in Worcester, Massachusetts. University Park was formed through a joint effort of Clark University and the Worcester Public Schools. This school serves students in grades 7 to 12. Seventy percent are low income, 50% are English language learners, and most of the students arrive at the school at least two grade levels behind. Despite all that, in 2004 not a single 10th grader in the school failed to pass the Massachusetts High School Exit Exam on the first attempt. Perhaps more important, they didn't just squeak by: 87% passed an advanced or proficient level. This school is now the fifth-highest performing high school in all of Massachusetts, far outperforming even schools that serve vastly more affluent students.

In other words, there are schools around this country, as I suspect is well known, that teach us that demography does not have to be destiny, that these students can in fact achieve. There are some who view these schools as flukes, or as schools that exist on the sheer force of some principal's will. They suggest that, since this could "never" be done on a broader scale, there is nothing really to learn here.

I have tried hard to understand why people need to respond to success among poor and minority children in that way. In that process, I have come to believe that many in our profession walk around with a kind of regression line in their heads. Why? Because we learned in graduate school that the overwhelming determinant of what is learned in school is socioeconomic status. As the number of poor students or students of color in our schools goes up, we believe that achievement will go down, and that there's nothing we can do about it.

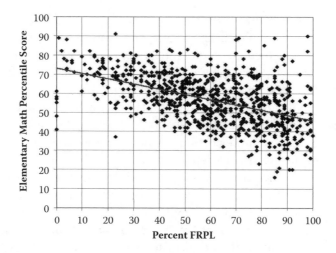

Figure 13.12   Poverty (free or reduced lunch program) vs. achievement in Kentucky Elementary Schools. Source: U.S. Department of Education, 2003.

That is the imaginary regression line. But here is a real one, drawn through actual Kentucky school data. On average, as the poverty level in the school goes up, its achievement goes down. Consider, however, only the highest poverty elementary schools, those schools in which between 80% and 100% of students live in poverty (Figure 13.12).

What did knowing that about them tell you about their student achievement? Literally nothing. As you can see within the group of highest poverty schools there are, some of the highest performing schools in this state, and some of the lowest. Equal poverty, along with very unequal achievement, means that what schools do really matters.

Data from many other states show exactly this same phenomenon. Yes, sometimes the schools show as high performers just for a year or two or in one grade, but not others. Yet there are other schools serving poor children that are high achievers across the board.

So assessment data are critical in signaling the urgency of the achievement gap problem, in helping people to see where we are today and how desperate a situation some students are in. But these same assessment data also show hope, even for schools and students in the most difficult circumstances.

From this combination of pressure to produce ever better results and evidence that we can in fact produce better results has come a renewed sense of focus, especially on the students who have up to now been left behind. I want to reiterate that being focused doesn't in itself necessarily mean doing things that are good for students. And it is certainly not a sufficient strategy for closing achievement gaps just to be more focused on the students who have been behind; there is abundant evidence around our country today that very focused people can often do things that are not so good.

I would like to make 10 suggestions that I believe would help us to use assessment results better in the effort to close achievement gaps. My first recommendation is simply that we should make better use of the assessment data we already have. We need to improve the quality of the primary assessment vehicles we already have, state assessments. We must also develop more assessments of the type that are even more useful for improving instruction. I acknowledge that many of the tests that states have adopted are far from perfect. As a very urgent priority, all of us need to work on that issue. Because, in fact, if people teach and can't see results occurring, that opportunity to improve learning is largely wasted. But I also believe that while we are working on that longer term problem, there are some things we can do with our existing assessments that will actually make them more instructionally sensitive. More transparency in assessment is one of the biggest problems we have faced. States have too often essentially hidden the criteria on which they base their assessment. The Education Trust just completed a 50-state study to answer the question: How accessible to classroom teachers is the information on standards that they need to have in order to teach effectively? In other words, do they have sufficient information to know that if they teach toward these standards or curriculum, students are likely to obtain positive results on the test? The answer, unfortunately, is that in only about five states is there sufficient information available to teachers. Again, one doesn't have to change the tests immediately to change this situation. A very important first step is thus to ask the question: Do our teachers have easy access to the kind of information they need to teach toward a clear goal and to expect that if their students actually learn it that it will show up on state assessments? That transparency should be a very high priority. If our teachers don't have this confidence, then we are never going to make the progress that our students so badly need.

My second recommendation is triggered by people who say that state accountability tests provide no information useful for instruction. And I know this is not true because all around the country I see schools that have worked very hard to take the information from their assessments and reorganize it in ways quite helpful to teachers. It is, for example, far less helpful to teachers to get only a report on how their grade level did last year than it is to get information on the entering class. Thus, as a high priority, one of the things that we need to do immediately is to reorganize the data from state assessments so that, as is already true in some school districts like Long Beach, California, teachers have a good initial profile of their students' knowledge and skills when they enter that teacher's classroom. And certainly some of the work the Grow Network (http://info.grow.net/) has done is particularly useful in that regard.

That is not to suggest, however, that information about last year's students isn't also useful to teachers. Certainly as we work with teachers around the country, we are finding that more and more are interested in a measure of the growth that their students have made on their watch. Again, good assessments are needed in order to do that. Thus, my third recommendation is that it is terribly important to teachers, and to the principals who need to work with them on whom they are going to teach, to have much better information on the growth that students make over the year, on exactly who is making growth, and on what that growth is, compared with students like them. It is only in this way that we can get ever better at both growing teacher skills and at improving the match between students and teachers.

My fourth recommendation concerns the role of parents and students. In general, we have left students and their parents out of the loop in most states. The good news is that this is beginning to change but not changing fast enough. Neither students nor parents in most places are yet getting meaningful information. "Passed" or "didn't pass" doesn't help you to know what to do. Some of the work with the Lexile ranking (http://lexile.com/) of reading difficulty is an example of information to involve parents. It shows parents how to get books and articles that their children can read. More effort is needed to translate this into meaningful steps students and parents can take. One of the most interesting insights from the El Paso Collaborative (Navarro, this volume) is that there are many people who thought poor or poorly educated parents could not actually do much themselves to improve their childs' achievement. But the fact of the matter is, when they get clear information about the kind of reading and writing that their children should be able to do, even the poorest and most poorly educated parents can in fact move ahead.

My fifth recommendation is that we inspire and inform others by studying schools that are unusually successful with certain kinds of students. When the Education Trust first started looking at state databases to identify schools that were doing an unusually good job serving poor students or students of color, we were very surprised to realize that most states don't do this routinely. That is truly unfortunate because those examples serve as powerful existence proofs in a state and as powerful aids to moving forward. A few years ago, the Ohio Department of Education launched a new kind of "schools to success" initiative designed to identify schools that were doing an unusually good job, especially with poor students, and then to help other schools to learn from those. Those can be very powerful learning tools in states, and it's a shame that more states don't do what Ohio has done.

My sixth recommendation is to replace myths with facts. There is a very powerful rumor out there that the best way to produce growth on standardized assessments is to teach narrowly to the test. The research actually and very clearly says otherwise, but the rumor persists. We need to debunk that misconception not just with the kinds of research that are very hard for teachers to make sense of, but also by analyzing and understanding the actual classroom practices of individual teachers who produce unusual growth in their students' learning. The good news I have seen, especially work in Chattanooga, Tennessee, and in Houston, Texas, is that the teachers who are producing the most growth on standardized tests are also the very teachers who you would want to teach your own children. These are exciting active classrooms at the elementary level. They are by no means bereft of art and music. They are lively classes with students doing lots of good work. Teachers need to see more of such examples, but they can't unless we connect the assessment data to conduct detailed studies of what they actually do.

My seventh recommendation is to mine assessment data over time to determine what kind of growth is possible for schools and students. Until we understand more about what kind of growth both at the child level and at the school level is possible over time we have no way to determine whether or not NCLB's goals are realistic. Over the past few years we have certainly amassed sufficient data to address this issue in a more rational way, to move beyond politics and into the realm of solid data and clear concrete examples of success. We need to mine our data to do that.

My eighth and ninth recommendations concern the need for more diagnostic and benchmark assessments. We need to develop tests that will help teachers understand more about what their students know, so that they can plan instruction more effectively, especially for English language learners. Teachers need to have more regular feedback about student learning. While much of that needs to be done by them and for them, not all of it does; and good benchmark assessments steeped in curricula that provide teachers with more regular and more feedback, and that provide administrators a way to identify when students are struggling before they fail the test at the end of the year, are hugely important. Michael Barber developed the Blair Education Reforms in Great Britain. He had done work with the rail system and healthcare. One of the things he said that I think is very important is that in many ways education is the hardest area of all to move, not because educators are less smart or less willing to change, but because the feedback cycle in education is so long, compared to crime rates or infection rates in hospitals or train schedules. With these other areas, it is possible to tell within a month whether interventions have made a difference or not. One of the things benchmark assessments do is give us a way to shorten the feedback cycle so that we will no longer have to wait 15 months to know whether what we did worked.

Finally, my tenth recommendation is that we need to do a lot more work on making assessments meaningful for students. That is especially true for assessments at the end of high school. There is a movement, most of it led by high school principals, to ensure that students have a reason to take their assessments seriously and that they realize benefits from them in terms of college or jobs. We have the technical knowledge to do that, and we need to make it a faster priority.

Let me end with some good news from NAEP. The most recent long-term trends results for 9-year-olds show record performance for all groups of students (white, Latino, African American). These data show higher performance than ever before and the smallest black/white gaps in reading and mathematics that we have ever had in this nation's history. The same thing is true of the Latino/white gap; we now have the smallest Latino/white gap in fourth grade reading and mathematics that we've ever seen in this nation's history. The bottom line is that when we really focus on something, we're likely to make some progress; and the question is, if we bring together all of what we know, can we make faster progress still?

References

Idaho Department of Education. (2005). *Native American Indian Education*. Retrieved July 6, 2006, from http://www.sde.state.id.us/Dept/

National Center for Educational Statistics. (2000a, August). *NAEP 1999 trends in academic progress: Three decades of student performance.* Retrieved July 6, 2006, from http://nces.ed.gov/pubsearch/pubsinfo.asp?pubid=2000469

National Center for Educational Statistics. (2000b, August). *NAEP 1999 long term trends summary tables.* Retrieved July 6, 2006, from http://nces.ed.gov/nationsreportcard/nde/

U.S. Department of Education. (2003). *National longitudinal school-level state assessment score database.* Education Trust analysis of data. Retrieved July 6, 2006, from http://www.schooldata.org

Endnotes

1. The No Child Left Behind Act of 2001, Pub. L. No. 107-110, §115 Stat. 1425 (2002).

Author Index

Subject Index